Don Quixote

AND THE DULCINEATED WORLD

Don Quixote
and the Dulcineated World

by Arthur Efron

UNIVERSITY OF TEXAS PRESS, AUSTIN & LONDON

International Standard Book Number 0–292–70148–9
Library of Congress Catalog Card Number 71–165908
© 1971 by Arthur Efron
Printed by The University of Texas Printing Division, Austin
Bound by Universal Bookbindery, Inc., San Antonio

PREFACE

Very few scholars or critics today find in *Don Quixote* a notable force of critical hostility toward the cultural norms of its national-historical setting. The following statement by a recognized expert is a rarity, and it is made in full awareness that it differs with accepted interpretations: "*Don Quixote* is, among other things, a tremendous protest against the moralistic assurances of Counter-Reformation Spain."[1] My own view is that the novel's "protest" is indeed tremendous, both in spread and in depth. It can only be called radical. The context of what it is against, moreover, is much wider in scope than what can be conveyed by designating a single nation at a single period in history.[2] In important ways, it is against our own epoch.

I deliberately emphasize the negative in making such a statement, for it would not do to disguise my sympathy with the negative values that, as I hope to make clear, are central to the novel's creative achievement. In the ensuing pages, I do not attempt to employ neutral language, which may displease the reader who has faith in the possibility of such language. One Hispanist has commented that obviously I do not "like" *Don Quixote*, and that I should recognize that, all personal preferences aside, Don Quixote acquires a certain amount of dignity by virtue of his willingness to die for his ideals. I cannot believe, however, that there would be any benefit in my practicing the intellectual dishonesty of pretending that my readings of the novel have left me with more affection for a character-as-person than I actually possess. Nor, for that matter, can I agree that willingness to die for a cause automatically confers dignity. Indeed, it is the automatic connection of sacrifice with positive value that is precisely one of the things I believe the novel is questioning. If this connection cannot be questioned, and in some instances (including the present one) rejected, then it must be that the heroes of all melodramas, of even the crudest cowboy film, have "dignity." One can even say that there is a burden of proof on the critic who finds the example of the cowboy film irrelevant, for, as Salvador de Madariaga has seen, the books of chivalry that inform Don Quixote's famous madness were "the melodrama of the age." And the "spirit of melodrama . . . lives now in the film and the serial novel."[3] Indeed, at least one manifestation of that spirit can be traced back to Don Quixote, for he himself, as well as chivalry in general, is a source for the cowboy hero.[4]

I have worked within the assumption that the way to deal responsibly with the evidence of the text is not through the use of a speciously neutral viewpoint, but by subjecting my treatment of such evidence to continual cross-criticism from the best of the alternative critical readings of Don Quixote.

Most of my many quotations from and references to the text of Don Quixote are taken from the translation by J. M. Cohen, The Adventures of Don Quixote, which is published by Penguin Books (1950). The "very considerable achievement" of Cohen's translation has been noted by H. B. Hall,[5] who reviewed the work in Bulletin of Hispanic Studies. Hall even judged that in this translation, "on the whole, the extremely difficult task of reproducing the various levels of dialogue has been skillfully accomplished." But my use of Cohen's translation should not be construed as a denigration of the final importance of the Spanish text. I do believe it is necessary to recognize, with E. D. Hirsch, that not all literary texts are equally "language-bound,"[6] and I certainly do not think that any major elements of Don Quixote have ever been demonstrated to be untranslatable. But I recognize that there will be some differences between Cohen (or any available translation) and the Spanish; my point is that it is quite possible to write literary criticism of the *Quixote* in English, and that the discernible differences in translatable quotations have, at best, minimal importance for the specific context of my present argument.

I have taken one further precaution: Professor Mack Singleton, distinguished Cervantist in the Department of Spanish and Portuguese at the University of Wisconsin, has been good enough to review for me once again all the quotations taken from Cohen's translation and to note any discrepancies in them. As a result, I have been able to reconsider the critical implications of certain passages and have revised my remarks accordingly. Professor Singleton has also furnished the prose translation of the two stanzas quoted from Don Quixote's poem in part 1, chapter 26 (page 43 below).

I also follow Professor Otis H. Green, who states in his work *Spain and the Western Tradition: The Castilian Mind in Literature from "El Cid" to Calderón* that "the text of *Don Quixote* is so well known and so readily available that I do not give the Spanish text of my quotations from it."[7] I shall insert a limited number of Spanish phrases whenever they appear to me to be unusually important in themselves, and I shall quote, very occasionally, from other translations of the *Quixote*, when these appear to me to have come closer to the appropriate English nuance. All parenthetical page references within the text refer to J. M. Cohen's translation, *The Adventures of Don Quixote*.

The notes themselves are intended as extensions of my argument and as indications of how I would pursue the problems in *Quixote* criticism and in critical theory that are connected with that argument.

For the Spanish text, I have chosen one more convenient to those wishing to read *Don Quixote* in its original language than are the usual multivolume scholarly editions. Spanish citations are from *El ingenioso hidalgo Don Quijote de la Mancha*, Prólogo y Esquema Biográfico por Américo Castro (Mexico City: Editorial Porrúa, 1960). As a reviewer of Cohen's translation observed, in the standard scholarly edition by Rodríguez Marín, almost all the thousands of notes on *Don Quixote* bear "not on its meaning as such, but on linguistic usages or allusions no longer current."[8] Leland H. Chambers has noted that Rodríguez Marín's appreciation of Cervantes "has not extended far beyond" some rather localized "linguistic considera-tion."[9] In view of the persistent failure of the major critical editions to prove of positive assistance to criticism, I have found it better to consult them silently, while citing an edition that is not as cumbersome.

I wish to express my appreciation to the Research Foundation of the State University of New York for awarding a summer grant that saw me through some of the essential writing of this study. I am also grateful to Leon Livingstone for reading the manuscript and offering a number of valuable suggestions and objections. Mack Singleton has my warm thanks for similar assistance at a later stage, as well as for his detailed advice concerning translations. To Professor Wayne Burns of the University of Washington, who greatly helped me to realize the critical importance of the somatic basis for Sancho Panza's common sense, I owe a large intellectual debt; it is a debt that extends well beyond any single idea or insight. And my wife, Esther, helped in innumerable ways, none of them more vital than by managing to stay so un-Dulcineated.

I wish to thank the following publishers for permission to quote copyrighted material: Penguin Books, Ltd., for kind permission to use, throughout the present study, passages from J. M. Cohen's transla-tion of Miguel de Cervantes Saavedra, *The Adventures of Don Quixote*; (Penguin Books, Ltd., 1950); Princeton University Press, for permission to quote from Erich Auerbach, *Mimesis: The Repre-sentation of Reality in Western Literature*, translated by Willard R. Trask (copyright 1953 by Princeton University Press; Princeton Paperback, 1968), reprinted by permission of Princeton University Press; and St. Martin's Press, Inc., Macmillan and Co. Ltd., pub-lishers of *Imperial Spain: 1469–1716*, by J. H. Elliott.

CONTENTS

Don Quixote
AND THE DULCINEATED WORLD

Ideals and Fictional Probing

Dubious Brotherhood

In *Cervantes across the Centuries* (1948), a collection of essays marking the quadricentennial of Cervantes' birth, the editors make the modest enough claim that "thanks to the work of a whole brotherhood of students and lovers of Cervantes, we are now in a position to discern some of the meanings of Spain's first genius."[1] My own starting point must instead be the anomaly of a great classic that is even yet misunderstood; the "sensitive objective criticism" that the editors commend cannot in my opinion be fairly said to exist in what has been written about *Don Quixote*.[2] The present study accordingly offers a reinterpretation of *Don Quixote* that I believe is fundamentally incompatible with the conclusions of nearly all *Quixote* critics.

A reinterpretation of so large a work requires its supporting evidence in the form of explication, and this I shall attend to, though never, I hope, in such page-by-page fashion as to bury the book. At the same time, I shall often have occasion to allude (both in the text and in footnotes) to the "brotherhood" of Cervantes critics. In other words, I have attempted an explication that is also a confrontation with the main critical opposition it can be expected to encounter. Often it is of necessity a confrontation with the forms of argument *Quixote* critics have used. Whenever such attention to critical premise has led me into fundamental problems of literary criticism, I have pursued the discussion to whatever lengths I thought necessary for the creation of a viable criticism of *Don Quixote*. It may well be that Cervantes' masterwork makes demands upon us that will seem to require a serious shift in some of our more readily accepted critical ideas; if so, we must be ready to let that happen.

The confrontation may profitably begin with a sketch of the three established, but I think dubious, critical approaches to *Don Quixote*, and with a brief examination of some of their implications. In the most pervasive of all approaches to *Don Quixote*, the Knight is regarded as being in some sense the locus of positive value. Depending on the particular bearings of the critic and the period in which the critic writes, Don Quixote may be described in positive terms because of his role as restorer of traditional cultural values, or because of his idealistic opposition to the values of his social environment, or because he is seen as an example of modern rather than medieval man, creating his individual personality with the strength of his own will and imagination rather than carrying out the role that his society has defined for him. These descriptions constitute what I shall call the *idealist* reading. Some would call it Romantic, for it developed under the impetus of that change in literary sensibility which often placed premium value upon the idiosyncratic and, if necessary, impractical assertion of self against society.

Second, there has long been a less popular stream of criticism that has taken the Knight for a man with good intentions that require purification under the pressure of reality. The proponents of this view do not dismiss or minimize his errors of perception, but concentrate upon the impurity of his ideal; for Don Quixote exhibits certain suspect traits, such as the urge for fame and the tendency to dictate an irrelevant idealism out of the past onto his own world. In this view, characters like the Priest, the Canon, and the Man in Green often serve to suggest a realistic standard of values and become standard-bearers of the author's viewpoint as well as of the Counter Reformation, to whose values the author is assumed to have subscribed. Slowly in the course of the novel Don Quixote is brought to realize the truth and beauty of this realistic norm, and at his death—a favorite scene for this approach to the novel—he fully accepts it. Variations within this approach include those which make the standard a more universal one of Christian Realism,[3] rather than its special Counter Reformation embodiment, and those which stress the social milieu as norm, thus pointing out the historical irrelevance of knight-errantry in a world that really belongs to the middle class. Soviet critics tend toward one variant,[4] Catholic critics toward another. Essentially, this is a *cautionary* interpretation; for although it ultimately judges the novel in terms of ideal values, just as the idealist interpretation does, it emphasizes the ways in which the protagonist of the novel is, until the very end of the book, out of step with these values, however well-intentioned he may be.

Finally, there is what might be called the *perspectivist* interpretation. Here the critics refuse to see Cervantes or the novel as endorsing either the real or the ideal (however those maddening terms are defined), but find that the novel shows an inevitable tension between these two perspectives, each of which appears in some way to have its claim to being an ultimate reality, and each of which is interpreted as part of the inherent human condition. Perspectivism ultimately assumes that life is the interplay of a number of equally real levels of reality. It is a view of life the reader of modern *Quixote* criticism will immediately recognize, although its prevalence is somewhat deceptive. There has been much discussion of Cervantes' baroque style, his doubleness, his "equívoco," and his perspectivism, but few of the critics who use these terms prove upon examination to be sticking to them as a final basis for judgment. Usually, but not always, critical practice indicates a choice of either the first two readings.[5]

Each of these three broad approaches is obviously connected at many levels with the critic's or the reader's particular grasp of life itself. My own reading is no exception. The novel is rich with connection, and I would not wish to deprive it of its very life.[6] But I shall attempt to avoid the arbitrariness or circularity of argument that maintains that the novel is based on beliefs about life whose truth *must* be self-evident. It is no good to decide beforehand that one's basic beliefs are out of reach of the novel's critical exploration; indeed, to state such a ground rule for criticism is to state a platitude. Yet it is a rule that is regularly violated, so frequently that its violation may be regarded as a chronic need of *Quixote* critics.

Many readings from the idealist position, for instance, decide with Turgenev that regardless of Don Quixote's comic mishaps, "the ideal itself remains in its untarnished purity."[7] Others repeat that no matter what happens to Don Quixote his "inner dignity remains unassailable," or that his ideals are simply "basically attractive," or that the material world is to be regarded as both Don Quixote's and our own nemesis.[8] Thus, by means of some prior commitment on the part of the critic, Don Quixote's struggle becomes unalterably identified with all that is worthwhile.

Benedetto Croce spelled out the philosophical and psychological assumptions behind these views when he wrote that all of us are in a state of unshakable sympathy with Don Quixote simply because life is itself a process of necessary illusions. "Every man," Croce argued, "no matter how wise he may be or think himself to be, is always wholly enveloped in illusions," and the most we can do is to become "philosophically aware of the logical process whereby all this is proved necessary."[9] But I shall not avail myself of the wisdom proffered here, or of the assumptions involved, because to do so is to abort any open inquiry into the novel. This sympathetic defense of idealism by means of imposition soon leads, for example, to trying to take straight all the comic and satiric qualities of *Don Quixote*. The kind of criticism that finds support for the ideal of virginity in the

discussion of the problem of the disequilibrium created by
ixote's sallying forth. Cautionary critics frequently do just
when they simplify the problem of Don Quixote's freeing of
ey slaves by emphasizing that the galley slaves were after
ubtedly "guilty criminals," or when they reduce his whole
c imitation into a case of the "pride" inherent in "imitative
(rather than of the desire to obey the will of God), or when
y to explain the drubbings Don Quixote receives as suitable
ment" for this "pride."[13] The cautionary reading thus tends to
rowly moralistic (unlike the idealistic approach, which at
as more expansive moods and aims) and eventually runs into
emma of proving that Cervantes has merely constructed a
f predetermined experiences for his hero, designed to punish
ure" him of chivalry-as-disease. If this were actually the case,
Quixote would scarcely deserve its repute as a great novel; it
be a moral treatise of a crude and sadistic kind, as indeed
Madox Ford suggested it to be.[14] And Cervantes would be not
t novelist but merely a more clever constructor of cruel *burlas*
are his own creations in *Don Quixote*, the Duke and Duchess
t 2.[15] The cautionary approach usefully alerts us to the possi-
that Don Quixote's upsetting of everyday routines in his fictive
y may be destructive of positive values embodied in that so-
but too frequently this sort of criticism has assumed beforehand
ny such disturbance is wrong in itself.

e effects of perspectivists upon critical predispositions are more
ult to describe and to counter, though they are hardly less
tionable. The idealist tends to assume the unassailability of the
t's ideals, the cautionary critic tends to identify with whatever
aced in resistance to the Knight, but the perspectivists reflect
re complex philosophical position, in which life is approached
series of indissoluble tensions. The dean of perspectivists,
rico Castro, has in fact developed a theory of Spanish history
hich unresolved conflict within the individual sense of identity

passage concerning "virgins in the
by some rogue or by a boor with
monstrous giant, never slept a nigh
at the age of eighty went to their
mothers that bore them" (76;* "com
is certainly to be avoided. For it is
the cost of being completely obtuse to
Rather than seeking insulation again
receives in a comic world, it is bette
that Cervantes continually abjures su
ness runs riot in ridiculous and hum
high-minded hero then tumbles and
self."[11] It is proper to attempt to sup
emerges from the total context still e
are shown by the novel to be superior
invent a protagonist who is immune fro
a set of values that one refuses to conc
and, if need be, rejected within a great

If one abides by the cautionary inter
Hispanists do), it is equally possible to
critic seriously expect to comprehend th
ing out that Don Quixote is not a true
gone through the proper chivalric initiat
somehow does take to the road in *Do*
narrow to quarrel at this level with hi
knight, just as it is surely petty to rem
The Courtier it is specified that "one mu
hence the "imitation of a doughty knigh
suited to an impecunious middle-aged
the everyday world's stock classifications

---

*All page references in the text of this stud
Saavedra, *The Adventures of Don Quixote*, tra
worth, Eng.: Penguin Books, Ltd., 1950) an
the publisher.

off oper
Don Q
that, as
the gal
all und
chivalr
desire"
they tr
"punish
be nan
least h
the di
series
and "c
Don (
would
Ford
a grea
than
of pa
bility
socie
ciety,
that

Th
diffi
obje
knigl
is pl
a m
as
Am
in w

is the key factor in Spanish character.[16] The Spaniard (and Don
Quixote is one of Castro's important examples) could not rely on
given absolutes and universals of conduct but had to establish his
identity in the self-created perspectives of his own life existence.[17]
Castro is thus able to put Cervantes among the direct forerunners
of Kierkegaard, Heidegger, and Ortega.[18] Indeed, if one consults
the aesthetics of existential critics, one soon finds that any real conflict must remain unresolved. "I acknowledge," Murray Krieger
writes, "that . . . I must deny that the existential world—the world
of felt human experience—can be anything less than a bewildering
complex of seeming contradictions. Given this sort of world, how
can any more systematic view of it . . . avoid, in its inadequacy, doing
this world a grievous injustice?"[19] Similarly, Heidegger argues that
a work of art is based on a *Riss*, a kind of essential strife, which is
revealed in the work not so as to lead to "insipid agreement, but in
order that the strife should remain a strife." The conflict within a
work should be disclosed but "should not be resolved."[20]

Perhaps these conclusions are the logical ones that much of recent
aesthetics must eventually reach; at any rate, they are congenial to a
great many of the intellectual positions found within the modern
temper. For if resolution of any kind would imply the grievous injustice of insipidness to specifically existential temperaments, it
would also be undesirable to many other writers on literary art.
Dorothy Van Ghent argues in her chapter on *Don Quixote* that
within the novel "perspective is achieved by consistent organization
of extremes of difference," and that the various perspectives revealed
in the novel are "constantly reversible." Were this not so, Van Ghent
feels the book would be some sort of "manual of moral *exempla*."
Similarly, W. K. Wimsatt, Jr., points out that recent literary theory
in general emphasizes "the reconciliation or ironic preservation of
warring interests and of the opposite views of the world from which
they arise" within the work of art. Northrop Frye sees *Don Quixote*
as an "ironic compound" of parody and romance and argues that a

satirist cannot legitimately allow the standards of sense experience to determine value in satire—to do so would be to oversimplify the value of those perspectives which deny the primacy of the senses. It would appear that, according to Frye, the "compound" cannot be dissolved, nor can it reach any other resolution than that it is in fact a compound. The modern temper may recognize that Don Quixote represents one kind of life and that Sancho Panza opposes him in many important particulars, but it gravitates toward a refusal to choose one or the other. Yet what if the novel should imply a choice? Would this automatically make it bad art? We would be disposed to say yes, for, as Lionel Trilling has so well intuited, "we believe that ethical dilemmas, confrontations of opposing principles of conduct, do not—because they should not, because they need not—exist."[21]

Yet there is much to say against this predisposition on our part. How likely is it, actually, that in a series of conflicts stretching over some 400,000 words the perspectives remain entirely "reversible" or even of approximately equal value? Is it really true that a work that brings its complex and interrelated components into resolution rather than leaving them in ambiguity,[22] paradox, or perspectival balance, is thereby a lesser work? To maintain this position on philosophical grounds seems to me most precarious. Such an approach to literature would slight all works that are responsive to what John Dewey called, in *Art as Experience*, "the consummating phase of every developing integral experience."[23] And it would require that all artists inhibit themselves; as Harold Rosenberg points out with regard to the Action painters: "To maintain the force to refrain from settling anything, [the artist] must exercise in himself a constant No."[24] Finally, and most important, to accept as unquestionable the creed that life is the unresolvable tension of intersecting perspectives is to come to the text of *Don Quixote* with a predisposition too formidable for the novel to overcome if it should happen not to operate within that creed. And I shall maintain that the novel does not fit the creed at all.[25]

Another Approach to Don Quixote *as Unique Novel*

All three of these established approaches to *Don Quixote*, it seems to me, are rather weakly supported by the text. At the very least, I would maintain that there is a fourth basic approach, in which the opposition between the Knight and the surrounding milieu is seen as a false one, not because Cervantes or the novel is relativistic or perspectivistic, but because there is no such fundamental opposition. The conflict is a comic battle of nonessentials, and in this battle resides the basis for a judgment of the novel. The unrecognized agreement between the two sides of the opposition, combined with an endlessly elaborated playing out of the surface conflict, finally shows that the seemingly radical stance of the Knight is merely an exaggeration of the life-denying idealism to which the members of the Knight's world (with the important partial exception of Sancho Panza) already ally themselves.

The fictional reality that Cervantes makes apprehensible in his complex way is one in which what I call *Dulcineism,* or *the belief that human life is satisfactorily conducted only if it is lived out in close accord with prescribed ideals of the received culture,* has succeeded in capturing and enfeebling its many adherents. Dulcineism is thus a name for some of the broadest effects of acculturation. By it I mean to indicate all those effects in which human choice is pointed toward a predetermined conformity with set patterns of thought, emotion, or behavior and is conceptualized in sharply outlined ideals, such as chastity, marital fidelity, justice in accordance with fixed rules, loyalty to one's social class, courage and suffering as automatically positive values, and, finally, an unquestioning faith that underlies continued adherence to the whole complex of accepted ideals.[26] The concept is necessarily broad (it expresses almost the total sweep of interests in the novel's fictional society), but it is not merely a catch-all; it excludes those aspects of culture which provide areas of genuine "negative freedom," that is, areas in which individuals are able to discover their own preferences, whether these happen to be compatible with received ideals or not.[27] But in *Don Quixote* Dulcineism has no opposition outside some aspects of Sancho Panza, the rich comic perversity of the fiction itself, and the smothered counterimpulses of the adherents. As I shall attempt to show, Dulcineism is able to maintain so pervasive a grasp upon the novel's characters because it involves a drastic idealization of sexuality. And this idealization is brought out in its clearest form in the relationship of Don Quixote to Dulcinea.

If Dulcineism attains nearly all its desired goals, within the world of the novel, it is clear that the novel cannot be seen in any of the traditional interpretations, which find that *Don Quixote* is the conflict of real and ideal or that it redefines them both as perspectives of the manifold real. Conflict, in these senses, disappears. Idealism, by the force of its own psychological, literary, social, and cultural weaponry, has possessed all the characters (except, again, Sancho and, in a very special way, the Duke and Duchess); the sense of an opposing "real" is transformed by the novel into a critical orientation that has no connection with the society of the novel itself. The opposing "real" is the critical art of Cervantes, expressed through his comic juxtapositions, through the critical voice of Sancho, and indirectly available through the narrative method Cervantes chooses to employ. If the novel shows (as I shall maintain) that Dulcineism debilitates any kind of bona fide truth-seeking, any chance of male-female contact, or any relationship on a person-to-person basis, it also shows that there is no living space in the society of the novel for the critical thought that is magnificently created in the necessary implications of the reading experience itself.

Thus I would revise the conclusion of such an observer as Arnold Hauser, who finds that *Don Quixote* is "the novel of alienation *par excellence.*" For it is not true that, as the novel proceeds, "the complete alienation of its hero from his time and environment emerges more and more distinctly." On the contrary, what emerges is Don Quixote's kinship with his world, and any quality of alienation is delivered into the lap of the reader. The novel in this sense becomes a prime example of what Hauser discovers in certain "Mannerist" works, which "because of their imperfection and inherent meaninglessness . . . point towards a fuller and more meaningful whole, which is not there for the taking, but has to be striven for."[28] And the impetus that makes "meaninglessness" apparent, as well as a "meaningful" wholeness desirable, is ultimately the creative art of Cervantes, exercising its potentialities for freedom of imagination over the course of a beautifully executed, gigantic novel.

In order to bring my own reading of that novel into focus, I find it necessary first to describe something of the way I conceive the book to work. *Don Quixote,* as Thomas Mann wrote, "is indeed a strange product: naive, unique, arbitrary and sovereign in its contradictions."[29] No single concept of genre can hope to encompass *Don Quixote,* and it will be well briefly to outline here the complex fusion of novelistic realism with other literary modes that I shall assume, throughout this study, makes up Cervantes' masterpiece.

Cervantes seems to me to be creating meanings through several kinds of juxtapositions. We are to connect together, and to consider together, the *contexts* of his many situations, their thematic connections with one another, their implications for the development of continuous fictional characters,[30] and—perhaps most important— their clashing or discordant qualities, both within single situations and over the range of related episodes. (Admittedly, most of this would be granted as part of the usual reading process in novels; no claim is made here of an innovation in the study of the techniques of fiction.) But Cervantes is also something of a *satirical* novelist, and so the loose term *juxtaposition* may be appropriate for suggesting his great sense of contrast and contradiction, his genius for bringing the apparently unimpeachable ideal into a desperate conflict situation and often for palpably undercutting that ideal or even exploding it.[31] He is also something of a comic novelist, despite critical efforts to purge away the comic quality of the book.[32] Philip Rahv's observation concerning fiction criticism of recent decades is relevant: ". . . critics are disposed to purge the novel of its characteristically detailed imagination working through experiential particulars—the particulars of scene, figures and action: to purge them, that is to say, of their gross immediacy and direct empirical expressiveness." The gross immediacy of those places in which Sancho acts as garrulous comic undercutter of idealism comes to mind here, as well as the particularity of scenes, which is so often distanced in critical attempts to support a philosophy of perspectivism.[33] It is better to start with some theory of literary openness, as Ricardo Quintana suggests, regarding the work of another satirist, Jonathan Swift:

> Once the situation has been suggested, once its tone, its flavor have been given, it promptly takes command of itself and proceeds to grow and organize by virtue of its own inherent principles. It is a state of affairs within which, as we mistakenly put it, "anything can happen"—mistakenly because everything that does happen is instantly recognized as a part of *this*, a unique situation. . . . In short, the situation may be thought of as a kind of chamber within which ideas and emotions are made to move and collide at accelerated speed.[34]

However different from Swift he may be, Cervantes does create an enormous juxtaposition of elements that continually collide with each other. Out of these many collisions comes an overall, highly critical, illumination of an immense range of values.

The basic process of the novel involves juxtaposition within chapters, paragraphs, and sentences, extended finally to situations and whole underlying attitudes. It is characteristic that when the Man in Green (who is still suggested, sometimes, as one of Cervantes' indications of a norm for the novel)[35] is asked by Don Quixote to describe his way of life, he includes an assertion that cuts away its own ground: "I share my goods with the poor, without boasting of my good works for fear of letting into my heart hypocrisy and vain-glory, enemies that subtly seize upon the wariest heart" (567). This statement comes a little too close to claiming that "everyone is conceited except me" to be taken straight. In the case of Don Quixote himself, such verbal undermining of professed ideals, heightened immeasurably by the contexts of the situations in which he is likely to apply his program of Dulcineism and still more by the revelation of the workings of his mind in his continuing dialogue with his companion-critic Sancho Panza, goes beyond irony; it becomes an ultimately overwhelming reversal of the honorific status of the ideals themselves.

If this claim holds true, then we must recognize the hopelessness of all idealist criticism that attempts to lift these ideals out of context, to restore their customary glitter, and then employs them for a reading of the novel. It is no help to be told, to take another representative statement, that Don Quixote's "*ideals* are, after all, reasonable. It would be a more rational world if courtesy, gallantry, and noblesse oblige were universal."[36] On the contrary, if one accepts a reading experience of *Don Quixote* as any kind of evidence, one would have to conclude that a world of such idealistic proportions would be quite unreasonable, as well as terribly unfeeling. It is because Don Quixote's ideals must focus upon a supremely ideal woman, and because their overall novelistic fate is to be revealed in all their programmatic and mechanical similarity to the ideals of many other characters in the novel, that I have chosen the intentionally ill-sounding term, *Dulcineated*, to describe the world these ideals create.

We may take as an introductory sample of the text one of the lesser juxtapositions in one of Don Quixote's most renowned utterances, his advice to Sancho on the subject of being a good governor: "Firstly, my son, you must fear God, for in fearing Him is wisdom and, being wise, you can make no mistake" (738).[37] Now there is something in the tone and placing of the final element in this sentence that juxtaposes itself in a parodic manner with the first two elements, something that makes the proffered wisdom appear somehow ridiculous. Perhaps that is why Samuel Putnam placed an annotating footnote two-thirds of the way through the sentence, rather than at its end. And if we read the three biblical references Putnam suggested as sources, we find that none of them contain Don Quixote's absurdity of wisdom's openly offering infallibility: "The fear of the Lord is the beginning of wisdom; a good understanding have all those who practice it" (Psalms 111:10); "The fear of the Lord is the beginning of knowledge; fools despise wisdom and instruction" (Proverbs 1:7); "The fear of the Lord is the beginning of wisdom, and the knowledge of the Holy One is insight" (Proverbs 9:10). To ignore the juxtaposing of advice with its reductive *but logical* conclusion in Quixote's sentence is—however obvious it may be to say so—a way of distorting the meaning. The novel creates a shattering clarification of the nature of the wisdom in Quixote's whole speech. It is not endorsing the advice, as critics have usually believed.[38] The speech is given form only as a series of comic juxtapositions, which in turn assures that a parodic interpretation of this one statement is appropriate within the context Cervantes provides.

This slight example may be contrasted with the most extended one of all, what George Meredith called "the juxtaposition of the knight and squire."[39] This is the one opposition that proves to be real rather than sham, despite Sancho's eventual acquisition, in some degree, of his master's way of perceiving reality. The fact that Sancho does give his master much opposition and resistance in a great many passages in the story is the one thing that is obvious and has probably always been granted by the common reader. Yet the professional critic, such as Joaquín Casalduero, is likely to claim that Knight and squire "are of the same nature with a difference in proportion."[40]

It is of course insufficient to appeal to the testimony of the common reader, even if that testimony could be recorded. The common reader, like everyone else, could be wrong. And perhaps the most crucial point the present study attempts to support is a denial of something the common reader has probably always accepted: that the clash between Don Quixote and his fictional social environment is based upon a fundamental opposition. Outside the clash with Sancho, this first impression of the novel does not lend itself to support. Instead, this impression must give way, on the showing of the novel itself, to the discovery of similarity between the Knight and his world.

The very fact that Don Quixote can become an innocuous parlor-knight at a ducal palace for some fifteen or twenty chapters in part 2 is itself indicative of the nonessential conflict between Quixote and the characters he confronts. The bandit chief Roque finds him "entertaining and sensible" and sends him on with hearty recommendation to his respectable friends in Barcelona (865). It would be too convenient to assume, as idealist critics have done, that the Duke, the bandit chief, and the Barcelona gentry merely fail to perceive their conflict with Don Quixote. More likely, there is little conflict to perceive. At least as early as the Knight's removal, by cage, from the inn to the village (part 1, chapter 46), Don Quixote assumes a primarily passive role. In part 2, he seldom attacks anyone, and he wins the praise of all beholders for his wisdom. His apparent opposition to the ways of his world increasingly becomes unthreatening entertainment, joined in by one and all, and contentment with the appearance of idealistic achievement is as fully characteristic of the Knight as of the people he meets at the ducal palace, in Barcelona, or on the road. There is a tacit accommodation between ideal and appearance, rather than the indignant implication that the mere mortals of the novel have failed to live up to their ideals. The overt content of the ideal code, as this study shall attempt to show, is finally less important than its psychological value as an inhibitor of all forces that might point behavior away from what the code suggests, toward the spontaneous, the physical, the natural.

The nonoppositional clash of Knight and milieu is developed throughout the novel. Like part 2, the earlier narrative also has qualities that imply compatibility rather than conflict. The kind of substitution suggested in Cardenio's donning first the Priest's and then Dorothea's clothing (255, 273), which Dorothea in turn had put on as a disguise, is an interchangeability of characters rather than simple comic repetition. There is much knockabout, bloody conflict, of course, but such conflict does not necessarily imply a conflict of values. In his essay on laughter, Bergson classified such scenes as the brawl among the mule driver, Maritornes, the innkeeper, Sancho and Don Quixote (part 1, chapter 16) as manifestations of the snow-ball effect found in many comedies. But this classification is too general. The Knight's action in that scene reveals more than that he mechanically mistakes all women for princesses of chivalric lore, and the novel's treatment of violence is more than comic "reality" hitting back. The scene has to be connected with the later brawl, in the same inn, over the barber's basin taken for Mambrino's helmet, and with the eventual institutionalized violence of the robber gang in part 2, chapter 60, and of the naval skirmish in part 2, chapter 65. That later skirmish is almost candied over with sentimental, quasi-chivalric effusions, but there is enough of Sancho present and enough funded effect from previous passages in the novel to reveal violence as an underside or complement, not an opposition, to Dulcineism. Within the life dictated by Dulcinea, the novel shows a need to be bashed, a need to be saddened, and a need for lashing and chastising.

The adventure of the Basque (part 1, chapters 8–9) is a brilliant early example of compatibility in conflict. Quixote, under the illusion that he is rescuing an abducted princess, first attacks a party of travelers. He knocks down a monk who is, in fact, not a member of the traveling group and then explains his gracious mission to the lady in the coach, while two servants of the monk pummel Sancho for attempting to rob their master according to the rules of errantry. Meanwhile, Quixote gets into a fight with a Basque who has been accompanying the lady's coach and who thinks, because of dialect difficulties, that Quixote has called him "no gentleman." It does not require much to set a fight going between this Knight on a valiant mission for his ideal lady and this man who is touchy about his manliness. Quixote finally agrees to spare the Basque's life, at the request of the now truly distressed lady, although the Knight requires as a condition that the Basque go at once and prostrate himself before Dulcinea. This kind of interchange among the opponents and in the components of a conflict seems less arbitrary as the novel develops toward a view of conflict as having surface implications only.

We must also notice that juxtaposed directly over the narrative surface of this fight with the Basque is the comic chapter break between chapters 8 and 9, caused, the narrator tells us, by the loss of the manuscript of *Don Quixote* itself. By breaking his chapter at the moment in which the conflict is at its climax, Cervantes mimics the use of cumbersome organization in chivalric romances, which frequently ended a narrative unit in mid-action.[41] But then, in his own role as narrator, Cervantes proceeds to lament the split.[42] He cannot understand how the manuscript of Quixote's adventures could have been cut off at just such an important point. This, he says, "caused me great annoyance." How could "such a gallant history" be "left maimed and mutilated?" The word "mutilated" ("estropeada") jars a little with the repeated professions of pleasure in "this delightful story." It subtly calls attention to the fictional situation itself:

> . . . we left the valiant Basque and the famous Don Quixote with naked swords aloft, on the point of dealing two such furious strokes as, had they struck true, would have cleft both knights asunder from head to foot, and split them like pomegranates. At this critical point our delightful history stopped short and remained mutilated ["quedó destroncada"] . . .

The Basque's head, however, is no pomegranate, for when Quixote, after the chapter break, strikes him, he begins "to spout blood out of his nostrils, his mouth, and his ears" (78). Quixote then stands over him, "looking on most composedly." Quixote by now has been literally mutilated himself, with the loss of half an ear. The whole juxtaposition of chapter break and fight inevitably suggests some displacement of value, from concern for physical pain to delight in the telling of its details, and from Quixote as a reader of chivalry books to the audience of *Don Quixote* as readers of a story about a man who is much more disturbed at his smashed helmet than at his slashed-off ear (81).

Beginning with scenes like this one, in which the Knight's particular obsession is exposed in an uncomplimentary comparison, the novel moves and expands to the point where the exposure can absorb such items as Don Quixote's discourse on Arms and Learning, his

advice to Governor Sancho Panza, the fictional society's acceptance
of that advice as a form of wisdom unsullied by the Knight's madness, and the "delighted" readers of part 1 who are discussed and
often encountered as fictional characters in part 2. The virtues admired and found delightful by the society turn out to be just the ones
at the basis of Don Quixote's madness. Many characters are shown
to be involved in their own idealist literature, imitating and accepting the fixed values of that literature in their own lives, particularly
in their loves. And so, if Don Quixote's madness may be said to be
the attempt to bring romance to a dull world, it must also be said
that he finds a world deeply engaged in dull romance that is basically
compatible with his own chivalric models. No one would accuse most
of the main characters of being narrowly realistic. They are instead
enveloped in a dream world comparable to Quixote's own and hence
exposed to the same danger of being satirically undercut or comically
exploded.

Two chapters after the adventure of the Basque, Cervantes intro-
duces the first of his "interpolated tales," the pastoral story of Chrysostom and Marcela (part 1, chapters 12–14). But the interpolation is
more properly called a juxtaposition, an immediate instance of the
condition lamented by Don Quixote in his famous Golden Age
speech (part 1, chapter 11), the pestiferous ubiquity of love in
modern times. In the last half of part 1, a number of idealistic love
(and war) stories are juxtaposed with one another and with Quixote's stay at the inn. And also occurring at the inn is a series of disputes, a "tangle of quarrels" ("máquina de pendencias") and a
"labyrinth of confusion" (408) over the arrest of Don Quixote, the
settling of a hotel bill, the ownership of a packsaddle, and the marriage of a rich man's son to one of the fair beauties staying at the inn.
It is necessary to regard these components in the light of the fusions
and collisions provided by the text rather than as separate strands
that merely chance to intersect. In part 2 an even closer interfusion
of side adventures is attempted, as the narrator correctly points out
(745–746).

For critical purposes, all this interrelation can be adequately described only in a study having scope enough to demarcate the collisions as they occur in a nine-hundred-page novel and to deal with enough of the juxtaposition to minimize distortion by means of selective focus. In plan, this study will attempt to do that, beginning with an examination of the main character, then proceeding to the secondary character and the nature of his relationship with Don Quixote. We shall go on finally to treat the expansion of the novel's implications within the other members of the Dulcineated world, which, in turn, will mean dealing at least occasionally with implications for our own world, Dulcineated as it also is.

Américo Castro has noted that Cervantes' accomplishment in *Don Quixote* put the author so far ahead of his time that his novel had to wait centuries before the rise of Romanticism made it possible even to begin an investigation of its portrayal of inner life.[43] I will go one step further and suggest that this first of the great novels has achieved its long popularity and acceptance as a classic in spite of, rather than because of, what it embodies. To make this claim for *Don Quixote*, in the terms which I shall employ, is indeed to deny that the other three extant kinds of *Quixote* interpretation are viable. I do not mean to deny that each of these readings has a certain amount of initial plausibility, or that there are works of literature that will sustain more than one relatively adequate interpretation. But for reasons I hope to make clear, the readings that I have called, respectively, the idealist, the cautionary, and the perspectivist should be regarded as seriously inadequate, and either the present interpretation or others yet to be discovered should be considered.

 CHAPTER TWO

The Benumbed Knight

A Problem of Quality

In *Meditations on Quixote*, Ortega y Gasset at one point comes to consider the Knight as hero. Ortega's conception of the hero, like so much else in the *Meditations*, is memorable and pertinent:

> . . . it is a fact that there are men who decide not to be satisfied with reality. Such men aim at altering the course of things; they refuse to repeat the gestures that custom, tradition, or biological instincts force them to make. These men we call heroes, because to be a hero means to be one out of many, to be oneself. . . . The hero's will is not that of his ancestors nor of his society, but his own. This will to be oneself is heroism.[1]

To see Don Quixote as a hero worthy of Ortega's description is not an unlikely position for a critic to take. Don Quixote certainly does reject biological instinct in himself and gives every appearance of going against the conventions of his society. Certain features of the plot help to reinforce this obvious impression. For one thing, Don Quixote is a character almost free of family relationships and is thus able to take to the road in the manner of someone entering freshly into the social world. Further, the very location of the bulk of the episodic adventures, in the open countryside, gives an impression of freedom from the restrictions of social life, and particularly from the close demands of city life.[2]

Yet I would maintain that on balance the impression of Don Quixote's free choice in heroic endeavors must be classified as an impression only, an impression undermined in comic ways as well as in more indirect ways. The forces of custom and tradition, and the will of his literary ancestors, ultimately do direct the Knight in so great a degree that, although his characterization is fully individualized, he cannot be said to merit the honorific use of the term *individual*, much less *hero*. There may finally be some irreducible difference between Quixote's ardent acceptance of fixed, ideal values and the similar but cooler acceptance by the characters he encounters, but there is no indication in the novel that the difference is great enough to pass the threshold beyond which "the course of things" must be altered. The case for Quixote as hero in opposition to existing reality can at first be sustained by the mere fact that Quixote is constantly clashing with other people, both physically and verbally. But at a more pertinent level, the case meets what is eventually established as an insuperable barrier: the fact that the Knight's manner of being himself is (whatever else it may be) a manner of imitation. He lives according to books. And how can a detailed acting out of roles learned by rote ever be accepted as a bona fide form of being oneself?

Coleridge (in a passage that in a sense anticipates Ortega) once said that Don Quixote manages to take on an allegorical role without "losing the least trait of personal individuality," and Coleridge's fellow Romantic, Hazlitt (anticipating Américo Castro), thought that the characters in *Don Quixote* are "strictly individuals"; their "actions and manners" arise not from their surroundings, but "out of the peculiar dispositions of the persons themselves, operated upon by certain impulses of imagination and accident."[3] These are generous estimates, but if anyone attempts to say how they are to be understood, he will be confronted with a complete impasse. Behavior so obviously imitative in the characterization of Don Quixote is finally recalcitrant to being redefined as self-realization. The problem requires one to prove not merely that Don Quixote departs from the unexciting routines of daily life, but that the departure amounts to a qualitative difference from routine living.

No one has been more influential and more insistent than has Américo Castro in the view that would take Don Quixote's actions as personal and original rather than as merely traditional and imitative. Yet Castro's reasoning is far from persuasive. He argues that a character in acting out a role taken from a chivalry book is thereby making that role his own and is thus not merely reading passively.[4] He argues that there is a whole Oriental tradition of the written word that infuses Cervantes' novel with the concept of book as direct "incitement" in a person's existence.[5] And such acting out, such incitement, is of course bound to be intense.[6] A character who reads about and then imitates a type of behavior undergoes a sudden transformation "into an individual animated by the most unexpected motives and challenges." Chivalry is no illusion, because no separation of reading material and life is to be assumed: ". . . a person reveals his individuality while incarnating the living substance of the book into his own life."[7] The incitement from books (as one critic has expressed it) "creates a totally new private ego" in the character.[8] Castro urges us to note that Don Quixote does not merely imitate any single chivalric model; he debates with himself, for instance in the Sierra Morena (part 1, chapter 25), over how best to combine the roles of Amadís and Roland, and which of these to make dominant. Moreover, so many of the people that Don Quixote meets eventually parallel his living out of romance that it can be said that he has in a sense created the Golden Age of which he speaks in part 1, chapter 11.[9] Or so Castro maintains.

The dubious nature of these arguments may perhaps be made clearer if we take this hypothetical example: suppose one day I read a book (say, any one of the James Bond thrillers), and then the next day I go out into public view and begin a complete acting-out of the behavior prescribed in that book. To be sure, I would not be reading passively, and I would experience with great intensity. I might conceivably even be responding to the Oriental tradition of the living challenge of the written word, though I would hardly be thereby establishing the *value* of that tradition. Certainly my actions would be real and not illusions. Suppose I even combined roles I found in Dale Carnegie, Norman Vincent Peale, and "My Most Unforgettable Character." And suppose too that a great many of the people I encountered responded favorably to my behavior and even began to imitate it themselves. Would any of this really establish my "individuality"? Would anyone but the psychologically incurious accept my behavior as evidence of a suddenly acquired, totally new ego?[10] It would seem that all I would have accomplished would have been the carrying out of a vast amount of imitative behavior: that is, I would have reflected quite faithfully just what I had found in the book or books, and I would perhaps have induced other people (who needed little inducement) to do the same. To maintain that whatever I do in such a situation is highly individualistic merely because it is unexpected in terms of my previous life is surely an obtuse, nominalist approach to individuality, just as the emphasis on the combination of various imitative roles is a kind of illusory pluralism. In the Sierra Morena, it is Don Quixote himself who points out that there is no real variety in this sort of pluralism: ". . . all my actions, past, present and future," he announces, are not only rationally justifiable, but also "conform in every way to the rules of chivalry. For I know these rules better than any knights who have ever professed them in the world" (201).

Despite all critical discussion of "individuality," following rules is approximately what Don Quixote comes to, even though he follows some rules that are not taken from chivalry books so much as they are derived from the Bible and the Church. As William Entwistle pointed out (but did not develop), Don Quixote is a "mighty pedant, with rules for everything, even for falling in love."[11] And this pedantry does not decrease over the course of the action. Very late in the novel, when Quixote is captured by a band of robbers, he falls into "the gloomiest and most melancholy expression that sadness itself could assume." But his sadness, as he himself explains, is not due to being captured; it is due to having broken the rule that requires a knight-errant always to be prepared for danger (857).

In general, we would not go far wrong to take the hint given us in part 2 by the Man in Green, who says to Don Quixote: ". . . I believe that if the ordinances and laws of knight-errantry were lost they would be found in your worship's breast, as in their proper repository and archive" (579). We are left with the unexciting conclusion that the man who has soaked himself in chivalry books and who sets out to imitate chivalry books does pretty much imitate chivalry books. The process is no more self-realizing than is St. Teresa's progression through eighteen years of carefully controlled pious reading. "All that time," the saint tells us, "except immediately after taking Communion, I never ventured to start praying without a book. My soul was as much afraid to engage in prayer without one, as if it had to fight against a host. With this protection, which was like a companion and a shield on which to take the blows of my many thoughts, I found comfort. . . . But always when I was without a book, my soul would at once become disturbed, and my thoughts wandered."[12] Neither St. Teresa nor Don Quixote allow their thoughts to wander very far from the rules. Nor do the other characters (except, again, Sancho).

The qualitative difference from routine living that would be necessary for establishing positive value in Don Quixote's form of social deviation cannot, then, be based on Ortega's requirement of a man who refuses to follow custom or tradition. Far from it: certain customs and traditions (rules) seem to infuse Quixote's actions and motives so deeply that it is doubtful if he can ever be extracted from the role of chivalric actor that he seems to have taken upon himself. Perhaps, however, a shift of emphasis is in order; perhaps it will be hypothesized that following certain rules, or taking up a certain set of duties, or adopting a certain pattern of life is genuinely ennobling, if not especially individualizing. It is self-development, if not total self-definition. We need not assume that my hypothetical case of an ardent imitation of *How to Win Friends and Influence People* is actually qualitatively equivalent to Don Quixote's own project of chivalric imitation. But how are we to judge that project's quality in terms appropriate to the novel?

The novel itself suggests an approach to this difficult question. At one point in his many attempts to defend the value of his devotion to Dulcinea, the Knight asserts that her factual existence is not the real issue, for she is "the daughter of her works" (681).[13] In other words, she is as valuable as are the results produced by her function as an imagined object for devotion. The novel, in fact, contains a number of Don Quixote's attempts to demonstrate that Dulcinea is not merely good by assertion, but good in her works. "I am not trying to make anyone believe me wise when I am not," he tells the Barber, at the beginning of part 2. "I am only at pains to convince the world of its error in not reviving that most happy age in which the order of chivalry flourished" (477).[14] The Barber had been teasing the Knight with a story of a madman who, convinced that he was Neptune, impotently threatened to rain on Seville. The Knight's answer is not a retreat to pure faith; he does not say that he does not care whether he is impotent to produce results or not, but rather that his way of life would produce excellent results if only the world would listen.[15] Later on in part 2, the Knight realizes that he cannot convince the Man in Green or the "majority of people in this world" of the actual existence of knights-errant, but he does resolve to "make you see how beneficial and necessary knights-errant were to the world in past ages, and how useful they would be in the present, if they were in fashion" (583). And after going to the rescue of a distressed damsel who is actually part of a puppet play, the Knight is quick to assert that this is part of the demonstration: "I should like to have before me at this moment all who do not believe . . . that knights-errant are useful in the world" (642). He is mortified (part 1, chapter 31)

when the lad Andrew, beaten the worse because of Quixote's interference, bitterly rejects an attempt to have himself used as part of the
evidence for "the importance of knights-errant in the world to redress
the outrages and wrongs which are committed here by insolent and
wicked men" (273). And Quixote here admits that he should have
managed the redressing more sensibly (275). Only when also mortified by the Priest's quite fictitious account of the damage done by the
galley slaves that Don Quixote had freed does the Knight resort to
the claim that he has "no concern or duty . . . to investigate whether
the distressed persons . . . are brought to that pass, or suffer that
anguish, for their crimes or for their whims."[16] In point of fact,
Quixote had briefly but rather impressively interviewed the chain
gang before releasing it and had come to the conclusion that the
sufferings were undeserved.

The righting of wrongs is a serious business and is admittedly
subject to some test of actually being in the right. The claims that
knights-errant could be of use to the world are also subject to test
within this particular fictional society, as are the Knight's many
claims that he has been made greater as a human being or lived a
fuller, more meaningful life of values since beginning on his sallies.
He argues to the Canon that "since I became a knight-errant I have
been valiant, courteous, liberal, well-bred, generous, polite, bold,
gentle and patient, and an endurer of toils, imprisonments and enchantments" (442). He desires, he tells Sancho, to "write his name
in the temple of immortality, to serve as a pattern and example to
future ages" (422).

The Knight is not anxious to have his faith in Dulcinea reduced to
a mere fideism, although he does not, it is true, care to insist that she
herself exists. And the novel gives us ways to come to terms with the
claims made, both for the internal ennobling of Don Quixote that his
love for Dulcinea is supposed to produce, and for the external effects
(or rather, would-be effects, since he often lacks strength to carry out
his intentions) of the Knight's interferences in the name of his ideal
woman.

The Impulsion toward Stock Appearances

The internal ennobling of the Knight is not as difficult to examine as one might suppose, because the endlessly disputable territory of the good life is for him a clear, well-fenced pathway: "I know that the path of virtue is very narrow," he tells his niece, "and the road of vice wide and spacious" (507). For the follower of rules, the path of virtue is an arduous but conceptually settled endeavor. Not only the rules of chivalry but also its categories and its vocabulary are a part of the endeavor. The internal ennobling to sensibility and imagination should be somewhere discernible in the speech of Don Quixote, if it exists. The speeches should go beyond what can be literally traced back to such sources as chivalry books. Yet one finds few serious critical attempts to make the necessary discriminations. Although there is no shortage of critical comment concerning the world of subjective reality or the voluble rhetoric that the Knight can call into service, it is difficult—and critical practice here belies critical claims—to find any speeches of the Knight's that are not pastiches of literary materials. Even the aggrieved speech he addresses to the peasant girl whom he thinks to be Dulcinea enchanted is little more than a well-structured concatenation of stock chivalric phrases.[17] "And you, O perfection of all desire! Pinnacle of human gentleness! Sole remedy of this afflicted heart, that adores you!" Quixote's speech culminates in offers of utter "submission," "prostration," and "humility," which, after all, were inherent in his own virtuous subordination to the rules of chivalry from the outset. The Knight's usual juxtaposition of ornate language with finally fairly simple concepts is given a relieving comic coup-de-grâce here as the girl not only rejects his attentions, but refuses even to allow the Knight to help her remount: "For, stepping back a little, she took a short run, and resting both her hands on the ass's rump, swung her body into the saddle, lighter than a hawk, and sat astride like a man" (530). This burst of unpredictable vitality—which evokes from Sancho a delighted exclamation—has its comic effectiveness because it is juxtaposed with the expectations of the Knight for still another chivalric set speech from his lady. Here reality proves more interesting than the ideal.[18]

The well-known scene in which Don Quixote amazes his squire by describing in great detail the two armies that he sees instead of two herds of sheep kicking up the dust is a case in point (134–137). It is this description which Unamuno calls a "world of reality," although in his commentary, he does not describe a single detail in that world.[19] This is hardly surprising, for the world created is quite stereotyped. The explanation that Don Quixote gives to the question of why the two armies are battling is a thoroughly stock one: the Moorish king of army A refuses to change his religion in order to merit the hand of the beautiful daughter of the Christian king B.[20] Therefore, there is war. Some of the warriors' shields are described, but entirely in terms of chivalric formulae. The description is filled out with a wealth of ethnic and geographical type-casting, including "faithless Numidians, Persians famous for their bows and arrows," Arabs "with no fixed abode," and Scythians "cruel as they are fair": "in short, all whom Europe contains within its boundaries" (136–137). The "world" created here is scarcely a creation at all; the images and concepts from some predetermined life are a drastic reduction of the possibilities of reality rather than an imaginative transformation.

Long lists of praises for the virtues of Dulcinea and for the Knight following in her wake have a similar stock quality. Her beauty is "superhuman," according to the Knight, "for in her are realized all the impossible and chimerical attributes of beauty which poets give to their ladies: . . . her hair is gold; her forehead the Elysian fields; her eyebrows rainbows" (100). He contemplates her as a lady possessing "spotless beauty, dignity without pride, love with modesty, politeness springing from courtesy," and so on (680–681). These listings are in fact compilations from the love literature of the late Middle Ages,[21] but, when run together in one man's speeches, they are juxtaposed into absurdity and come out sounding more like assigned exercises in some school of oratory than like expressions of

felt devotion. I can imagine a mind concerned only with verbal performance rattling off a string of apostrophes in the manner of this ex-
cerpt—"O my lady Dulcinea del Toboso, sum of all beauty, summit
and crown of discretion, treasury of grace, store of virtue and, lastly,
pattern of all that is beneficent, modest and delightful in the world!"
(391)—but I find it hard to conceive of the Knight's mind actually
going behind the words that he speaks and connecting with the
qualities given.

This fascination with noble-sounding words, to be rolled off the
tongue at any of a thousand automatically appropriate moments, is
an important indication of the lack of depth in the Knight's offering
resistance to the customs of the everyday world. As Ortega pointed
out (a decade after *Meditations on Quixote*), Don Quixote's mind
is full, not of ideas, but of "paragraphs of stereotyped quotations";
outside this "mass of hackneyed thought . . . his mind is empty."[22] The
problem of the quality of inner and outer life is nullified by the
Knight himself, who opts for verbal surface and chivalric appearance. Despite the vast intellectual and emotional energy required
for the creation of a totally imaginary lady, the creation of Dulcinea
is carried out with regard for the real existence of neither Aldonza
(the peasant girl upon whom she is superimposed) nor any woman
at all. (It might, in fact, be described as the attempt to imagine the
human female right out of existence, to expel her from experience.)
Similarly, if there is any further depth of character or idiosyncrasy
to any of the knights Don Quixote imagines to be fighting in the
battle of the sheep, we do not hear of it; for Quixote, the surface details of pageant are enough.

Because of this indifference to the real, Don Quixote's unimaginative perceptions do indeed become "real"—that is, all the reality he
is capable of apprehending—just as the unimaginative perceptual
screen imposed by the other main characters (particularly the idealistic lovers) becomes quite "real," inasmuch as it blots out any other
possibility of the real. "Appearance"—which Dulcinea's adherents
agree to accept as the real—becomes enough for fulfilling both real

and ideal categories. It is the undeclared, built-in decomposition of idealism that underlies all the declared ideals, and that serves to prevent a recognition of their bankruptcy by the characters. The movement from everyday routine toward ideal life, which Quixote in large measure and other characters in smaller degree attempt, is in compass of the novel shown to be a way of keeping up an appearance of great and courageous involvement in human possibilities when in fact it is the sterilization of reality.

A homily by the Knight that seems to be designed to show Sancho how silly it is always to desire fame, "even if for nothing good," soon comes around to extolling the desire for fame itself, juxtaposing examples from European history (Caesar crossing the Rubicon, Cortés burning his ships in Mexico) with examples of the endeavors of knights (516–518). To be *known* as a hero is as good as being one, and, when in part 2 Cervantes uses the astonishing device of having characters who have "heard" all about part 1 come up and greet Quixote as a hero, it is not for the Knight to notice that these people usually conceive of him as a man with a reputation for madness.[23] The fame that he seeks is based only on the appearance in which the hero is presented in chronicles. It is not necessary, Don Quixote tells Sancho, to report the hero's humiliating defeats: ". . . there is no reason to record these actions which do not change or affect the truth of the story, if they redound to the discredit of the hero. Aeneas was not as pious as Virgil paints him, I promise you, nor Ulysses as prudent as Homer describes him" (488). In an earlier passage, he tells Sancho that to achieve a reputation for certain virtues it is necessary to imitate Aeneas and Ulysses, but that Virgil and Homer did not portray these heroes "as they were, but as they should have been, to serve as examples of their virtues for future generations" (202). His trip aboard the stationary wooden horse, Clavileño, Quixote can truthfully put forth as "courage, courage!" (733). And his being greeted with pretended honors by boys who see a sign reading "This is Don Quixote de la Mancha" pasted on his back can evoke from Quixote only genuine self-congratulation: "Great is the prerogative that lies in knight-errantry, since it makes its professors known and famous through all the ends of the earth" (870–871). Lip service becomes indistinguishable from the stock virtue for which it is designated.

The resuscitated Knight from the past who upholds standards that appear to be impossibly strict for his social milieu thus turns out to be the standard-bearer of the ordinary, the trite, the cliché. He has gone out of his mind in order painfully to imitate heroes (thus engaging in an imitation that might be thought to promulgate the growth of traditional masculine virtue) and has achieved the alloted fame—which is here revealed to be just as good when totally bogus! Cervantes in his indirect way conveys a sense of being very "knowing" about heroism and reveals it as an empty, as well as a self-emptying, tradition that is, as the examples from Homer and Virgil show, by no means limited to the heroes of chivalry.[24]

To be sure, being the standard-bearer of elaborate triteness is not easy. Quixote goes through trials and sufferings, but he does so with good faith that these will be rewarded with recognition of his prowess and virtue, just as the idealistic lovers suffer in the name of their own similar stock virtues. When the Ducal pair adulate Don Quixote for his entertainment value to them, he is unable to discern that they are not true believers in errantry. But, in context, this is due not merely to his trusting nature; it is also because there is no very great distance between himself, an achiever of the superficial, and them, inheritors and adulators of the superficial.

At the Ducal court, Quixote is fussed over, sprinkled with scented waters (and so are the Ducal pair sprinkled); Quixote feels for "the first time that he was positively certain of being a true and no imaginary knight-errant, since he found himself treated just as he had read these knights were treated in past ages" (667). The Duke and Duchess, after all, are lords of the realm, kin to those kings, queens, princes, and princesses who figure so prominently in Don Quixote's whole chivalric project from the very beginning as the validating personae who will receive the victorious knight and set fresh tasks for him. Such validation is only fitting in a personal mission that is defined externally to the person, defined through the stock prescripts to which the Knight is so thoroughly addicted. The great faith that the Knight has in the "outstanding virtue" of the hero-rulers like Caesar and Alexander (484) and his belief that "it is only right, then, for every prince to think more highly" of knights-errant than of courtiers (504) are corollaries of his dream of entering, by means of emulating stock but sacrosanct virtues, the lineages of the great (505–506). And, as he explains to his niece, those outside the great lineages merely exist, "since they have achieved no form of greatness that entitles them to praise."[25] To be entitled to praise is the point, rather than the seemingly objective tests of greatness and fame to which Quixote alludes in this speech to his too skeptical niece: ". . . the only families ["linajes"] which have a claim to greatness and fame are those who show it by their virtue, by their riches, and by the liberality of their members" (506). Although the Knight does go on to say that wealth alone is not a sufficient cause for greatness, later on he is so impressed with Ducal riches and generosity that he is unable to perceive the most open contradictions. Hence, even after being subjected to sadistic pinchings and scratchings at the Ducal court, he can express his desire to leave only in stock terms, not in any critical view of his stay: ". . . he thought himself guilty of a great fault in permitting himself to be shut up in idleness amidst the countless luxuries and delights[!] which the Duke and Duchess lavished on him in his character of knight-errant" (833). For a knight, of course, is not supposed to indulge in "ease, luxury, and repose" (96). The Duke's challenge of a duel is waived by Don Quixote —surely the one time in his career that the Knight turns down such a chance—because of the generous treatment the Knight feels he has received: "God forbid . . . that I should unsheathe my sword against your most illustrious person, from whom I have received such favors" (836). At the Ducal court and all through part 2, in fact, the usefulness of knights-errant is indeed proved by Don Quixote; as his aristocratic host in Barcelona, Don Antonio Moreno, points out, there is a "pleasure afforded by his extravagances" (892). At the Ducal palace, Quixote bests a puritanical ecclesiastic in a verbal encounter (676) —and then temporarily displaces him as a household guest. Apparently Quixote's society needs people who will indulge elaborately in social deviation, but leave the status quo untouched; in him it has found its man. Inevitably, it has also helped to define the quality of his inner achievements.

To believe in conflict when there is none, to believe in the existence of accomplished chivalric feats when all that is involved is a re-labelling of established values, is to take a view of the world that D. H. Lawrence was long afterwards to describe as that of the "mental-lifer." For the mental-lifer, the rule is "Out of sight, out of mind." Or, as Lawrence phrased it in *Lady Chatterley's Lover*, "Sufficient unto the moment is the *appearance* of reality."[26] And, as Lawrence would also have recognized, in a world of mind, body must suffer. We shall in fact discover that the basis of the social world of *Don Quixote* is the denial of body.

Toward Perpetual Bondage

In fulfilling his preposterous role as the attainer of ideal appearances, Don Quixote undergoes pain, sadness, and suffering. More than a few readers have identified with the sad Knight for his very suffering, and many have felt pity for his numerous physical batterings. Unamuno even thought that the whole process of undergoing ridicule, which the Knight endures, is a model for all those of us who wish to partake of "the tragic sense of life."[27] (For cautionary critics, the Knight's physical batterings are merely a harsh form of "comedy." But Cervantes goes far beyond the point of comic impact in his exploration of Quixote's physical pains.) Here at last one expects the positive quality of the Knight's quest, which I have so far found to be quite lacking, to shine with the clear moral light of victimhood and perhaps with the wisdom that is said to emerge from suffering.

When we examine the Knight's experiences of pain in their various contexts, however, we soon discover that there is a sought-for element in them. Further, we find that the Knight's evaluations of his pains always subordinate them to the greater good for which the experience is presumably being undergone. He does not mind being dubbed knight by the innkeeper, with "a sound blow on the neck, followed by a handsome stroke on the back with the Don's own sword" (45); he is as oblivious to the pain here as he is to the pain he has caused the mule driver whose head he has just smashed open (44). When beaten so badly by Toledan merchants that he is unable to get up, he decides "to resort to his usual remedy, which was to think of some passage in the books. Whereupon his madness called into his mind that part of the story of the Marquis of Mantua, when Carloto left Baldwin wounded. . . . It seemed to him to fit his present plight to a T; and so he began to roll about on the ground with every sign of intense pain" (52–53; "con muestras de grande sentimiento"). The expression of the required chivalric suffering, the "sentimiento," supersedes the actual pain. The pain itself is not allowed to penetrate into critical contact with his ideas (which it could do simply by suggesting the question, what price chivalry?).

After being toppled and bruised in his encounter against windmills, Don Quixote is most upset at the loss of his lance, for which he consoles himself by deciding that a replacement can be found in the manner of the famous knight Diego Pérez de Vargas, the "Moor-Pounder" (69; "Machuca"). When Sancho then suggests that he must be hurting, Quixote agrees, but says, "And if I do not complain of the pain, it is because a knight-errant is not allowed to complain of any wounds, even though his entrails are dropping out" (69–70). The dream of the magical "balsam" is an expression of the knight's valuation (or devaluation) of the physical body as material for the chivalric project, for with the help of the balsam the body could be sliced and smashed again and again (81). After the beating from the Yanguesans, Quixote defends his painful journey with such arguments (developed at some length here in chapter 15) as that "wounds dealt with instruments which are accidentally in the hand do not disgrace a man," and (more positively) that "wounds received in battle . . . rather confer honor than take it away" (116, 117). The pain of losing several teeth is really too much even for Quixote and he does complain (141), although he goes on (142) to assure Sancho that in the laws of errantry there are ways of adjusting "everything" ("que modos hay de composición en la orden de la caballería para todo"). After being strung up by the wrist, strappado fashion, for some time, he calls for help, but he is concerned not with having been cruelly hurt, but solely with ensuring that those who have witnessed this episode shall not think him "rightfully enchanted" (396). The three women who weep for his being abducted and carted off in a cage are assured by the Knight that "if these calamities did not befall me I should not consider myself a famous knight-errant" (419). Before long, the would-be knight-errant is battered into unconsciousness by a group of penitents, but his first words upon regaining his senses are: "He who lives absent from you, sweetest Dulcinea, is subject to greater calamities than these." Only then does he mention his shattered shoulder (455). Loyalty to Dulcinea is thus instantaneously applied to the experience of pain.

Only Don Quixote could regard being trampled by a herd of swine as "Heaven's just chastisement on a conquered knight-errant" (907). Not many chapters previous to this mishap, Quixote had also been run over by a herd of bulls, but his "vexation" in that instance had quickly been channeled into a plea for Sancho to undergo some "three or four hundred lashes" in order to speed the promised disenchantment of Dulcinea (846–848).

The instances of the swine and the bulls are both handled by Cervantes under a comic dispensation in which no very severe injury is sustained by the victim, who just gets up and goes on to the next thing. But this is not the case with an assault by a less powerful breed, a batch of cats that are sicked upon Quixote at the behest of his lovely hosts, the Duke and Duchess. The adventure of the cats leaves Quixote with a bandaged face. Yet even here his comments are not directed at the pain, but at the possible chivalric honor due him for fighting off so many cats single-handedly (764), and his main distress seems to be his unseemly appearance after being bandaged. He stays in his room for some days before venturing out again (772).

These examples show that Cervantes is not only creating the chivalric pattern of pain for a purpose, but is also creating contexts by which the pattern is revealed in its own involuted absurdity: constant appeal to the purpose blots from consciousness the full perception of the pain. Hence the ostensibly heroic choice of a trial by suffering vanishes like so much else in Don Quixote into stereotyped system. Pain thus becomes one more of the elements suffused with the unremitting critical light of Cervantes' novel.

The sought-for element is very much present in the knight's "sad" quality too. Sadness is only superficially caused by the "enchantment" or by the unavailability of Dulcinea; it is a role that is sought, and made sure by an ever-receding imaginary lady. In fact, when Sancho at first attempts to draw the Knight home by means of simply telling Don Quixote that Dulcinea has sent for him and awaits him, the Knight refuses to comply: ". . . he was determined not to appear in her beauteous presence until he had done deeds worthy of her favor" (250). When spirited off in the cage by the Priest and the Barber, he is said to be consoled by the (mock) prophecy that he will be brought to Dulcinea, who will then marry him and produce "the whelps, his sons, to the everlasting glory of La Mancha" (417). But this "miraculous mating" (as the Barber describes it) does not seem to hold Quixote's interest for long. He prays that the prophecy be fulfilled, but goes on to say that in any case he will count his imprisonment as a good: "But, however that [the outcome of the prophecy] may be, I shall account the pains of my prison glory, these chains which bind me comfort, and this litter upon which I am laid no hard field of battle, but a soft couch and happy marriage-bed" (417). A little later, he allows Sancho to persuade him to go back to his village and plan a new expedition, apparently forgetting all about the prophecy and its promised union with Dulcinea (455).

Prior to Dulcinea's "enchantment" (again due to a ruse by Sancho) in part 2, Quixote is seeking her out, not especially as a love object, but so that she may bless him in his endeavors of knighthood (515, 524), although he is also interested in an elaborate decoding game by which he will interpret whether Dulcinea exhibits any of the signs of love that chivalric ladies are supposed to display (525). He waits for Sancho's return "full of sad and troubled fancies" (525) rather than with a lover's hopefulness; he continues his waiting by "uttering countless amorous lamentations" (527); and he is ambivalent in his response (happy-sad) even when Sancho tells him that Dulcinea is on the way: "See that you do not deceive me, or seek to cheer my real sadness with false joys" (528). Quixote is already laboring in the role of the sad knight before the enchantment. Later on he can lament still more hopelessly: "I shall live in perpetual tears till I see her in her pristine state" (682).

This sadness is all part of the chivalric project, and in no way crippling to his pursuit of it; sadness and chivalric joy are juxtaposed. In fact, a few chapters after the enchantment scene, in which he swears that now he is "the most unfortunate of men," Don Quixote is in a state of extreme elation over his success in one of his adventures (560, 562). The sadness is likely to return at any time, but its quality is hardly that of the authentic suffering it first appears to be. For example, some earthenware jars made in Dulcinea's village are sufficient to recall her to his mind, but only in terms of the opening lines of Garcilaso's tenth sonnet. In those terms, she is "the sweet pledge" ("la dulce prenda") of his "great bitterness" (580; "mi mayor amargura!"). The fact that Dulcinea appears in the Knight's Montesinos cave vision still in her rejecting, duping, and enchanted form (621–623) does not detract in the slightest from the great delight that the vision gives him. And when, in one of the elaborate Ducal *burlas*, a girl pretending to be Dulcinea speaks only long enough to deliver a vituperative speech at Sancho, in which she demands that he at once "lash, lash, that thick hide," Don Quixote is obtuse to the possibility that his "sweet pledge" has turned out to be something of a bitch (702), just as he fails to draw any conclusions from the fact that she appears side by side with another figure who is "the very shape of

Death, fleshless and hideous" (699). At the very end of the novel, it finally becomes evident that Dulcinea will never be disenchanted, that she will never appear (930–931), but Don Quixote just moves on to fresh plans to adulate her in his projected pastoral adventures (933). There is no clear implication in the text (despite a frequent critical disposition to find one) that Don Quixote's death is caused by a realization that Dulcinea is mere illusion.[28]

The implication that Don Quixote's pain and sadness involve an abdication of self and not self-assertion is reinforced by another sub-theme (which accords well with the tendency to submit to pain), the tendency to submit to events themselves. Rocinante chooses the road that the Knight will take (164);[29] any boat found along a river bank is a requirement for the Knight to get in and let it take him where it will (477, 656); knights-errant are required to battle their enemies "in all perils and on all occasions" (503); every knight has to defend the honor of "all women of whatever rank" (200). In a plot summary of a book of chivalry, Quixote lists, as part of the "universal delight" that the tale affords, the action of the knight who obeys a command from some hidden voice to plunge into a lake of boiling hot pitch, full of serpents, snakes, and lizards: "No sooner has the knight heard this dreadful voice than he abandons all thought for himself, and without reflecting on the peril to which he is exposing himself, or even easing himself of the weight of his ponderous armor, he commends himself to God and his lady, dives into the middle of the boiling lake" (440). This notion of the plunge is repeated in the address to Dulcinea that the Knight makes before entering the cave of Montesinos—"I am about to cast myself, to plunge and bury myself, in the abyss which opens here before me" (613)— an action calculated to be most pleasing to Dulcinea. Once in the cave, he claims to have been "suddenly and involuntarily" put into a deep sleep, and awakens to meet the enchanted inhabitants. Soon Montesinos indifferently explains: "How or why [Merlin] enchanted us no one knows, but that will be told in the course of time, and before very long now, I imagine" (617).

This pattern of submission is continually juxtaposed with the evidence of the Knight's stock mentality to imply a spurious air of openness to his wanderings. He will make no choice; he will let fate itself send him the adventures he wishes. But, at the same time, he carries about with him a set of attitudes that makes all adventures into repetitions of the same worn patterns.

If this openness toward chance and adventure is deceptive, so is the element of choice that Don Quixote appears to exercise in his selection of possible patterns to imitate from among his chivalric heroes. The direction to which Quixote gravitates in these choices becomes a curiously circuitous path toward still more pain. Cervantes of course knew his chivalric sources thoroughly, minutely; and yet, in one of Quixote's defenses of the way of pain and suffering, the Knight offers as evidence to Sancho the story of how Amadís was once given two hundred lashes with the reins of his own horse (115). This incident, as John Ormsby pointed out, is not to be found in the *Amadís* cycle.[30] And we notice later on that lashing becomes a special interest of the novel, an obsession of Quixote's. (To be sure, the Knight is *directed* to develop his interest in lashing; it is part of the scheme to disenchant Dulcinea. But there is a thematic intersection in this choice of method that is made highly significant in the novel's context.)

This deviation from source has some bearing on our understanding of the Knight's character, since it shows him choosing in the direction of pain, even beyond the demands of his chivalry books. But another change is equally important: in chivalric literature it is the custom of maidens in castles to strip the visiting hero of his armor and to bathe him. (In fact, the late chivalric romance tended to feature a hero who was erotically adventurous—much to the distress of moralist readers.)[31] Now Don Quixote is aware of the chivalric custom of being stripped and bathed (39, 441), but he himself resists it with determination when the occasion arises—twice—at the Ducal palace (669, 748).[32] Quixote's exercise of choice is toward the chaste, ultimately even toward the ascetic.[33]

It is relevant to recall here that, prior to becoming a knight, Don Quixote had admired the peasant girl Aldonza for some twelve years, although he saw her (and apparently from a distance) only four times (208). The Knight makes this admission in chapter 25 of part 1 as part of an interchange between Sancho and himself regarding the act of penance Don Quixote is to perform in honor of Dulcinea, a project that will enable him, he thinks, to "attain the utmost perfection and renown of which a knight-errant is capable" (201). In this chapter, Sancho's delight and amazement in discovering that there is a real girl, Aldonza (whom Sancho knows), behind the image of Dulcinea, is juxtaposed with the Knight's determined (and predetermined) arguments that show his own need for some act of self-immolation, some demonstration of fidelity to Dulcinea, irrespective of what Aldonza may happen to be like as a person.[34] The ladies of chivalry, Quixote explains, were not "really flesh-and-blood ladies ["damas de carne y hueso"]. . . . Most of them were invented to serve as subjects for verses, and so that the poets might be taken for lovers, or men capable of being so" (210; "por hombres que tienen valor para serlo").

In determining the precise form of penance required by this particular dream woman, Don Quixote is able to exercise a degree of choice in selecting from chivalric patterns. He debates quite seriously with himself whether to imitate "Roland's downright madness or Amadís' melancholy moods" (214). To imitate the former would involve butting his head against rocks, and otherwise inflicting injuries upon himself, whereas the latter calls for efforts limited mostly to verbal actions. And, for once, Don Quixote chooses the less physically painful course of action. He recites a great number of Ave Marias, and (in place of Amadís' being shriven by a hermit priest) he writes a great number of verses. But the apparent choice of lesser pain is deceptive. His madness (and the accompanying ritual of submission to the ideal woman) is not to be taken as simply suicidal. The imbibing of pain is to be far more extended and involuted; and it is defined with increased precision in this particular scene.

The one Don Quixote poem given here is a parody by Cervantes, but it should not be dismissed simply because it is in that category; some of its details show Quixote, alone in the mountains—one of those rare times in the novel when Sancho is not with the Knight—revealing more about the nature of his need for Dulcinea than he usually does. The poem is a lament for the absence of Dulcinea, but it leads up to an image of love as a whip:

> Hirióle Amor con su azote,
> No con su blanda correa;
> Y en tocándole el cogote,
> Aquí lloró Don Quixote ...

("Love struck Don Quixote with his lash—not with his soft strap; and when love touched the back of his neck, then Don Quixote wept.")

This is another early premonition of the lashing that will become so important in part 2, as well as a significantly painful imagery of love, selected from many poetic conventions. The middle verse of the poem is even more interesting, because it seems to hint at an admission of a reversal in the chivalric or courtly pattern; the penance is not really an approach to Dulcinea, but a retreat from her:

> Es aquí el lugar adonde
> El amador más leal
> De su señora se esconde,
> Y ha venido a tanto mal
> Sin saber cómo o por dónde.

("Here is where the most faithful lover hides from his lady; and he has to come to such great misfortune without knowing how or along what road")[35]

Thus the adventure in the Sierra Morena seems to reinforce further the Knight's penchant for painfully attaining an ideal that is all appearance; "Amadís of Gaul," Quixote knows, "achieved an unrivalled reputation as a lover" (215) through such verbal penances as Quixote chooses to perform. But the poem itself suggests that beyond the formula by which a Knight is not to reach the object of his desires there is a wish to keep away from any such object.

In the Sierra Morena, Quixote is alone and free from such resistance as he meets from other people throughout the novel. A comparable passage, and one that delves even more directly into his deepest wishes, is the vision in the cave of Montesinos, which is either the knight's improvisation or pure dream. More likely it is a dream, because the powers of improvisation needed seem to be quite beyond anything displayed elsewhere by Don Quixote in the novel; moreover, his own later questions concerning the truth or falsity of what he has seen in the cave never imply a concession of improvising (637, 735, 874),[36] though they would be compatible with the hypothesis that he has confused a dream experience with waking reality.

Presumably, the wish-fulfillment in dreams is not absent from Don Quixote's unconscious any more than from anyone else's, and presumably his subconscious is capable of envisoning Dulcinea in her disenchanted, loving state. But of course no such thing happens; she is envisioned in just the opposite mode—rejecting, mocking, and in cheapened circumstances—*but the Knight is well satisfied with the vision all the same.* It is, he declares, "the sweetest existence and most delightful vision any human being ever enjoyed or beheld" (614). Yet he goes on immediately to juxtapose a renunciation of life's pleasures with a full list of the miseries he has seen: "Now, indeed, I positively know that the pleasures of this life pass like a shadow and a dream, and wither like the flowers of the field. Oh, unhappy Montesinos! O gravely wounded Durandarte! O luckless Belerma! O tearful Guadiana, and you, unfortunate daughters of Ruidera, who show by your waters what tears your fair eyes have wept!"(614). This overall evaluation of the vision indicates that the statement he makes to the dreamed Dulcinea ("I am grieved in the spirit at her troubles") is, as it appears to be, *pro forma,* for certainty he is not grieved by the vision at all. The more likely point, once again, is the vow to keep going in the quest for disenchantment: "I swear . . . not to rest, and to travel the seven portions of the earth more diligently than did Don

Pedro of Portugal, until I have released her from her enchantment" (623). To which Dulcinea's messenger replies, "All that and more your worship owes my lady."

This infinite regress into endless servitude instead of movement toward fulfillment is exactly the spirit of the major episode of the Montesinos vision itself, the story of Durandarte. Durandarte has been lying in a state of deep-freeze, enchanted since the battle of Roncevalles, in an alabaster sepulchre that displays not the usual replica of a knight made of brass, marble, or jasper, but one "of pure flesh and bone" (616). Some wish of Don Quixote's own for the metamorphosis of living body into totally dormant substance is suggested by his glowing description here; he is well aware of the displacement of marble by marblelike flesh. The reclining knight's heart has at his own request been cut out by his friend Montesinos, who, after thoughtfully salting it so that it would not smell, has presented it to Durandarte's lady, Belerma. That this is the true and "delightful" consummation of Durandarte's dream is indicated by his laconic reaction to the possibility of never being disenchanted: "Patience and shuffle the cards" (618).

This aphorism in turn functions dramatically, in the Montesinos vision, as the signal for the introduction of a procession of "most lovely women," all of them sobbing and groaning. The women are members of a perpetual-grief society, centered around the lady Belerma who carries the mummified heart; led by her the women hover in mournful dirge, four days a week, over the knight Durandarte's "body and afflicted heart" (618–619). Participation in a procession of this kind is the highest attainment possible for a woman in the Dulcineated world. And Durandarte's encasement in a coffin, his heart finally cut out, his body neither eating, sleeping, nor defecating (620)—physical aspects of life that Quixote denigrates— is revealed here in the Knight's unconscious as the height of chivalric manliness, the dream or archetype or self-image behind the appearances of virtue that obtain in Quixote's daylight world.[37]

Manuel Durán, a critic who has recognized that the central details of the Montesinos vision are so brutally antipoetic that they render utterly absurd the Knight's idealistic loyalties, goes on to say that this only redounds to the Knight's favor. For Don Quixote comes out of it all with his faith still far greater than his doubts. Indeed, according to Durán, Quixote is not only fending off the social world and the world of physical reality; he is now also fighting the revelations of his own unconscious mind, which have shown that even his ideals do not exist in their reputed inner purity. In this interpretation, Durán is echoing Salvador de Madariaga's contention that although Don Quixote is aware, finally, that he has an "inner enemy," an undercurrent of doubt concerning his whole way of life, he is nonetheless more admirable for fighting off this doubt.[38] Loyalty to the ideal of conscious will power can go no further than these two critics carry it. In a conflict between ideal and real (or spirit and flesh), ideal and spirit must win out by sheer force of will—or so they would have it—even if the illumination that the particular fiction gives is plainly to show that what is being won is perpetual bondage to prescribed forms of pain, sadness, suffering, and self-evasion.

One must return to the scene itself. As Durán himself points out, the symbolic action of the scene shows the absurdity of the main chivalric ideals. Why, for instance, should a Belerma mourn constantly for a Durandarte when she could instead be at his side, a few paces away?[39] Cervantes has created a grotesque revelation; Belerma and Durandarte, like Quixote himself, are evading the self-knowledge their various situations afford. Their personal commitments to defend the truth of cultural ideals become entangled instead in avoiding truth entirely. Faith becomes, in Cervantes' novel, bad faith, and loyalty to one's ideal image becomes disloyalty to one's total self.

That joy may come out of sorrow and that suffering lovers somehow suffer *toward* something are themes of Western literature from Aeschylus on through Tasso and beyond.[40] And in the Knight's fictional milieu, we find analogies outside chivalry, as in his own statement that "whosoever humbleth himself, God doth exalt" (85), and "penances . . . are all good" (626). *Don Quixote* explores this theme (or bundle of themes) in the specific context of what the theme becomes when it has been thoroughly acculturated and standardized—in other words, when it has become Dulcineated, if, indeed, it ever was anything else. Like the ideals of the Knight, his pain and his sorrow exist only so that they may be perpetuated further. They become goals in themselves, stock roles blithely masquerading as the height of life's possibilities. The possible emergence of real value from the experience of pain—and I have no intention of issuing some sort of blanket condemnation of such a possibility—is thus truncated. Dulcinea has converted it to a prescription.

The Psychology of Renunciation, and Three Stubborn Women

One would gather from criticism that Don Quixote's progression toward bondage is inexplicable in psychological terms.[41] Most commentators see the Knight either as the assertion of the personality free to take its own road to fulfillment or (as in the cautionary readings) as an object suitable for reformation to solid Christian mores. Few critics venture even the defensive statement one finds in Erich Auerbach's *Mimesis*:

A modern psychologist might find . . . explanations of Don Quixote's strange madness. . . . But this sort of approach to the problem has no place in Cervantes' thinking. Confronted with the question of the causes of Don Quixote's madness, he has only one answer: Don Quixote read too many romances of chivalry and they deranged his mind. That this should happen to a man in his fifties can be explained—from within the work—only in aesthetic terms, that is, through the comic vision which came to Cervantes when he conceived the novel: a tall, elderly man, dressed in old-fashioned and shabby armor, a picture which is beautifully expressive not only of madness but also of asceticism and the fanatic pursuit of an ideal. We simply have to accept the fact that this cultured and intelligent country gentleman goes suddenly mad—not, like Ajax or Hamlet, because of a terrible shock—but simply because he has read too many romances of chivalry.[42]

Now it is true that the *donnée* of the novel is a fictive kind of madness, not something for a merely medical diagnosis.[43] Moreover, Quixote's derangement is so nearly the central *donnée* of the book that it does little good to attempt to explain it in any psychological detail. One can only see what Cervantes does with his *donnée*, and at that level psychological explanation is very feasible. There are quite "within the work," and having an undeniable (though possibly not conscious) "place in Cervantes' thinking," psychological implications that are surely as clear as any such implications can ever be in a novel. To ignore them avoids the basic implications of the novel, and requires a suppression of the critical intelligence itself. Rather than being the machinations of the modern psychologist, psychological explanation is only the result of not trying to fend off psychology when reading the text. Why, after all, should Cervantes be less able to intuit a psychology in depth than his contemporary Shakespeare was able to do, say, in *Othello*?[44]

Don Quixote struggles desperately to attain a fame that is little else than a conventional badge of merit, handed out in almost flagrant indifference to the fact that it is all a matter of appearance. Yet his struggle involves great self-sacrifice and certainly does not involve an *awareness* of the ludicrous combination of ideal goals and surface fulfillment. The novel finally equates goal and appearance, and Quixote even manages to state the equation at times, but this is all one can say insofar as "appearance" is to be taken as his motivation. The novel juxtaposes not only overt ideals and their covert transformation into the goal of appearance, but also the deeper portrayal of what Don Quixote does to himself.

What appears first as the *donnée* of a character with a merely typological manner of perceiving (the limitation to the rules of chivalry and to other cultural prescripts of a more general, Christian, and European origin)[45] is eventually carried to such lengths that one realizes the nature of its psychological energy. For Don Quixote to expend such enormous energy in order to remain imperceptive is very hard work. It is repression. And Don Quixote becomes the first "real" character in fiction, not only in the usual honorific sense, which implies a character who is drawn with full complexity, but also in the sense of having a realistic psychological basis for his typological behavior. If he could but devote even a fraction of his psychic energy to seeing rather than to denying the bearing of his actions and speeches, he would dissolve in an instant the shallow appearance of success in preserving the integrity of ideals. But to come to such recognition would imply a radical denial of his whole pattern of life, just as it would imply a denial of the culture around him.

A project calling for rigid adherence to a set of stock responses and of submission to pain for its own sake necessarily implies some massive self-denial within the character himself. In Don Quixote there is, to state the case flatly, a denial of all sensual pleasure, especially of erotic pleasure. He is the attainer of the merely verbal pleasures of being adulated and accepted as the knight he wants to be, a man who can be *called* courageous, virtuous, and deeply in love. The enormously prestigious received cultural values that define the good man as the unselfish one are shown at work in the Knight's personality, producing a selflessness in him that approaches the impossible goal inherent in a morality of sensual renunciation.

The novel makes evident the futility of such a goal, not because the goal is unattainable, but because it is shown to be stultifying. (I of course do not mean that *Don Quixote* is a recommendation of a countercourse in virility for the aging Knight. Renunciation has gone so far in him that such advice would be beside the point.) The novel is therefore inextricably engaged in the most radical kind of culture criticism. Not only do the cultural ideals extract the painful repressive costs that Freud was later to outline; they also stand revealed as creators of a way of life that is farcical, incurably superficial, and, in the overall critical context of the novel, clearly not worth maintaining. And because this world of superficiality shows every sign of nonetheless maintaining itself indefinitely, an inflexible comic character like Don Quixote, who embodies the ideals in all their essential arbitrariness, is perfectly apt.

Don Quixote's program of renunciation is made manifest by the novel. Indications are more clear than the listing, among other goals of errantry, the desire to "slay indulgence and lust," along with the other deadly sins (518). In his defense of knight-errantry against the accusations of uselessness made by the ecclesiastic at the Ducal court, Quixote, in one of the passages usually cited as showing his mental and rhetorical prowess, declares: "I am in love, only because knights-errant are obliged to be so; and being so, I am not one of those depraved lovers, but of the continent and platonic sort" (675). The ecclesiastic had not mentioned love, but the explanation is given without asking. For Don Quixote, it represents an obvious merit. Don Quixote declares that he has never had a thought of marrying (608), but this is only consistent with his Dulcineism. Aside from his repeating the happy ending in the plot summary of the chivalric tale (441–442) and his hopes for getting his lineage started, the novel is remarkably sparse in statements showing the Knight's hope for union with his lady. When Quixote rejects the offer of marriage with Dorothea-Micomicona, he seems to be ready to kill Sancho for daring to disagree with his decision (262–266);[46] but there is no direct statement that he intends to marry Dulcinea. Only assertions of continued obedience and loyalty are to be found: "For, so long as my memory is engrossed, my heart captive and my mind enthralled by that ["a aquella"] . . . I say no more; it is impossible that I could so much as think of marriage, even with the Phoenix" (263; ellipsis in the original). Quixote's rage at Sancho at this point may also be connected with the *way* Sancho has described Dorothea: "I wish all the fleas in my bed were as good" (262). Don Quixote is deeply concerned too that, in the recording of his exploits, the chronicler take care not to impugn his celibate love (485–486), and he is much reassured when informed that this hope has been fulfilled (487). His vow of penances that he takes because of the loss of his helmet (81–82, 142)—a loss he interprets in his own way—is also clear in its emphasis upon sexual denial: the Knight vows "not to eat bread at table, nor lie with his wife—and some other things" (82; the other things are never specified). The same vow is alluded to favorably by the Knight in his Montesinos vision, just before his own vow of endless questing.

In Don Quixote's apostrophe to the Golden Age, so often cited as the embodiment of the better world he wishes to resurrect, he is careful to insist on propriety: "Then did the simple and lovely shepherdesses go from valley to valley and from hill to hill, with their tresses loose, and without more clothes than were needed to cover modestly what modesty requires, and has always required, to be concealed" (86). He goes on to say that these girls could give up their virginities by their own "will and desire," but the language he chooses is heavily moralistic: "y su perdición nacía de su gusto y propia voluntad." He then goes on to indicate, through his choice of words, that sex is a kind of disease one has to do one's best to fend off: "But now, in this detestable age of ours, no maiden is safe even though she be hidden in the centre of another Cretan labyrinth; for even there, through some chink or through the air, by dint of its accursed persistence, the plague ["pestilencia"] of love gets in and brings them to ruin despite their seclusion" (86). Shortly after this, Quixote hears of a woman who is considered just such a plague-bringer (94) because her beauty is the excuse for men to become pastoral, suffering lovers, but when he realizes that Marcela is really fanatically pure, a women who has vowed never to marry any one but "to live in perpetual solitude" until only "the earth would enjoy the fruit of [her] chastity and the spoils of [her] beauty" (109), he immediately comes to her rescue. Quixote declares this woman worthy of a special distinction, "for she has proved that she is the only woman living with such pure intentions" (110). He even attempts to seek her out and "offer her all the service in his power" (111). Three chapters from the end, the Knight is still living in a world requiring correction for its unfortunate sensuality. In response to two paintings, one showing Dido and Aeneas, and the other the Rape of Helen, he regrets that he could not have been on hand to avenge these ladies, although there is "one noticeable difference" in the two pictures: "Helen went with no very ill grace, for she was slyly smiling to herself, but the fair Dido was shown dropping tears as big as walnuts from her eyes" (924). But Don Quixote does not wish to see this difference; to him the true goal of all women is conventional purity, whether the women happen to agree or not.

Only Sancho would consider describing Don Quixote's lady in physical terms, rather than literary ones (262); only the dim-witted coiners of epitaphs could think to remark on Dulcinea's high bosom (459, 460). Sancho's claim that the supposed princess Micomicona is really not a princess, because, if she were, "she wouldn't go kissing with somebody in this company every time anyone turns his head, and round every corner" (413), provokes Don Quixote to such rage that he actually dismisses Sancho on the spot; he is only dissuaded when Dorothea urges that the kissing was undoubtedly some illusion fomented by evil enchanters (414). A princess obviously could not be kissing.

Quixote attains his goal of being one of the "platonic sort" of Knights, but only by settling for the painfully preserved appearance of chastity, much as his other attainments are eventually shown as mere appearances. Cervantes shows that it is a self-denigrating task for the Knight to attempt to smother his sexual feelings for various women, even toward the unattractive old waiting-woman, Doña Rodriguez, or toward the flat-nosed, large-mouthed Altisidora (753), whose appearance is something like that of the peasant girl Quixote has pronounced unutterably ugly in the episode of Dulcinea's enchantment. Finally Quixote is able to lay claim truthfully to the *record* of chastity in and for itself: the conventional definition of chastity is thus fulfilled.

The episodes in which Quixote comes into contact with real women are the novel's way of showing the significance of his platonic renunciation in terms of internal cost. They are also vital to the novel's meaning because they show that the Knight's dedication to Dulcinea is an act of will that does not represent his entire self. Only a *portion* of Don Quixote has "created" Dulcinea and the role of following her demands; the huge remaining segment of the follower of Dulcinea—

namely, his body—is repressively omitted from the project except as material to be painfully eliminated. "Leave me in peace, unwelcome thoughts," Quixote says (872), but somehow they never do. From the first encounter with Maritornes (122–123), from the Altisidora and the Doña Rodriguez episodes, a pattern emerges: the Knight convinces himself that these women wish to sleep with him; he steels himself to resist, and then half completes his own wish by violating his resolution at the same time that he repeats it. The pattern is analogous to the idealistic love scenes in other sections of the book. It shows a failure to do more than deform sensual impulses in the attempts to extinguish them.

In the first Maritornes episode, it is made clear that, although Don Quixote steels himself to resist, "deciding in his heart" to remain faithful to Dulcinea, it is he, more than Maritornes, who initiates the action. He "stretched out his arms to receive his beauteous maiden"; then, "gripping her tight," be begins a set speech on why he cannot satisfy her desires. The carrier discerns that Maritornes is trying to get away while Quixote is "trying to hold her." Quixote refers, in fact, to his interchange with Maritornes as "sweet and amorous colloquy" (125), and, as he leaves the inn, he emits a "sigh which seemed to be torn from the depths of his bowels, and which everyone thought must be from the pain in his ribs" (129). But the sigh is for the inn-keeper's daughter, whom he imagines to have been the princess he had addressed when grabbing Maritornes.[47] The first Maritornes episode thus is the closest Quixote comes in the novel to allowing his impulses, which evidently would override the decision he thinks he has made in his heart, to struggle free. The rest of the time, he manages to make his set speeches do their duty in keeping him split between impulse and action.

His success is shown in the Altisidora episode. Several of its details indicate that the effort involves both exporting his Dulcineism to others, whether they appreciate it or not, and deluding himself about the nature of the encounter. Quixote is determined to resist this young girl, no matter how beautiful she may be (772). And he does resist,

but only by going through an elaborate exercise in self-control. After
hearing Altisidora's song, he bemoans the sad fate of being sexually
irresistible and asserts that "for Dulcinea alone I am dough and sugar
paste, but for all others I am flint . . ." An indication of the intensity
of his struggle is given in another of the comparisons he uses (for
once not a chivalric formula): ". . . I must be Dulcinea's—roasted or
boiled . . ." Even these assurances to himself need to be topped with
a nervous action: ". . . he banged the window to and, fretful and
heavy-hearted, as if some great disaster had befallen him, lay down
on his bed" (754). And on another evening, he composes a ballad for
the enamored girl, full of advice on the dangers of love, on the ad-
vantages of sewing as a counterirritant to idleness, on the shallowness
of infatuations, and, of course, on Dulcinea's supremacy (762–763).
Explaining the episode to Sancho later on, Quixote asserts in typical
juxtaposition that love observes no bounds in its desires *and* that
Altisidora admired him for his chastity and good behavior (841).
The standardized nature of all this moralizing and its affinity with
renunciation of the sensual are plain.[48] The Knight's dream of
Dulcinea is just a few steps away from what his society would in
any event prescribe for every girl, and this is brought out further
when Don Quixote—after being told flatly that Altisidora had only
been pretending in all her protestations of love—merely repeats
without change his advice that she be put to work and kept out of
trouble (918–919).

Don Quixote's missions, which are all parts of his attempt to bring
back what he regards as a Golden Age, follow a chivalric program
designed to "defend maidens, relieve widows, and succor the orphans
and the needy" (87; the virtuous Marcela, incidentally, is an orphan).
The case of the widow is mentioned in Quixote's speech on courage:
"It is a braver sight, I say, to see a knight-errant succoring a widow
in some lonely spot than a courtier knight wooing a maiden in cities"
(578). The preference for the nonerotic is carried out in the Knight's
actual contact with a widow, Doña Rodriguez, the waiting-woman
at the Ducal palace. But the widow is herself so concerned with

sexual purity that she and Quixote have trouble even staying in the same room.[49] At the beginning of the scene (part 2, chapter 48) Quixote is still afraid that it is Altisidora who is trying to get into his room, and he delivers aloud a speech of fidelity to his Dulcinea, in order to discourage the young girl. But instead of Altisidora, the waiting-woman, dressed with "a white pleated veil, so long that it covered and swathed her from head to foot," enters. Quixote himself is "enveloped from head to foot in a yellow satin quilt, a nightcap on his head," and with bandages on his face, the result of his recent misadventure with the scratching cats (773). After assuring each other that they are not phantoms from purgatory or other apparitions, they also have to reassure each other of asexuality: ". . . I must inform you," Quixote announces, "that I am good for no one, thanks to the peerless beauty of my lady Dulcinea del Toboso."

But despite the waiting-woman's reassurances, Quixote is troubled by "a thousand thoughts" concerning the danger he is in; he is very concerned lest this temptation "arouse my sleeping desires and cause me, after all these years, to fall where I have never stumbled" (774). Even the thought that after all Doña Rodriguez is white-veiled, fat, bespectacled, and hence unable to "arouse any lecherous thought in the most depraved breast in world" does not suffice; he has to get assurances again (775), for, as he admits finally, "I am not made of marble nor you of brass . . ." After all these preparations, the two of them walk chastely, hand in hand, "from the door to the bed." Dulcinea has become quite abstract since Quixote's admission that she is based on the peasant girl Aldonza in part 1, chapter 25,[50] but here in part 2, chapter 48 the gross demands of the human body are still as insistent as ever, once there is the slightest chance of their being wakened.

The denouement is comic, for the waiting-woman is trying to undo a seduction, not provoke one. By part 2, chapter 60, Sancho can declare with truth, as the Knight once more takes up the cudgels for still another seemingly betrayed (and actually lethal) maiden: "My master's a very good hand at matchmaking" (859). Even Don

Quixote's legal will, sometimes exhibited as evidence of his recovery into sanity, is hardly free of the matchmaker's mentality, for it specifies that his niece shall be disinherited if she marries the wrong kind of man (938). (Or, perhaps the will amounts to the novel's delayed joke; by proscribing any male who even so much as knows "what books of chivalry are," Quixote is ruling out all the eligible males in the novel's fictional context.)

It is finally curiously appropriate for Quixote to go to the rescue of an enchanted "Antonomasia," a maiden whose name itself is a figure of speech that substitutes for a proper name (716). The Lady Belerma, in the cave of Montesinos, is willing to parade in endless grief for her disemboweled knight, Durandarte. Dulcineas, Antonomasias, and Belermas are very much needed by the idealist mind as guarantees of that perpetual distance from the flesh which it seeks. And in the fictional society of the novel the pressure toward becoming the ideal woman is applied to any real women who happen to appear. Cervantes easily violates any naturalistic probability by having so many of his female characters appear as stunning beauties— and then shows that such beauty makes no difference anyway. The beautiful maidens—the one intimation, in the fictional milieu of the novel, that an age of deeply pleasurable romance could still be created (I am indebted to Wayne Burns for this observation)—are treated exactly as if they were standard candidates for marriage. The creation of Dulcinea is a great act of nonimagination, an assertion of the arbitrary and uniform where all variety would otherwise be.

The famous passage in which the Knight, hard pressed by Sancho's questioning, admits that in his imagination he draws Dulcinea as he would have her be (210) is preceded by an anecdote that subtly illustrates the opposite of his own position:

Once upon a time there was a beautiful widow, young, gay, rich and not a bit prudish, who fell in love with a stout and lusty young lay-brother. His superior heard of it and addressed the good widow one day by way of brotherly reproof: "I am astonished, madam," he said, "and with good reason, that a woman of your quality, beautiful and rich as you are, should have fallen in love with such a coarse, low, ignorant fellow as So-and-So, seeing that we have so many graduates, divinity students, and theologians in this house, and you could pick and choose any of them like pears, and say: "I like this one and not that one." But she answered most gaily and impudently: "You are much mistaken, my dear sir, and very old-fashioned in your ideas, if you think I have made a bad choice in that fellow, idiot though he may seem, seeing that for all I want of him he knows as much philosophy as Aristotle, and more." (210)

But it does not follow, as Quixote himself thinks, that his Dulcineating of Aldonza the peasant girl is similar in nature to the reasons given by the young widow, unless one holds that it is quite the same thing to value people *for themselves,* apart from their roles as graduate or divinity student, as it is to value them *for their fulfillment of abstract requirements,* which Aldonza, in herself, does not meet.

Yet it could hardly be otherwise under the reign of Dulcinea. If life requires a channeling of all its energies into received cultural values, there could be nothing more threatening to such a channeling than sexuality. As a theological commentator on *Don Quixote* reminds us: ". . . sexual instinct revolts against the limitations of morals."[51] What Don Quixote does is expressed through his particular form of madness, but the most basic psychological level that Cervantes shows in him is a kind of renunciation that Quixote shares with any number of other characters and that is (as Freud showed) an inevitable part of the making of culture, at least as the term *culture* has been understood. Whether the renunciation is admirable or worthwhile or not is a question it will not do to discuss in general. One can only say that Cervantes has brilliantly shown it to be quite worthless within the context of his own novel.

Hence it is not just Don Quixote who is mad. Nor does the novel allow us to think that this madness is a higher form of wisdom. So fully does it show that Don Quixote's way of life is a denial of all personal emotion and individualized desire that it renders untenable this standard Romantic interpretation. For if Romanticism was the demand, among other things, for a high valuation of intense personal urges and, eventually, for their fulfillment, Dulcineism is the plainest example of pseudo-Romanticism. Cervantes, in creating a comic-satiric critique of the emotional elaboration of well-gilded stock responses, was being more Romantic than the poets of the nineteenth century were quite prepared to dream. And what was later to be considered the Romantic "Will" of Quixote is given its severest deflation, within the novel, through his three encounters with live women.

Maritornes, Altisidora, and Doña Rodriguez are placed within the novel in such a way as to invalidate the philosophical pretensions of the idealist reading, just as the overall pattern of superficial appearance becoming the novel's overbearing reality also invalidates that reading. It will not do simply to quote Heidegger on the way Being and Appearance are "changing unceasingly into the other," as a recent existential-phenomenological critic of *Quixote* has done. Being and appearance, at least within this novel, are not as manipulable as such critics would like them to be. Don Quixote's bodily being is finally intractable to idealization; no amount of devotion to Dulcinea is ever able to subdue the offending flesh. The attempt to effect such a victory over the flesh places the Knight within a psychological role that cannot be disguised by any arguments (however interesting or attractive) concluding that "el espíritu es libre y se crea sus propias posibilidades."[52] *Don Quixote* may indeed be a novel whose subject is what is traditionally called "spirit," but, if so, it refuses to follow the critics in making spirit the essence of man.

Changing the World

Still, from Don Quixote's own point of view, and from that of many of the novel's critics, there is finally a justification for Dulcinea's works, or at least for her intentions, that allows us to dismiss or discount her preference for stock response and her basis in a psychology of renunciation. To defend the helpless is an impulse one dare not cynically disregard, particularly since that impulse may lie behind the greatest ideal of all, that of justice. Give up the impulse toward even the "hare-brained justice" of Don Quixote, G. K. Chesterton wrote, and you give up "our whole social ideal."[53] And Turgenev, too, felt that the Knight's unhesitating and even thoughtless sense of mission was identical with the essential human drive that allows civilization to progress. The fact that young Andrew gets beaten all the worse for Don Quixote's efforts does not matter, Turgenev thought, for were a man to think out his idealism before acting, he would be as hesitant as Hamlet and perhaps would never make a move.[54] The same assumptions seem to inform Dorothy Van Ghent's attempt to salvage some shred of ideal justice from the Knight's disastrous meddling in the case of Andrew. But despite Van Ghent's intimidating claim that we should be reduced to a brutal level were we to renounce "justice" in this scene,[55] the novel makes it impossible to discount the youth's screams, especially when Andrew himself later curses Quixote and points out that if there had been no interference he probably would have received a mere "dozen or two of lashes" and been paid his wages too (275). The ideal of justice, to the extent that it is involved in this scene, is a satirically shattered ideal. To hold onto it is what is really brutal.

There is one great scene, though, where the Knight's urge toward defense of the helpless is more efficacious: his freeing of the galley slaves in part 1, chapter 22. The appearance of these chained men is a distinct challenge to Quixote's whole project, since he has just reiterated, in a lengthy discussion with Sancho (165–171), that eventually it will be the Knight's pleasure to present himself for service to some king and, in fact, to become a king himself. It now becomes clear that the king does not live by chivalric values at all; he uses brute force on men, as Quixote immediately notices (171). Yet Quixote's investigation does not show the majority of these men to have been particularly harmful to others. Their crimes are mostly petty and civil, but their punishment amounts in some cases to "civil death" (176). A man who stole a basket of linen, for instance, later confessed under torture and received one hundred lashes plus a three-year sentence in the galleys. Gines de Pasamonte is going to the galleys for ten years—which would be recognized by contemporary readers as a virtual death sentence. The slippery Gines is unforgettably described as chained with cruel caution: "... he had a chain on his leg so long that it was wound right round his body, and two collars about his neck, one secured to the chain and the other of the kind they called a *keep friend* or *friend's foot*. From this two iron bars reached down to his waist, with two manacles attached in which his wrists were secured by a heavy padlock, so that he could neither lift his hands to his mouth nor bend his head down to his hands" (175).

What is unique to the scene is that Quixote seriously inquires into all this; he does not just employ stock response. He discovers not only that force is being used, but that these particular men are quite arbitrarily selected by the king for such treatment: "... possibly it is only lack of courage under torture in one, shortage of money in another, lack of friends in another—in short, the unfair decisions of the judge —that have been the cause of your undoing and of your failure to receive the justice which was your due" (177).[56] He even reasons with the guards: "... these poor men have committed no wrong against you ... it is not right that honorable men should be executioners of others, having themselves no concern in the matter. I make this request in a calm and gentle manner" (178).

But of course the guards are in no mood to listen, and Quixote has to release the prisoners by using force. And he manages to do it without seriously hurting anyone. It is presumptuous of cautionary readers to say that in taking this action Don Quixote is engaging in an "extreme perversion" of his ideals.[57] The ideal of justice is after all based on the correction of inequities ("the defense of the helpless"), and what better time to correct than when men victimized by a legal manifestation of justice are on the way to the galleys? Nowhere in the novel do we even learn of these men committing further crimes (except for Gines' partly comic theft of Sancho's ass), though it would have been a simple enough thing for Cervantes to have inserted such a report had he really been interested in such a primly moralistic point. The Priest's story of depredations committed by

Don Quixote's released prisoners (258) is a trite invention that serves to embarrass the Knight and thus to entertain those characters whose mockery of the Knight only conceals their deeper agreement with his values. Gines the ass-thief turns up in part 2 as a puppet-show master, a turn of events that one might feel is a comical but successful rehabilitation. On the other hand, the established forms of justice acquire an unpleasant tinge, to say the least, from such details as the member of the Holy Brotherhood who is very quick to bash in Quixote's head in reprisal for a verbal affront (126–127), and the gruesome vigilante hangings of scores of bandits (856). In overall context, the release of the galley slaves remains as a great moment for the Knight, one with which readers have been indelibly impressed.

And yet it is his only such moment, for reasons plain to see. The released prisoners do not consent to go down the main roads and present themselves to Dulcinea. This promptly enrages Quixote, who reacts like a modern liberal upon discovering that victims are not angels. Quixote's rage serves to release the slaves' own considerable violence, and the chapter ends with Quixote and Sancho in sad shape indeed. The next chapter begins with the Knight swearing off this kind of direct action: "I have always heard, Sancho, that doing good to base fellows is like throwing water into the sea. . . . let this be a warning for the future" (181). This willingness to learn from a single unhappy experience is certainly not Quixote's characteristic reaction. What has set him against his own earlier impulse to free the men, and thus made his brief foray out of the world of stock response seem worthless, is the same thing that characterizes him throughout: the test of Dulcinea, a test the galley slaves have failed. The Knight's command that these men go to Dulcinea, which at first looks simply like a sudden recurrence of his madness, is shown in the extended context of the novel as fully characteristic of the Knight.[58] The aftermath of the release of these galley slaves causes a comic double-take to occur (retroactively)— a refocus on the release episode. We realize that all along, in questioning the prisoners on the justice they have received, Quixote is keeping in unspoken reserve his assumption that it is "true" justice—that is, service to Dulcinea—that these men really should receive, and that the human impulse toward equity of treatment which Cervantes evokes so powerfully in the scene is for Don Quixote not at all identical with the ideal of justice, any more than it is identical with the justice being executed by the king's guards. Quixote's ideal woman is the most important thing in his life, and he cannot but choose her side in any conflict, even if any of his actual accomplishments are thus lost. As a result, there are no accomplishments, no one who is actually helped, unless (as in the case of Marcela) the victim happens to be quite Dulcineated already, or unless (as in the case of Basilio) Quixote can at least pretend that this is so.

So thoroughly does Dulcinea become the determination of justice that, when late in the book Don Quixote encounters another group of galley slaves, he does not respond to their plight in the least (879–881). He is, on the contrary, happy to be along for the ride, "delighted to find himself treated in so lordly a fashion" by the slave commander, a "Valencian gentleman of quality" who lavishes compliments on Quixote, the great knight-errant. Galley slaves are "base fellows," not noble followers of Dulcinea, and the king is not to be reproached for his treatment of them. The defense of the helpless is of course not renounced; it is merely incorporated into the Knight's painful lip service to idealism. And in Cervantes' novel that is all "justice" can be, inasmuch as there will only be various manifestations of Dulcinea's demands on one side (whether by the Knight or by one of his admired kings or princes), which will be called "justice," and occasional "spontaneous" comic reversals on the other.

What remains from the novel and the great galley-slave scene of part 1, chapter 22, is not some ethereal remnant of the ideal of justice, but the impulse toward immediate equity of treatment that the scene evokes both in Don Quixote and in many a reader.[59] To hope, compulsively, that this impulse will somehow, in some universe, be satisfied by some combination of Dulcineated hero and Dulcineated social system—that is, to hope for "our whole social idea," as Chesterton called it, to be fulfilled—is a hope that the twentieth century still retains. Such gullibility far outdoes anything Sancho Panza displays in his hope for an island of his own to govern. But *Don Quixote* does not encourage this hope for a happy outcome to Dulcinea's project; in fact, the novel identifies such a hope as part of a covert desire to subordinate the impulse toward human equity beneath some banner of idealism guaranteed to thwart it.

I believe that the procedure I have followed in analyzing this scene is warranted and indeed demanded by the novel itself, if we expect to make contact with it in terms suitable to its enormous imaginative reach. We need not assume that its special context has absolute relevance for any situation in which we may ever find ourselves; we need only grant that, despite the many differences between a great many of our present situations and that of the fictional world of *Don Quixote*, there is also some basic similarity and hence relevance. Do we not in fact as twentieth-century readers subscribe faithfully to the ideal of justice and hence to its various legal manifestations, despite all its shortcomings? And do we not in fact habitually ignore or discount the glaring illumination of that ideal which Cervantes gives us?

It is not a distortion to say that Cervantes challenges us to give up "our whole social ideal" and to find some other way to make life tolerable. He is as controverting here as he is in challenging our whole concept of imagination.[60] We have thought that the man who sacrifices his selfish bodily needs and who contacts through imagination the literary traditions that embody the ideals his society has sadly forgotten or betrayed (or never really practiced) is thereby engaging in an act of transcendence of the everyday world. But despite the apparently rich mixture of heroes and ideals that Don Quixote manages to contact, his life does not lead to enrichment, either in his inner world or in daily social life. Instead, Cervantes shows both Quixote and his world on a path of perpetual bondage, controlled by the ideals rather than benefited by them. As it turns out, there is much more potential and critical resistance to the stifling nature of Dulcinea's world in Sancho's earthbound body and less constricted mind than there is in the soaring Quixote.

If Dulcinea can be evaluated by her works, her works must, on the showing of the novel, be those of automaton thinking, imperceptiveness in the face of sought-for pain, a degradation of anguish to a sought-for and conventional sadness, an uncritical acceptance of anyone who has the look of nobility about him, and a radical devaluation of the human body. The critic's defense of Dulcinea must be based on mere dogmatism, and that defense is as unanswerable as it is out of contact with the novel and its many juxtapositions. Not all obsessions are magnificent. Cervantes makes us see that the Knight's obsession is quite deadly, and Cervantes does not stop with the Knight.

These implications are serious ones, and, for idealist, cautionary, and perspectivist critics, they seem to be less acceptable than death itself. Nonetheless, the novel is hardly tragic; some of its many comic explosions I have pointed out. The novel is satiric and, in the case at least of the Montesinos cave, grotesque. The depth and complexity of its vision of life testify that at least Cervantes as novelist could joyously shatter Dulcinea's cage and disenchant himself. Such disenchantment, it is true, it not compatible with the greatest of Christian imperatives; the gentle comedy that so many have tried to find in *Don Quixote*, in which laughter becomes the outer binding of love for the object laughed at, is scarcely to be located in the overall novel. Cervantes instead proves the truth of Hobbes's scandalous definition of laughter as a "sudden glory" in the laugher[61] and shows that loving acceptance of Don Quixote is ultimately loving acceptance of perpetual grief for the sake of Dulcinea. But readers have been averse to the novel's implication that Dulcinea is dead weight; hence, unlike the man in the well-known William Steig cartoon,[62] they have not yet noticed (with a predictable gasp) that Cervantes has sawed right through the chain by which the weight is attached.

CHAPTER THREE

The Possibilities of the Squire

Critical Juxtaposition

By creating Sancho—that frequent voice of critical opposition to Dulcineism—at the Knight's side, Cervantes effects a continual crossing of opposite currents and enables the novel to work its criticism of all that Quixote stands for in a fictional atmosphere that is immediately vivid. What could otherwise conceivably be taken as the Knight's mere slips of the tongue or as harmlessly contradictory statements become instead, under the strong critical powers of Sancho, immediate preliminary indications of the ultimate urge toward total obedience to Dulcinea's appearances, an urge that the novel reveals in all its levels. Sancho begins and keeps going and often presses very far a criticism that the responsive reader is impelled to test and work out, even when Sancho is not actually speaking.

What is especially unparaphraseable about Sancho is that his critical powers often can not be identified with any conscious effort on his part. John Ormsby was not far off when he said that "Sancho's mission throughout the book" is to be "an unconscious Mephistopheles, always unwittingly making mockery of his master's aspirations, always exposing the fallacy of his ideas by some unintentional *ad absurdum*, always bringing him back to the world of fact and commonplace by force of sheer stolidity."[1] The squire, in his several ways, delivers objections to the Knight's pursuit of Dulcinea that even the Knight, for all his encyclopedic command of the chivalric rationale, cannot answer.

Sancho cannot be understood as an average peasant in historical time. He is too extraordinary.[2] Even aside from his unstoppable flow of proverbs—which he uses critically, not just at random—Sancho often exhibits a free mind at work, but a mind that is somehow not identical with what is called rational thinking. What begins as the comic *donnée* of the wise fool becomes in Sancho a unique blend of his (and our) enjoyment of a critical freedom fused with the enjoyment of creature comfort.[3]

Sancho is the one man in the novel who shows an ability to enjoy food and sleep and to take notice of such role-playing females as Dorothea and Altisidora as sexually attractive women (262, 920). For there is a fund of common sense in Sancho, if common sense may be defined as that which instinctively resists dogmatic faith in the virtue of sensual renunciation—the very faith that is conveyed by Dulcineism. He is the one person not fascinated with the workings of Dulcineism. Such sequences as that showing Sancho's failure to stop eating all during the wedding of Camacho (part 2, chapters 20, 21) do not illustrate his gluttony as much as they show his ability to avoid involvement in what we shall find to be a complex variant of the love rituals of Dulcinea. The Knight and the other idealists would not miss this wedding for the world, just as the Knight, Canon, and Priest are delighted with a goatherd's stylized tale of pastoral love lamentations, to which Sancho does not care to listen at all (445).[4] Sancho does unashamedly prefer eating to such listening. But is there any reason, in the novel, for him to prefer otherwise?

Quixote elaborately explains the commonplace of death as the great leveller (538–539), but he cannot see any connection between this and his own speeches glorifying chivalric as well as military combat. Sancho quickly expresses the same commonplace (539), but lives in such a way as to make the most of what life he has. Even his eating is, in a sense, a critical act.

Sancho's mind is not only in touch with his body; it is not understandable apart from his body. His descriptions of Dulcinea, for instance, in hyperbolical terms of physical vitality, are memorable in their crudeness:

O the wench, what muscles she's got, and what a pair of lungs! I remember one day she went up the village belfry to call in some of their lads who were working in a fallow field of her father's, and they could hear her as plainly as if they had been at the foot of the tower, although they were nearly two miles away.   (209)

She was over the crupper of the saddle in one jump, and now without spurs she's making that hackney gallop like a zebra.   (530)

This sense of joyous physical reality is quite beyond Quixote; and Sancho's expression of such a world inevitably throws a glaring illumination over that sad pursuit of a physical nothing which Dulcinea provides for the Knight.

To be sure, the mere juxtaposition of a bodily point of view with an idealistic one does not produce automatic victory for the former. The novel gives ample scope to work out the conflict at leisure. But it does work it out, and the vindication of sense over soul that idealist and perspectivist critics seem to dread does finally occur.

This is true even if sense sometimes errs. Sancho certainly errs in his estimates of the realistic possibilities of certain situations, as in the case of the fulling mills (part 1, chapter 20) or in his habitual inclination to advise Don Quixote not to attempt battles against superior numbers. The comic realism of the novel does not employ an everyday sense of probability. But it would be a much greater error to conclude from this that in the novel "anything goes," that

Sancho is finally as fallible as his master,[5] or that (as Aubrey Bell remarks), since nothing is certain, everything is possible. This conclusion is a misappropriation of Dostoyevsky and reflects not the novel, but Bell's own idealist belief that, "if the senses deceive the soul, the soul will not deceive the senses . . ."[6] The case is rather that Sancho is not *ultimately* deceived by his senses in the novel, and that his errors are corrigible in the light of further knowledge. He learns, for instance, that the fulling mills are not monsters and has a laugh. Quixote, however, requires perfect knowledge of Dulcinea's truths and therefore must construct more and more devious explanations (in the form of alleged enchantments) to explain each of his upsets. Accordingly, he even tries to forbid Sancho from laughing or criticizing. At the end, it is Quixote who is deceived by a quest for Dulcinea, upon which he is utterly dependent but from which he gets nothing that the novel suggests to be an enrichment of his life. Sancho enjoys himself much of the way, reaps a number of real rewards, and lives on. The senses (contrary to our usual assumption) provide more enduring knowledge than do the transcendant ideals.

Even before the squire begins to scatter his proverbs, he shows an ability to resist the Knight's creed of renunciation. The resistance may take the form of fairly clear argument:

"For I would have you know, Sancho, that wounds dealt with instruments which are accidentally in the hand do not disgrace a man; that is expressly laid down by the law of the duel. . . ."

"I don't care a hang, down here [on the ground], whether the beating was a disgrace or not, but I do mind a lot about the pain I got from it, and that's likely to stay as deeply in my memory as it bit into my back."

"For all that, brother Panza," replied Don Quixote, "let me tell you that there is no memory which time does not efface, nor any pain that death does not destroy."

"But what misfortune could be worse," replied Sancho, "than one that waits for time to efface it and death to destroy it?"   (116)

Here again the resistance is based on the reality of physical, sensory experience, as it is in his refusal to forget the blanket-tossing, a painful fact that he insists upon recalling. Sancho's statement that "it would not be right for me to destroy myself for someone else's good" (706) is vastly removed from either Dulcineism or "greediness." Nor is it "cowardice" to say that one will not be guided by the rules of knight-errantry in quarrels and fights:

... I am very peaceable by nature and all against shoving myself into brawls and quarrels. But as to defending myself, sir, I shan't take much notice of those rules, because divine law and human law allow everyone to defend himself against anyone who tries to harm him.   (71)

... I intend to use all my five senses to avoid being wounded or wounding anyone.   (163)

At times, he can express the same attitude in religious terms: "There's no reason, sir, to take revenge on anyone ... for it's not right for a good Christian to avenge his injuries. ... it's my intention to live peacefully all the days of life that heaven grants me" (537–538).

The critical impact such a position may have on Dulcineism is well explored by Cervantes. Sancho's arguments against the Knight's futile defense of the sexual honor of a certain fictitious, chivalric lady are so devastating and are pursued so well to their conclusions that Quixote finally can only say, "Once more, Sancho, be quiet" (200–201). In other words, although Quixote argues doggedly in this sequence, Sancho forces the Knight back into tacitly admitting that perhaps Dulcinea cannot meet a test of works.[7]

Even the Knight's highly developed rationalization of enchantment as an explanation for the yawning discrepancies between chivalric fiction and real event is eventually penetrated by Sancho. Sancho's argument is based on a physical test—the enchanted do not defecate and therefore Quixote could not be enchanted—and proves far more fundamental than the juxtaposed arguments of the learned Canon of Toledo, who is, for all his protesting, on the side of Dulcinea (part 1, chapters 47–49). Here Sancho not only catches the Knight in the contradictions of his own chivalric system;[8] he exposes the complete indifference to the physical that is the system's hidden corollary, and he even seems momentarily to rock the conviction of the Knight, whose reply in terms of pure faith ("I most certainly know that I am enchanted, and that is sufficient to ease my conscience, which would be greatly burdened if I thought that I was not under a spell . . ." [434]) seems to satisfy himself only in part. Immediately after delivering this profession of faith, Quixote does consent to try Sancho's scheme of escaping from the cage where he is enchanted, although escape from enchantment is, by the rules, an impossibility.

Quixote's anger at the proverbs of his squire, ostensibly because of their irrelevance or because of his own resentment that a squire should be able to make wise statements, is most definite when Sancho has said something embarrassing to the mystique of Dulcinea. When Quixote is lecturing Sancho on the need for circumspectly idealistic behavior in his high new role as governor, Sancho responds with a string of proverbs that includes the following segment: ". . . the rich man's foolishness passes for wisdom in the world; and since I shall be rich, and a governor and liberal as well, which I intend to be, no one will see fault in me. Make yourself honey and the flies will suck you; you're worth as much as you've got, as my old grandmother used to say; and there's no getting revenge on a well-rooted man" (743). It is at this point that Don Quixote denounces proverbs. The out-of-earshot, out-of-mind trick that Quixote is attempting may work for him, but, in a responsive reading experience of the novel, Sancho's puncturing of the whole moral rationale behind his apprenticeship to a follower of Dulcinea is great comedy and clears the air. The idea that a governor will be an efficient man of justice if he studies the moral and practical precepts of an idealist was one that occupied some of the best minds of the Renaissance, but Sancho points out that holding power is a reality that makes a man independent of such niceties. It is Sancho who so memorably realizes that "there are only two families in the world, my old grandmother used to say, the *Haves* and the *Have-nots*" (600). The novel shows that Quixote makes himself palatable to the haves, in order to attain the illusion of being one of them; but his rationale of thus performing a moral service is dealt a rude blow in Sancho's crude "make yourself honey and the flies will suck you." Sancho has elsewhere brought this crude fact to the attention of his betters, as in his sharp reactions to similar homilies concerning governing with justice, on the part of the learned Canon: ". . . I've as large a soul as the next man," Sancho tells the Canon, "and as stout a body as the best of them, and I'd be as good a king of my estate as any other king; and being so, I should do as I liked; and doing as I liked, I should take my pleasure; and taking my pleasure, I should be contented; and when one's content, there's nothing more to desire; and when there's nothing more to desire, there's an end to it" (443). The Canon is able to argue back only half-heartedly.[9]

The thoroughness of Sancho's critique of Dulcineism can be suggested by examples like these, though of course the actual reading experience of Sancho juxtaposed with Quixote cannot be duplicated in paraphrase. The Knight's ostentatious offer of equality during dining (premised on the acceptance by Sancho of the basic inequality of master and man) is shown up in its triviality by Sancho's response: "I thank you . . . but I must confess to your worship that so long as I have plenty to eat, I can eat it as well, and better, standing by myself, as seated beside an Emperor. . . . So, dear master, let the honors your worship means to confer on me for being a servant and follower of knight-errantry—which being your squire, I am, be exchanged for something of more use and profit to me" (85).[10] Much further in the novel, the Knight's (as well as the Duke's and Duchess') fussy pleasure in polite table manners is deflated by an anecdote of Sancho's that brings back into view that some are haves, and some have-nots, all pleasantries between the two notwithstanding (670–672). The logic of pain leading to power is brought into precise focus by Sancho's definition of a knight-errant as one who "is beaten up one day and made Emperor the next" (119). The predetermined misfiring of an attempt to help the defenseless according to the rules of Dulcinea receives its apt epigraph in Sancho's slip of the tongue: ". . . the famous knight Don Quixote de la Mancha, who rights wrongs, gives meat to the thirsty, and drink to the hungry" (526).[11] At the Ducal palace, when Quixote praises the Duchess as "the sovereign mistress of beauty and universal princess of courtesy," Sancho reconciles this hyperbole with the Knight's usual adulation for Dulcinea, in a proverbial comparison that indicates how stereotyped this whole concept of beauty is: "It cannot be denied— in fact it must be declared that my lady Dulcinea del Toboso is very beautiful. But the hare starts up when you least expect it, and I've heard say that what's called Nature is like a potter who makes vessels of clay, and if a man makes one fine pot, he can also make two, three, or a hundred" (665).

Sancho's greatest single exposure of the stock quality of Quixote's love for Dulcinea occurs in his parody of the Knight's letter to her. Sancho forgets the text of the letter, but relies on memory. He tells Quixote that he repeated the letter to the parish clerk, who had written it down again and had commented that "he had never read as nice a letter in all the days of his life, although he had seen and read plenty of letters of excommunication" (267). Sancho's grotesque juxtaposition of love letter and letter of excommunication, however, does not trouble Quixote, whose letter is thus revealed in its affinity, not with love, but with Dulcinea's strategies for social control. By the time Sancho repeats the letter back to the Knight, it has changed wonderfully: "If I remember anything at all it's that *'suppressed'*—I mean *'sovereign-lady,'* and the ending: *'Yours till death, the Knight of the Sad Countenance.'* And in between I put more than three hundred *'souls,' 'lives,'* and *'dear eyes.'* (267–268). Don Quixote, however, does not object. Cervantes breaks off the chapter immediately after the above rendering and opens the next chapter in full focus on the reply: "All this does not displease me at all" (268).[12] In a love language made up of accepted literary formulae, nearly anything will do.

Sancho's conscious criticism of Dulcinea, which seems to be present, for instance, in his logical arguments against the enchantment in the cage, are thus parallelled and overshadowed by his semi-intentional acts of criticism, as in his slips of tongue or in his botching up Quixote's letter to Dulcinea. He is characterized as a man who *must* speak impulsively whatever comes into his head (265), and it is evident that his stringing of proverbs is not planned out ahead of time, as he himself makes clear in answering one of the Knight's pleas that governor-elect Sancho reduce his use of proverbs: "Let God look after that . . . for I know more proverbs than a book, and so many of them come all together into my mouth when I speak that they fight with one another to get out; and the tongue seizes hold of the first it meets with, even though it mayn't be just to the point" (742). This statement, corroborated by a great many passages, is candid enough. The proverbs allow Sancho a kind of freedom of response to situations, for they provide an uncensored, spontaneous quality.

Sancho's *conscious* mind, on the other hand, is often as conventional as anything in the novel. At the peasant level, too, Dulcinea has allies and has made her inroads. At the peasant level there are, predictably enough, evidences of an urge to restrict sensuality and regularize love. The Knight's explanation of why two armies fight, based on ethnic stereotyping of the pagans attempting to steal away the Christian king's daughter, is readily accepted by Sancho (though he soon comes to doubt the reality of his master's substitution of armies for sheep), and he is quite ready to join in the rescue efforts (135). The letter from Sancho's wife shows a concern and interest in the chances of proper marriage for certain deviant village girls, as one might expect in a traditional agrarian society (810). Shortly after receiving this letter, Sancho himself has a chance to comment on an instance of possible sexual irregularity. His Moorish friend, Ricote, is telling Sancho about his (Ricote's) daughter, who is thought to be in love with a Christian:

". . . Moorish women seldom or never have affairs with Old Christians, and my daughter, who, in my belief, cared more for her religion than for love, would not pay any attention to the young heir's attention."

"God grant you're right," replied Sancho, "for it would be bad for both of them." (822)[13]

This kind of set view is only to be expected, considering Sancho's social origin (and certainly the novel makes it clear that this origin is relevant to understanding Sancho even if he is not an average peasant). It does not need to be taught by the Knight.

Sancho is conventionally shocked when Quixote accuses him of not really fearing God (600), and portrays himself as one who firmly values soul over body (745), although the language, even here, is of the body: ". . . I love a single black nail's breadth of my soul more than my whole body . . ." His first reaction to the Knight's plan to free the galley slaves is utterly uncritical of the social order: "Consider, your worship . . . that justice—that is the King himself—is doing no wrong or outrage to such people, but only punishing them for their crimes" (171). Further on in the scene, however, after getting a closer look at the slaves, he feels sorry enough to give one of them a *real* (175), and in the second galley-slave scene late in the novel, he is able to voice a protest: "What have these wretches done that they flog them so? And how does this single man, who goes about whistling, have the audacity to whip all these people? Surely this is hell, or at least purgatory" (880). These reactions to the galley slaves (the last juxtaposed with his master's unfeeling approval of the scene) speak well for Sancho's ultimate responsiveness to experience, but there are equally evident gaps or short-circuits in this responsiveness. Fleeing in terror from his mock-governorship, he declaims a thoroughly stock *vanitas vanitatum* speech (813–814), telling himself that he should have remained a simple peasant. A few chapters further on, Quixote matches him by guessing that he has been cast into the pit for his sins (826). Master and man are drawing a conventional moral from Sancho's disillusionment at governing, but in fact that disillusionment was engineered entirely by the Duke.

Sancho's statements that he is through with governing are not his final word on the subject, however; later on he wishes that he could try it again (879), and still later he hopes to become at least a count (893). These second thoughts are generally ignored by critics, who have taken Sancho's trite lesson of vanity as their own moral, and who habitually emphasize his stock qualities at the expense of his main role of providing critical contrast with the Knight and with the Knight's values. Anxious to cut short the novel's critical treatment of ideals, critics cling to Sancho's sincere but conventional approval of his master's knowledge, goodness, and wisdom, and use that approval to eradicate all his opposition. But instead of operating as instructions for our reading of the novel, Sancho's pious declarations concerning his master are themselves subject to critical insight and demolition through his deeply physical grasp of the value of life in a life-denying cultural environment. His critical function in the novel far supersedes his role as citizen.

Resisting Dulcinea's Pressures

The tendency to ignore or discount the contrast of master and man is most acute in the critical fascination with the "quixotization"[4] of Sancho, that is, with his transformation into something of a Quixote. But this transformation is never complete enough to remove the contrast and is of no value in providing evidence for Dulcinea's works, since the addition of Sancho to Dulcinea's ranks (even if that event did occur) would further prove only Dulcinea's strength, not her value.[15]

That there is a real distinction here is brought out forcefully in the Knight of the Wood episode. In this sequence, the two squires, Sancho and his counterpart Thomas Cecial, hit it off companionably, discuss the strange predilections of their masters, eat and drink voraciously, and eventually fall asleep in the manner of earthy slobs, "grasping the almost empty bottle between them, with their meat half chewed in their mouths" (550). But pressures to be more chivalric are brought to bear on Sancho. In the next chapter the mock squire tries hard to induce Sancho into some sort of duel. Sancho, after comically reducing the challenge to a fight with soft pillows, is finally clear and precipitate in refusing any serious battle (553–554): "No, I tell you sir, I'm not fighting. . . . Let our masters fight and good luck to them, but let us drink and eat. For time takes care enough to rob us of our lives, without our going out to look for ways of ending them off before their due time and season. They'll drop off when they're ripe" (554). After resisting further provocations from the mock squire, Sancho climbs a tree during the duel itself. But then he re-enters his squire-role by suggesting to his master that the fallen Knight of the Wood be dispatched by thrusting a sword "right into this man's mouth." Quixote, incidentally, accepts this advice, for "the less enemies the better," and he has to be restrained from carrying it out (558). Shortly afterward, Quixote mentions his regret at being kept from the kill by his malign enchanters (563). The novel does not let us assume that quixotization is good; in this scene Sancho's realistic hedonism is plainly presented as a far more attractive attitude.

Sancho's quixotization is customarily substantiated on two grounds: that he comes to share his master's delusions, and that he doggedly continues to serve his master against all dictates of common sense. The sheer exposure to Quixote over nine hundred pages of adventures does constitute enormous pressure on Sancho to accept his master's delusions, and Sancho is far from being perfectly immune. To engage in disputation with the Knight over the spoils of the chivalric project requires, to be sure, a willingness to believe at least temporarily that such a project is a real possibility. But Sancho is at the same time probing; he is skeptical of the details, and he hardly accepts at face value the promise of being made a governor in a day. By chapter 26 of part 1, we can see that he does not expect the end to be achieved for a very long time; for by that time he expects to be a widower (220). The Priest and the Barber conspire to assure Sancho that his governorship is a real possibility, and it is little wonder that Sancho does not question their authority, particularly when the Priest himself promises to put in a plea for a governorship, rather than an archbishopric, for Sancho (220–221).[16] Sancho can go on believing in a governorship as a kind of wonderful bonus—but not as the only material payment for services that he is to receive. And in part 2, he is presented with sensible proof—the "governorship" of one of the Duke's "isles." That Sancho falls for the ruse is perhaps evidence of gullibility (though what peasant would claim to have been able to penetrate this well-engineered mock?), but hardly of chivalric delusion.

More serious signs of quixotization may be drawn from Sancho's gullibility in the episode of the wineskins (part 1, chapter 35) and in the surprising burst into chivalric formulae in his speech over the (illusory) death of his master near the end of part 1:

O flower of chivalry, whose well-spent life one single blow of a stick has cut short! O glory of your race, honor and credit to all La Mancha, and to the whole world besides, which, now that you are here no longer, will be overrun by malefactors who will no longer fear chastisement for their iniquities! O liberal beyond all Alexanders, since for only eight months' service you have given me the best isle surrounded and encircled by the sea! O humble to the proud and arrogant to the humble, undertaker of perils, sufferer of affronts, enamored without reason, imitator of the virtuous, scourge of the wicked, enemy of evil-doers, in a word, knight-errant, which is the highest that man can desire! (454–455)

This speech is stronger proof than Sancho's willingness to fight for ownership of a packsaddle on the grounds that his master won it for him in a "fair fight" (402); Sancho's material aim in that incident is too flagrant for the supposed belief in chivalry to be taken straight (as early as chapter 8 he had been trying eagerly to collect trophies won in "fair" fights). The eulogy is also stronger proof than his single use of the word "basin-helmet," which has been mistaken as a philosophical admission by Sancho that a barber's basin might really be a piece of chivalric armor, as Don Quixote insists.[17]

The eulogy contains its own characteristic undercutting. The Knight's unreasoning respect for those in power is brought into focus by the phrasing, "O humble to the proud and arrogant to the humble," and Dulcinea is also commented upon in the phrase "enamored without reason." But the quantity of chivalric praise, which sounds much like the Knight's own talk, and the belief in the isle as an achieved reality show Sancho at least partially succumbing to the master's vision. At the same time, one of the main reasons Sancho gives here for praising chivalry is that it pays off very nicely in material rewards.

There are other places where Sancho seems to be succumbing, as in the episode of the Knight of the Wood, where, despite his being able to see that the mock knight is really his old neighbor Carrasco, he remains of two minds, with an obvious leaning toward the chivalric interpretation: "He certainly looks like the Bachelor Sampson Carrasco, but perhaps if you kill him you'll be killing one of your enemies the enchanters" (558). And in the Clavileño episode Sancho seems not only to fall for the ruse of being transported through the heavens on a magical horse; he is even able to say that while in the stratosphere he was privileged actually to see the "seven little she-goats" and to play with them for three-quarters of an hour.

But Sancho's creation of a new constellation among the stars is hardly clear evidence that he has come to be as deluded as his master, because it cannot, in the reading experience of the novel, be separated from Sancho's role as an improvising liar who has to prevent his previous lies to his master from becoming known. Nor can we see much difference in imaginative quality between Sancho's seven playful, colorful she-goats and his usual language of physical energy; he is no more imaginative here than in describing Aldonza's lusty voice. It is equally implausible to say that Sancho's improvisation of three princesses out of three peasant girls, in order to satisfy his master's need to see Dulcinea, "commits" Sancho "inexorably" to his master's vision.[18] Sancho's ruse in this instance begins in the squire's designs for getting out of a spot, and maybe for getting out of all such future spots: "Perhaps if I hold out I shall put an end to his sending me on any more of these errands, seeing what poor answers I bring back" (527). Though Sancho carries out his ruse with obvious relish and goes beyond the strict needs of prevarication, he shows little further interest in this kind of invention.

The fact is that instead of inexorably joining in the Knight's kind of vision-making, Sancho explicitly gives it the lie. In spite of the Duchess' ability to get Sancho to all but believe in the enchantment himself (693), he soon reverts to amazement "at their insistence, in defiance of the truth, that Dulcinea was enchanted" (697). Sancho's basic attitude, under pressure to believe in the enchantment, is to refuse responsibility. As he tells the Duchess, ". . . if my Lady Dulcinea del Toboso's enchanted, so much the worse for her; for I don't have to take on my master's enemies, who must be plentiful and wicked. The truth may be that it was a peasant girl I saw. I took her for a peasant girl, and a peasant girl I judged her to be. But if it was Dulcinea it can't be laid to my account" (690). This air of detachment from any alleged commitment to Dulcinea is incompatible with Dulcineism; it is part of the novel's showing that Sancho is in continued contrast, even to the end of the novel, with his master.

Sancho sticks to his irresponsibility. When pressured by Duke, Duchess, and master, as well as by a bevy of mock-chivalric personages, to accept the role of a human whipping-block with magical powers of disenchantment, he eventually gives in, but only after ensuring that "lashes" that are just "fly-teasers" will count in the reckoning (704–705). He appears to assent to having magical powers in this lashing at one point (928), but the admission is juxtaposed with strong indications of disbelief or at least lack of cooperation: Sancho merely slashes the trees, not himself (923, 929). Indeed, he is as inventive in this role as at any time, ridiculing the sadistic implications of the concept of lashing by using hilarious mock-heroics. He insists on enduring thousands of lashes at a time:

"Stand aside a little longer, your worship, and let me give myself another thousand lashes at any rate. Then in two such bouts we shall have finished this job, and even have something to spare."

"Well, since you are so well disposed," said Don Quixote, "may Heaven help you. Stick to it, and I will stand aside."

Sancho returned to his task so furiously that he had soon stripped a number of trees of their bark, so severely did he lash himself. And once, raising his voice and dealing one of the beeches a tremendous stroke, he cried: "Here dies Samson, and all with him."   (923)

Similarly, when pressed into riding Clavileño in order to disenchant the mock-enchanted waiting-woman, only the threat that Sancho will lose his governorship is adequate to convince him to go on the ride (728–729).[19] Very late in the novel, in still another of the Ducal ruses, he is intimidated into accepting another sacrificial role as restorer of the dead. But Sancho soon recovers himself, loses his temper, and breaks up the ceremony with a great roar (913). Also late in the novel, he is still found in his characteristic role of satirically deflating Dulcineism, as he comments on the chaste pastoral dreams of his master:

My daughter Sanchica shall bring us our dinner to the fold. But mind out! For she's good looking, and the shepherds are not all simple. There are rogues among them, and I wouldn't like her to go for wool and come back shorn. . . . and a leap over the hedge is better than good men's prayers. (904)

These remarks produce from the Knight another request for a cessation of proverbial wisdom. Finally, in the deathbed scene, Sancho's sincere blubbering for his master is at once juxtaposed with his good cheer at the fine bequest that he will receive from the estate (938).

The interest in the bequest is on the whole more indicative of Sancho's motivation in following the Knight than is his groaning for his "dear master" (937). Sancho's few professions of love for his master, when seen in context, seem to be sincere gratitude for and approval of the Knight's generosity toward him. One of the strongest statements is the one he makes to the Duchess, who, in pretending to weigh Sancho's qualifications for governor, has just accused Sancho of necessarily being mad for following so mad a master. Sancho counters: ". . . I should have left my Master days ago if I had been wise. But that was my lot and my ill-luck. I can do nothing else; I have to follow him; we're of the same village; I've eaten his bread; I love him dearly; I'm grateful to him; he gave me his ass-colts; and, what is more, I'm faithful; and so it's impossible for anything to part us except the man with the pick and shovel" (687). The Duchess is unaware (but the reader is not) that just a few chapters back, where Quixote's fortunes seemed to be leading Sancho nowhere, Sancho had quietly determined to leave his dear master: ". . . he was looking for an opportunity of escaping and going home without entering into any reckonings or farewells with his master. But Fortune was kinder to him than he had feared" (662). The kindness of fortune referred to here is the Squire's welcome by the Duchess herself, which means to Sancho more opportunities for eating and drinking, for the "good living" he had found in other episodes (666). It is this good living which is decisive, because the appeal to Sancho's loyalty had already been played by Don Quixote for all it was worth (part 2, chapter 28) *prior to* Sancho's quiet decision to leave, and this appeal was not enough to entice him indefinitely. Similarly, in part 1, when Sancho first began to realize that knight-errantry was no longer in fashion, "he decided in his own mind to wait and see how this expedition of his master's turned out; and if the result was not up to his expectations, he resolved to leave Don Quixote and go back to his wife and children and to his usual occupation" (281). This time Sancho is kept from leaving because he is reassured—as when the pretended princess Micomicona tells him that he will become at least a count (319) —that his expectations will be fulfilled. In another episode, he is also quite ready to leave for good when he sees his master take to doing battle with lions (575), but, since the Knight actually outstares the lion, Sancho is quite willing to come back. These bits of evidence constitute Cervantes' very careful way of establishing that what holds Sancho to Don Quixote is not disinterested loyalty or spiritual involvement.

What seems to be Sancho's strongest statement of any that attest to his love of his master is his declaration to the mock Squire of the Wood that "there's nothing of the rogue in him [Quixote]. His soul is as clean as a pitcher. He can do no harm to anyone, only good to everybody. There's no malice in him. A child might make him believe it's night at noonday. And for that simplicity I love him as dearly as my heartstrings, and can't take to the idea of leaving him for all his wild tricks" (547). This statement is surely the most likely evidence of Sancho's love for his master, but even it is juxtaposed, after further discussion with the mock knight of the poor fare a squire receives, with Sancho's shrewd answer to a proposal that the two peasants simply return to their village: "Until my master gets to Saragossa, I'll serve him, and after that we'll come to some arrangement" (549). Sancho is leaving a loophole.

What is at stake in my noting these points in Sancho's character is not an attempt to reduce Sancho to purely material motivations. I simply wish to show that, although the professions of love and loyalty give good ground for saying that Sancho develops some affection for his master in the course of their wanderings, there are no grounds for interpreting that affection as unequivocal fealty, let alone as a sharing of Dulcineism. There is far clearer evidence for saying that the Squire is loyal to his master because of the prospects of material gain. The pattern is in fact established as early as the adventure of the fulling mills, when Sancho tearfully declares that he will serve his master even if danger is involved. This resolution—from which Sancho sometimes departs in the course of the novel—is made in the specific context of his overwhelmed gratitude for the favorable terms of Quixote's will (156–157).

It is necessary only to recall that Sancho, whose salary as laborer, at some time in the past, has been 2 ducats per month, plus food (653–654), receives a number of windfalls in the novel: 100 crowns from the adventure in the Sierra Morena, where his master goes in search of the super-chaste Marcella (186–187); a gift of 200 crowns from the Ducal treasury "to supply the needs of the road" (834); and a whopping fee of 1,850 *reales* for giving (or rather pretending to give) himself the lashes necessary to disenchant Dulcinea (921–923). In these fees, as well as in the gift of ass colts that his master promises and eventually gives him, Sancho takes great interest. He is shrewd enough to withhold all information of the 100 crowns he has picked up in the Sierra Morena from the Priest, who thinks Sancho is telling him everything there is to know (223). He raises the fee for being a whipping-block as high as he can make it go. And he tries to get a promise of regular wages from the Knight before setting out on the last sally, though he is balked by the fact that Quixote can easily get someone else to take his place (509–511). He also makes it clear that he will not go on that last sally unless his master does all the fighting (495).

Sancho is a man haunted, understandably, by the thought that he may be able to cash in on a sweepstakes ticket that would allow him to live a life of ease. As he vividly explains to the mock Squire of the Wood, he has only returned to the office of squire because he is "enticed and deceived by a purse of a hundred ducats which I found one day in the heart of the Sierra Morena. For the Devil's always dangling a bag full of doubloons before my eyes here, there and everywhere. At every step I seem to be laying my hands on it, hugging it, and taking it home, then making investments and settling rents, and living like a prince. And while this runs in my head all the toils I endure with my idiot of a master become light and bearable, though I know he's more of a madman than a knight" (547). And despite many professions to Quixote and to the Duke and Duchess of desiring to be only good, honest governor, Sancho's motives are very much those of gain. He says, in a letter to his wife: "In a few days I shall leave for my governorship, to which I go very anxious to make money, and I am told that all new governors go in the same frame of mind" (707). He is not pleased to say after his brief tour of duty as governor that "I've had no chance of taking bribes or collecting dues" (827). Notwithstanding Sancho's sympathy, upon direct contact, with galley slaves, he toys with the idea of being a slave dealer himself, should his governorship come through (254–255, 272).

The dream of the doubloons (which is not the same thing as belief in the promised island) is understandable enough, particularly
when we realize what the money would mean for Sancho's family.
His daughter, for instance, would marry easily and into wealth,
rather than have to begin saving for her dowry, at the age of fourteen,
by making bone-lace in exchange for the pittance wage of eight
maravedis a day (810). His wife's deep scruples concerning the in-
advisability of trying to rise too high from one's own station are
answered by Sancho's better knowledge that in this society appearance is all, an insight he has discerned for himself from the words of
a visiting priest "who preached in this village last Lent." "He said,
if I remember rightly, that what we see present and before our eyes
appears, stays and persists in our memories much better and much
more vividly than things past. . . . that when we see someone finely
dressed, adorned with rich clothes, and with a train of servants, we
seem to be moved and compelled involuntarily to pay him respect,
even though at that very moment our memory may recall to us
the low conditions we once saw him in" (501). No wonder Sancho
wants to try his luck at adventuring with his master when he sees
this kind of chance before him. And his wife's scruples vanish
in the joys of being able to play the great lady once Sancho seems
to have succeeded (part 2, chapter 50). The Knight's repeated
assertions that "a knight-errant, if he has two grains of luck, has
every potentiality for becoming the greatest lord in the world" (719),
backed up by the confirming statements of the Duke, the Priest,
and others—along with plenty of cash payments—are sufficient
to account for Sancho's apparent rashness in following Quixote.
Sancho's willingness to try the way of appearance-as-ideal is still
a quixotization, though of a very different sort than is usually as-
cribed to him. But when he finds that his particular governorship is
all verbal honor and great physical discomfort, he soon accepts an
opportunity to abdicate, helter-skelter. The world of appearance
alone is not enough.

W. H. Auden compares Sancho to "a man who had been sold a

nonexistent gold mine [but who] continued to believe in its existence after he had discovered that the seller was a crook."[20] Therefore Auden, like so many others, believes Sancho to be motivated mainly by other than material goals in accompanying Don Quixote. But the greatest nonmaterial interest of Sancho is not in going along with his master or with his master's values, but in exercising his own critical faculties, a talent that he indulges even at the risk of Don Quixote's reprisals. As for the nonexistent gold mine, Sancho manages to extract sizable amounts of gold from it, all the while resisting the considerable pressure that would make the sale final and binding.

Governorship: Promotion to a Lesser Life

Sancho's career as governor can support the claims neither of those who see him as an inherently wise ruler who puts to shame the Duke and Duchess,[21] nor of those who regard it as proof that peasants should stay in their positions in society. He is not a particularly wise ruler, though he exhibits a liveliness of mind that gives moderate comic delight. On at least one occasion, he bursts forth in one of his great, unparaphrasable comic moments. This is the case of the Perlerino family, to whose grotesque and meandering plea for a state subsidy Sancho listens with growing impatience and then explosively rejects (768–772). His peasant shrewdness is at times evident, especially in solving the case of false rape (798–799). But most of the other cases are decided on dubious bases, often reflecting not wisdom, but the impatience of a governor who is being starved. The bases for decision include: whether the plaintiff happened to arrive at dinnertime (780); whether the defendent is verbally adept (783–785); whether the disputant in a racket is, in the judgment of Sancho, an underdog (781–783). Yet all his decisions are hailed as wisdom of unheard-of caliber; his mediocre record is easily incorporated into a tradition that needs a stock of commonplaces to be embroidered with high praise. The praise begins in jest the moment he enters his village and ends in seriousness with a memorial to his wondrous ordinances—although those ordinances reserve the heaviest penalties

for singers of "lewd and disorderly songs" and impose nothing less
than the death penalty for the adulteration of wine (804). This
moralistic note also informs Governor Sancho's desire to cleanse his
realm of "every sort of impurity" and his penalty of ten years' banishment for a man who engaged in a petty gambling operation (781–
783).[22]

All the above cases are (unknown to Sancho) *burlas*, elaborate
practical jokes rigged up for Sancho's consideration and consterna-
tion by servants of the Duke. And when one real case does happen to
come to Sancho's attention, his conventional conscious mind, occupied with his efforts to improve his family's fortunes, at once exhibits
itself. This is the case of the adolescent brother and sister who are
caught out on the streets at night, acting guilty. We learn that the
girl has been shut up in the house for ten years by her father, who
did not even let her go to church, and that she had merely wanted to
see what was going on in her own village. Sancho listens to her confession of these "sinful wishes" (787) and her regret at being shown
up as a wicked "capricious girl" (788), but he can see in her flight
only a "childish prank." He sends her back home to her warden-
father with instructions not to act "so childishly" in the future. Sancho
agrees entirely with the local populace that the two youths are to be
admired for their "beauty and good breeding," presumably enhanced
in the girl by the decade of isolation. Governor Sancho's butler is
eager to have the girl for a daughter-in-law, while Sancho wishes his
own daughter to marry the brother. As for the father, Sancho is only
aware of him as a perfect "gentleman and an old Christian" (803).[23]
Taken all in all, it does not appear that Cervantes is proposing his
not-so-simple fat man as someone who can solve the still unsolved
riddle of how to sit in authority and at the same time be perceptive
and humane.

The inglorious outcome of Sancho's mock governorship is indicative of the extent to which he is in the novel for his function of providing critical opposition and resistance to the Knight. In the gov-

ernorship sequence, he is juxtaposed neither with the Knight nor with idealistic characters, but with *burlas*. These tricks are set up by the Duke and Duchess for their own inane purpose: to see how Sancho, who to them is merely a cute peasant, will act. They hope to build up a store of amusing anecdotes, and they are helped by the steward, who tells them all about it and more. "And in conclusion he gave them an exaggerated account of the assault on the isle, of Sancho's fear, and of his departure, from all of which they got no small enjoyment" (829). Like so much of the Ducal sequence, this episode indicates the pettiness of the great life of noble appearances that they lead and that Don Quixote venerates. But the main significance of the governorship is in its quality of anticlimax: Sancho has learned all a squire should learn, and he should by chivalric right be a notable governor, for "one who has been a good squire will be a good governor" (691). And yet as governor he is neither his full sensuous self nor a complete junior version of Don Quixote.

The latter is of course what he is supposed to be, if he has really learned his lessons. The Knight's two chapters of advice on governing, along with the covering letter forwarded to Sancho while he is in office (part 2, chapters 42–43; and Cohen, pp. 800–802), form a complete set of prescriptions for the demolition of Sancho. He is warned by Quixote to attribute his success not to his own "merits," but first to God, and "afterwards to the greatness implied in the profession of knight-errantry" (737). Thus begins a disparagement of Sancho's untutored self that progresses on through the advice and that amounts to a way of calling for the reduction of Sancho to a body-denying follower of Dulcinea. Quixote, in this sequence, sets himself up as Sancho's "Cato" (737), referring to a well-known collection of moral couplets already mentioned approvingly by the Duchess some chapters before (691). Then follows the nonsensical proposition I have already discussed that equates the fear of God with guaranteed "wisdom" (738). Next, another momentous piece of Renaissance guidance is introduced: Know thyself.[24] It is interpreted in typical picayune fashion here and further on, with the advice that Sancho had best remember his origin, rather than act the part of the frog who wanted to be as big as an ox, and that Sancho had best cultivate a "mild suavity . . . guided by prudence," so that malicious slanderers (who seem to take the place of malicious enchanters) will not be able to harm him. Then back to the sublimities; "virtue" is extolled for a few lines, since it has "intrinsic worth" and evidently does not require elucidation. It can be applied, however: if any of Sancho's relatives come and see him, he is to entertain them, not reject them, for God "would have no one disdain His creation" (738).

The application would be moderately impressive, perhaps, except that it is amplified by two more paragraphs that cancel it out. Sancho is told first that if he should take his wife with him, he must "instruct her, indoctrinate her, and pare her of her native rudeness" ("enséñala, doctrínala, y desbástala de su natural rudeza"); otherwise all his good work as governor might go to waste. Second, the Knight kindly envisions what steps would be taken if Sancho's wife were to die and had to be replaced by another one more fitted "to suit your office." These are strange words for someone who has just affirmed the inherent value of all those in God's creation; they sound more like the words of an organization man.

There follow various exhortations to be merciful, equitable, and just—a counsel of perfection—including one apparently designed to overcompensate for the chivalric custom, built into Sancho's training, of heeding the request of any woman who begged a boon in good tearful form; now such pleas are to be considered on their merits only. The first chapter of advice ends with a promise of the fine rewards to be gained from adherence to the virtues enumerated, including long life, great fame, and "indescribable" happiness—which seems to consist, among other things, of marrying one's children in accordance with one's own wishes. Aside from a little matter of wife-replacement, Sancho would enjoy a happy, or at least large, family life.

In the midst of these complete rules for the guidance of a governor's soul, Quixote also says, "Never be guided by arbitrary law . . ." Yet the entire sequence is not only arbitrary, but unthinkable as anything the novel could suggest as true wisdom. The procedure followed by Quixote is almost on a par with that jeered at in Cervantes' prologue to part 1, where the "friend" tells the author how to guarantee a reputation of solid achievement in his book by means of dragging in such quotations as "But I say to you, love your enemies." This wisdom is of the sort that you can come by "with a little bit of research"; it will enable you to quote "the words of no less an authority than God himself" (28).

But the advice to the governor-elect goes on with a chapter now devoted to the body, which of course is to be transformed with no regard for its own importance, but in terms of what appearance it will make. After a paragraph in which Cervantes' ostensible Arab author effuses over the immense wisdom Quixote has just displayed and is about to display (repeatedly invoked by critics as evidence of what Cervantes, and therefore the novel, means), Quixote arrives at his first momentous command for bodily health—"to be clean, and to pare your nails" (740). Next, Sancho is told not to dress carelessly, for "disorderly clothes are the indication of a careless mind," unless used as a disguise for cunning. Following this advice will at least give one that intelligent *look*.

After some notes on household economy, Sancho is transformed on other levels of the physical and impulsive life: he may not eat garlic lest he "reveal" that he is a peasant; he is told not to belch in anyone's presence (presumably you just hold it), and always to say "eruct" instead of "belch," for the simpler word is too vulgar, though "very expressive." Sancho accepts the correction but balks when told that he must also cut down on proverbs. There is further advice about riding a horse in a suitably staid fashion, and then some anticipation of Samuel Richardson and Benjamin Franklin: "Be moderate in your sleeping, for he that does not rise with the sun does not enjoy the day; and remember, Sancho, that industry is the mother of good fortune, and slothfulness, its opposite, never yet succeeded in carrying out an honest purpose" (742). One of Quixote's incidental maxisms, which occurs in the midst of all of this, is juxtaposed neatly: "all affectation is bad."

Sancho of course does not try to go very far in pursuing such an overall prescription for living. Had he allowed himself to be Dulcineated he would have been obliterated as Sancho. And yet, aside from the material rewards that Sancho is careful to extract, Don Quixote offers little else than this complete and utter Dulcineating. And since this involves the attainment of the appearance of virtue, it is not surprising that the one incident in which Sancho as governor does put his master's wisdom to direct use becomes something of an affectation. This is the case of the toll bridge, supposedly owned by a certain lord who would extract the death penalty from anyone who lies about his reasons for desiring to cross over. Confronted with a possible liar who could conceivably come under the penalty (but who could also be found not guilty), Sancho of course decides on the side of life rather than death. But he invokes his master's wisdom to do it: ". . . in this case I have not spoken out of my own head, for there came to my mind one of the many precepts my master Don Quixote gave me the night before I came to be made Governor of this isle; which was that when justice was in doubt I should incline to the side of mercy" (799). Something is missing from Sancho's voice here, and it is probably the raucous critical remarks he usually would make about such a preposterous case of life and death. He seems to see nothing amiss in the lord's insane ordinance of death for a fib. Yet this is the same Sancho who previously had been aware that "time takes care enough to rob us of our lives, without our going out to look for ways of ending them off before their due time and season" (554). When invoking the ideals of justice and mercy, Sancho indeed is not speaking from his "own head," and the resulting drop in vitality is noticeable.

One a Master, the Other a Man

The Knight's incurable tendency to relate not to people but to Dulcinea's ideals is carried through in the case of Sancho, the one extensive personal relationship in all of Quixote's adventures. Sancho, though acceptable as a droll and wayward peasant, is always none-theless the squire to Don Quixote. Sancho's *donnée* function of pro-viding enough practical guidance to keep the Knight from doing himself in is expanded thematically to show the displaced sensory side of one man's Dulcineism, Quixote's, emerging in the vassalhood of the squire. The squire, in a configuration sometimes spelled out and sometimes implied, becomes the "limb" for Quixote's disattached mind or head, in a Dulcineated social microcosm. Sancho is the fall guy who receives the physical pain along with or in lieu of the Knight (who, as we have seen, is purposely imperceptive about pain); be-ing a mere peasant, Sancho is not supposed to be fully susceptible to this pain.[25]

So Quixote explains in an early section, where Sancho's shoulders are pronounced to be less sensitive to pain than are his master's (115). In later discussions of the blanket-tossing, the embarrassment of the Knight at his failure to rescue his squire is rationalized—for his own benefit—into the specialization of mind and sense: ". . . I felt more pain then in my spirit than you did in your body" (482–483). Actually what he had felt was not pain, but rage at his squire's (not his friend's) mistreatment by the world, and perhaps even an im-pulse to laugh as Sancho soared above the blanket (131). But Sancho is not to suspect a lack of sympathy in his master; he is ordered to "Be quiet" about it (488). Sancho is expected in-stead to feel obligated to the unnecessarily sacrificing Knight, who stays awake at night "reflecting on means of sustaining, bettering and favoring him" (594); these "everlasting meditations" (656) are somehow payment for Sancho's own night of "pain." And, when the two companions suffer minor injuries in dismounting, the squire is expected to take the blame and "God's curse"; the fact that he himself had "remained dangling with his face and chest on the ground" (664–665) counts for nothing to Knight, Duke, or critic. Here the Dulcineated pain is presumed to apply to the man who can still fully feel pain.[26]

The final convolution is shown in the attempt to disenchant Dulcinea by lashing Sancho or having Sancho lash himself. The solution is prescribed by the mock Merlin at the Ducal court, who says it is "the universal resolution of all the authors of her sad misfortunes" that Sancho be lashed on his "two most ample buttocks" to the tune of 3,300 whacks (701). Among "all the authors" the novel would have us include not only Don Quixote but also the idealizing minds who have created the fictional world of chivalry, the Ducal servants who have unerringly gravitated toward this particular form of "disenchantment" and who stress Sancho's supposed gross insensitivity to pain, and the Ducal pair themselves, who are as usual "delighted . . . , for nothing promised them greater pleasure (705)." All these combined constitute a bit of "advice" (whip yourself) that Sancho is required to accept before he can receive the more polite advice on governing (elevate yourself) from his master alone.

Quixote, it is true, easily manages to convince himself that Sancho's hoax of fulfilling this prescription is as good as actual blood (and thus Quixote remains true to his preprogrammed world of ideal appearances), but the thematic import is to undermine the superficial appearance of an increased respect of master for man in part 2. For, although Quixote no longer literally strikes Sancho, as he had done in the first part, the "universal resolution" in favor of lashing is not a growth in ethical stature for the Knight, but a face-saving sublimation based upon his whole Dulcineated life project.

The inevitable climax becomes more and more clear as the novel approaches a finish; Don Quixote cannot sleep unless Sancho stays awake and gives himself three or four hundred lashes (847–848; see also 728). Quixote, "just as lovers feel" (922), cannot wait for nightfall, so that Sancho may proceed with the lashing; at one point Quixote attempts to pull down the sleeping Squire's breeches in order to administer the lashes himself. Sancho wakes up and Quixote argues: "Dulcinea is perishing; you are living in idleness; I am dying of desire, so pull down your breeches of your own free will, for it is my intention to give you at least two thousand lashes in this lonely spot" (855). When Sancho finally pays the debt of the lashes by pretending to lash himself and actually slashing the trees, the Knight stands in the distance, counting the strokes and mentally shuffling the cards, taking care not to "lose by a card too many or too few" (922). The indifference of Durandarte is here reincarnated. Quixote, however, "being naturally humane, and much afraid besides that Sancho might put an end to his life and he through Sancho's imprudence not attain his purpose" (923), postpones some of the lashing until another time. But this afterthought—coming after thousands of lashes have supposedly been delivered—is all too clear an index of the incredibly low priority Quixote assigns to human flesh. The culmination of the obsession with lashing brings an end to Quixote's rationalization of the head feeling more than the limb; it is now clear that Sancho can feel pain, but Quixote characteristically finds that he *should* feel it: ". . . you are a hard-hearted peasant, although your flesh is tender" (855); ". . . that flesh of yours—may I see the wolves devour it!" (901). This seems to be the ultimate point in the novel's exploration of the relation of master and man.

On the novelistic relationship of Quixote and Sancho, a discouragingly large mountain of criticism has accumulated. But most of it sentimentalizes this relationship, inflating the tolerance of Sancho for his master at the expense of examining the results of the two men's being together over the long ramble that makes up the novel. Mere proximity is confused with deep sympathy and understanding, words of affection with situational realities. Sancho's affection for his master has been grossly exaggerated by critics; the master's alleged love for Sancho is likewise often far from evident. It is usually documented with the instance of the regret he expresses when Sancho goes off to govern his island. No mention is made of the rest of the page in which he says that Sancho's absence "is not the principal cause" of his sadness, and in which he becomes quite upset at the Duchess' offer to have her maids attend and serve him "to his complete satisfaction" (748). It is Sancho's absence that makes the Altisidora episode possible. But, although his presence would have prevented that episode, it would also have had its drawbacks for the attainment of ideal appearances, for it is at the Ducal court that Quixote is most embarrassed by Sancho, who, he feels, may give away their true identities, and who had best be put out of the room entirely before he lets the Ducal pair see what "gross and peasant stuff" he, Sancho, is made of (669–671). Here, as earlier, Quixote has reason to fear that "Sancho would blurt out a whole pack of mischievous nonsense and touch on matters not wholly to his credit" (481). Perhaps what one can best say to those who find that Don Quixote loves Sancho as he "loves himself"[27] is that this conclusion might be true in the sense that Don Quixote does not love anyone's self at all.

The sentimentality that would confuse long proximity with depth of relationship is, I believe, at one point in the novel directly burlesqued,[28] in the comic hyperbole of a description of the relationship between Rocinante and Dapple:

Now the friendship between the pair was so rare and so strong that there is a tradition handed down from father to son that the author of this true history devoted some special chapters to it, but, to preserve the propriety and decorum proper to so heroic a story, omitted to put them in. Though at times he forgets this purpose of his, and writes that as soon as the two beasts were together they would start scratching one another, and that once they were tired and contented, Rocinante would cross his neck over Dapple's—and it would stick out by more than half a yard. Then the two of them would gaze fixedly on the ground and stand in that position for three days, or at least for so long as they were left, or hunger did not compel them to seek for sustenance. The tradition is, I repeat, that the author left in writing a comparison between their friendship and that of Nisus and Euryalus, and of Pylades and Orestes. And if this is true, it can be deduced how strong the friendship between these two pacific

animals must have been, to the wonder of the world and to the shame
of humankind, who are so little able to preserve friendships for one another. Hence the saying:
                'There is no friendship between friends,
                Men's sparring canes are turned to lances'
and that is the reason for that other song:
                'Twixt friend and friend the bug creeps in.'
    But let no one suppose that the author digressed in comparing the
friendship of these animals to that of men. For men have received many
lessons from the beasts and learnt many important things from them, for
example: from storks, the enema; from the dog, vomiting and gratitude;
from cranes, vigilance; from ants, thrift; from elephants, chastity, and
loyalty from the horse.   (540–541)

This passage is juxtaposed with what has just preceded, Sancho's
declaration that he is truly growing in wisdom because some of the
"muck"[29] of his master's conversation has stuck to his own "parched
understanding"—an example of vomiting-gratitude not likely to be
surpassed. The novel shows that it is the master's understanding that
is parched, so parched that his heart is indeed no bigger (as Sancho
puts it) than a hazelnut (525). Rather than demonstrating the great
internal benefits that a Sancho must derive from association with a
follower of Dulcinea, the novel shows that no such benefits are to be
had, and that only by resisting to whatever extent he is able can
Sancho preserve himself from being reduced to the numbed state of
feeling and perception that his master and the many idealistic characters represent.

    At the same time, it is clear than Sancho's resistance is not a
norm.[30] For although it makes the human body overwhelmingly
present in Don Quixote, even when Sancho is not immediately on
the scene, and thus invalidates all attempts to extract Quixote safely
from the context of destructive criticism in which he has his novelistic
being, Sancho is far too much a mixture of stock peasant consciousness and stubborn, brilliant, physiological independence to represent
adequately anything that might be called, in D. H. Lawrence's

phrase, "the life of the human body." The novel is showing that within the framework it explores there *is* no answer to Dulcinea. Sancho holds on to his own and betters himself, with his various monetary gains and his various ways of preserving himself from the kind of remaking Quixote would do to him. But the ways of Dulcinea are otherwise unchecked, as powerful as any that the critics could desire. The haves and the have-nots continue, just as the pattern of appearance-as-ideal goes on. The complete triumph of the haves is emphasized, late in part 2, especially when Sancho is shown sharing some cheese with the Duke's lackey. After devouring the cheese, the two of them "even licked the packet of letters" belonging to the Duke, "only because it smelt of cheese" (900). Sancho has avoided the pressure put upon him to be lashed voluntarily (701) and has illuminated Dulcineism with his penetrating critical light, but he is by no means entering into conscious opposition to the order of society in which he finds himself. It would probably be of no avail to do so, even though the novel—very much with Sancho's help— shows that order to be antipathetic and potentially deadly to everything Sancho enjoys.

CHAPTER FOUR

A World Already Conquered by Dulcinea

Dulcinea's Postconquest Poetry

On the level of immediate, surface action, it is not Sancho, but various others who resist Don Quixote: those who fight with him, those who attempt to bring him back to his village, or those who sneer at him. To accept this aspect of the text at face value, however, is to be deceived.[1] The clash is only Dulcineism engaged in a kind of family quarrel, and a not very determined one. Apparent clash recedes in favor of deeper reconciliation. After a critical reading, the clash should not control an interpretation of the novel any more than the many statements assuring readers that chivalry books are the only target.

Even Don Quixote's treatment at the hands of the Priest, the Barber, and the Bachelor of Law, all of whom try to get him to give up his chivalry, is not a conflict of values.[2] True, their opposition sometimes becomes quite unfair, flatly opposing Quixote's project without consideration of the psychological roots involved in it. And even though we must avoid taking at face value the Knight's appearance of undergoing great pain in his trials, every reader recognizes that at one level the other characters seem to take a certain amount of pleasure in what pain they believe themselves to be witnessing. There need be no great surprise that the undeniable masochistic element in Dulcineism is complemented by the appropriate sadistic element in the novel's other characters, even though such a gross psychological classification tells us little of the novel's specific qualities. The bloody fight between Quixote and the goatherd near the end of part 1, for example, is witnessed by the learned Canon, the well-read Priest, and the plain tough-guy troopers with ugly glee: ". . . with some help from the barber[!], the goatherd managed to get Don Quixote down, and rained such a shower of blows on him that the Knight's face poured blood as freely as his. The canon and the priest were bursting with laughter; the troopers danced for joy, and everyone cheered them on, as men do at a dog-fight. Only Sancho Panza was in despair, because he could not get himself loose from one of the canon's servants, who was preventing him from helping his master" (451–452). The reactions of the characters to Don Quixote's trouble tell against the cautionary interpretation, which would have us believe that Cervantes was positing the social background of Spain as a normative basis for the cure of the "mad" Knight.

It is more to the point to note how Cervantes exploits the comic openings of a realism that is not based on an ordinary sense of probability (as comedy is not). The flouting of "reality" by Don Quixote (as by many comic characters in literature) is in Cervantes' context of comedy met not merely with the usual hard outlines of the real world but with a world that does unexpected things and in which events transpire in an arbitrary way. Eventually, however, the two strands of arbitrariness complement and comment upon each other. They even congratulate each other, in a sense, only to be ultimately mocked from the critical perspectives provided by the novel itself.

Like a good comic character interested in a single stance toward reality, Don Quixote is ready to fight anyone who impugns Dulcinea in the slightest way, and thus he gets into frequent fights (at least in part 1). But, instead of creating a host of devoted enemies, he wins more and more acceptance. Moreover, those who set for themselves the task of curing the Knight of his chivalry reveal extended involvement in it themselves. The novel's first chapter tells us that even before his madness, Don Quixote often would have "arguments with the priest of his village, who was a scholar and a graduate of Sigüenza, as to which was the better knight—Palmerin of England or Amadís of Gaul. But Master Nicholas, the barber of the village, said that no one could compare with the Knight of the Sun" (32). And the first chapter of part 2 begins with an ostensibly diagnostic visit of the Priest and the Barber to Don Quixote, which soon wells up into a three-way discussion of the inner details of certain chivalry books. The facility with which such discussions are precipitated, the facility with which a number of characters can enter into lengthy masquerades of chivalry, amounts to a ritual celebration in acceptance of Dulcinea's values rather than resistance to them.

The Duke and Duchess (along with that apparently frustrated young girl, Altisidora) do most of the outright sneering at Don Quixote. The Duke's resistance to Dulcinea even takes form in his being "greatly amused" to hear of the mauling his own household had contrived to give the Knight (790). But *everything* amuses the Duke, or at least so he hopes.[3] The Duke is living comfortably the pretentious life of appearance-as-ideal—which is the kind of culture that is predetermined in Quixote's search for something, some all-accepted greatness, that could be presented as evidence of Dulcinea's works. The Trifaldi episode, ostensibly instigated for mere amusement by the Ducal pair, is a long drawn-out, unfunny joke concerning the alleged inherent ugliness (from a stock point of view) of all waiting-women.[4] Its upshot is that Sancho and Quixote are induced to ride on the mock magic horse Clavileño and are frightened by firecrackers hidden in the horse's tail, which the Duke and Duchess personally set off (732). Yet this hoax gives the Ducal pair something to weep over (726) as well as something to laugh about, "not only at the time but for all their lives" (735).[5]

The Duchess does not react to Sancho's various critical remarks, except with a cloying sweetness and a fascination with what she takes to be cute little peasants, the Panza family (792, 807). Although she shows no sign of understanding Sancho, she does seem to wish to mistreat him. She begins her acquaintance with Sancho by addressing him as brother (663), but, much like Quixote, she comes around to promising Sancho to find a whip that "will agree with the tenderness of your flesh like its own sister" (706). It is the Ducal mind (manifested through household servants) that hits upon the unfunny but symbolically appropriate project of lashing Sancho. Ducal resistance to Dulcinea turns out to be perpetual re-creation of some of Dulcinea's patterns for living, now revealed as titillations rather than heroic effort. Thus the similarity of Quixote and the other characters (except Sancho) is ultimately clear, whereas resistance to Dulcinea becomes more and more unclear, equivocal, and finally negligible.

This pattern is especially impressive in the case of the Ducal pair, because they plainly do not take Dulcinea seriously in their conscious minds at all. They are the people who do not need to dream of gaining the autocratic power held out as one of the attractive prizes in the chivalric game played by others; they already have such power. In one way, Don Quixote is in their employ from the very beginning of the novel, and the fact that they have such a tight hold on social power caustically contradicts his great claims for the transforming power of chivalric devotion. True to the patterns of ruling-class behavior, they think of little more to do with their social prominence than to continue ostentatiously and sadistically redramatizing the values of Dulcinea—especially the value placed on impressive appearance. When Quixote and Sancho are not available as objects, the regular servants (such as Doña Rodriguez) are. Dul-

cinea's world is here seen in its works; the painful efforts in acculturation produce expensively trivial results.

Similarity instead of opposition can be seen in another of the crucial areas where Cervantes is careful to show it: the sharing of poetic
standards. In the Knight's speech defining poetry, poetry is personi-
fied as a Dulcinea-like maiden, "formed of an alchemy of such virtue
that anyone who knows how to treat her will transform her into the
purest gold of inestimable price . . ." Such a maiden "does not care
to be handled or dragged through the streets. . . . She must be exposed for sale only in the form of heroic poems, piteous tragedies,
or gay and artificial comedies. She must not let herself be handled by
buffoons, nor by the ignorant vulgar, who are incapable of recognizing or appreciating her treasures" (568–569). Poetry is a way of
achieving fame second only to errantry itself, Quixote goes on to
say, and his defense of a young man's right to be a poet, even against
the contrary promptings of his father, is an illusory defiance of social
prescript, finally juxtaposed and cancelled by Quixote's advice that
the best way for the young man to win poetic fame is to allow himself to be "guided rather by the opinions of others than by his own"
(587). All these statements win the amazed approval of the would-
be poet and of his father (570, 587), but the novel is too firmly engaged in an exposure of the life of appearances caused by reliance
on collective opinion to allow this to be taken at face value.

In fact, the novel consistently juxtaposes poetry formed after a
Dulcineated model of purity with contexts that reveal its irrelevance
and ineptness within human situations.[6] Even the love lyrics of the
Renaissance poet Garcilaso are incorporated for stock purposes, and
not only in Quixote's nostalgic use of a couplet to reiterate "the sweet
pledge" of his bitterness at Dulcinea's enchantment. Garcilaso's pastoral sentiments are quoted by Don Quixote while he devises a suitable penance to be performed in Dulcinea's name: ". . . this is the
spot where the moisture from my eyes will swell . . . this little stream"
(205). His poem expressing the difficulties of reaching the "high

seat of immortality" (507) is used by Quixote in moralizing on the nature of good and evil, and it arouses the silly niece's admiration. Quixote replies to Sancho's realistic description of what Dulcinea, as a peasant woman, must be doing, by referring to Garcilaso's four nymphs, who have undoubtedly dressed Dulcinea in clothing "all of gold, silk, thread and pearls, plaited and interwoven" (515–516). When Quixote is supposed to be in his greatest distress over the enchantment of Dulcinea, his first words are a conceit on Fortune, from Garcilaso (529–530). Much further on, Altisidora coyly flatters him by using the formula from Garcilaso: "—— oh, harder than the marble to my plaints, thou stony-hearted Knight!"(917). Even the Knight finally asks if there is any connection between Garcilaso and the events he is called upon to commemorate (919)—perhaps Quixote's only flicker of enlightenment in his whole mountain of experience.

The affinity between Don Quixote's concept of poetry and the uses to which poetry is put by other characters is slowly made clear in side episodes that always lead back into the main pathway of Dulcinea. The Knight's urge toward Dulcinea is eventually an urge not to reach her or any woman, but to perpetuate an internal sterility of feeling and perception by living endlessly in the context of stereotyped sentiments and group approval. In the first of the pastoral episodes, there is a similarity between Quixote and the sad case of Chrysostom ("Grisóstomo"), who pursues an utterly antisensuous maiden, Marcella, with numerous complaints of rejection, sadness, and love lament. Quixote hears of this (to him) "delightful" story, and arrives just in time for the funeral of the young man, whose body is decked out not only with flowers, but also with reams of his own verses (102). Chrysostom's "Song of Despair," with its account of sorrows intensified "for greater torture" with "lumps of my wretched bowels" (104; or "wretched entrails" : "por mayor tormento,/ Pedazos de las míseras entrañas") "pleased all its hearers" (107)! It is a song in which Love is extolled as the tyrant of mandatory pain (106). The burial of Chrysostom is as delightful, when seen from the inside, and as sought for as Durandarte's perpetual enchantment in the cave of Montesinos, and in both cases the fact of death itself is completely lost sight of by the participants and bystanders, though Cervantes does not allow it to be lost on his readers.

But what is generally not recognized by readers is that the conventional poetry of Chrysostom is impossible to distinguish from what Quixote has extolled as great poetry. The poetry of *Don Quixote*, usually dismissed with embarrassment by the novel's translators and commentators, is equated by Quixote and the idealist lovers within the novel with the deepest of sentiment, the perfect expression of ideality. Sampson Carrasco, seen very literally, is the most determined of those who oppose Quixote, because he is the man who rides out and finally defeats the Knight in combat and forces him to return home. But Carrasco as poet is invited by the Knight to compose verses in honor of Quixote's departure from Dulcinea (496). True, he at first seems to have difficulty, but in his role as Knight of the Wood he masters the formula of devotion to a mistress who will "prescribe a law" that the chivalric hero can follow "unswervingly."[7] And, late in the novel, Quixote pronounces Carrasco a good poet (903), an opinion Carrasco can accept eagerly; he is glad to agree to go into the pastoral life with Quixote, "for, as all the world knows by now, I am a most famous poet. I will compose pastoral or courtly verses at every turn" (933).[8] The integrity of Quixote's feelings and those of the other characters is thus heavily impugned by Cervantes' equations of the obviously stock with the would-be deep and emotive.[9]

The Canon of Toledo initially appears to be opposed to the Knight's literary standards, but he is actually far more in agreement than not. The Canon wants his conventional virtues and vices (426) unencumbered with the improbabilities of knight-errantry. But his recommendations for factual as opposed to fanciful history include *El Cid* and the Book of Judges. Quixote is quite within the framework of the Canon's beliefs when he says later that the existence of giants is proved by the Bible (479).[10] The Knight, in his defense of knight-errantry before the Canon, is able to "mingle truth and fiction" thoroughly in his recounting of heroism as it is understood in history. For the Canon, this mingling is another occasion for being "amazed" at the Knight's knowledge of all knight-errantry (439). But the novel is exploring a fictional social context that relies on stories of exemplary heroes, whether they are purely chivalric or not.[11] The Canon's taste for safely moralistic literature is securely present in the Knight's chivalric project, and the narrow gap is narrowed still more by the Knight's approval, late in the novel, of a moral tract he finds at the printer's: "Books like this, numerous though they are, are the kind that ought to be printed, for there are many sinners nowadays, and there is need of infinite light for so many in the dark" (878).[12]

It has often been noted that a great many of the characters (Sancho and the Man in Green are the only major exceptions) are acquainted with chivalric literature. The Priest can string a list of chivalric references as fast as anyone else (255–256). The Landlord and the Innkeeper enjoy these tales, although they claim to be only entertaining themselves with them and, incidentally, providing entertainment for the hired help who hear them read aloud (41–42, 277, 279–281). The illiterate Maritornes has likewise enjoyed these readings. Even an overworked plowman is glimpsed momentarily as he sings a battle ballad from the Carolingian cycle (522–523). The Canon is sure that the tales are all "triviality and lies," but has tried to combine their ability to "delight" readers with his own dubious standards of realism: he has written one hundred pages of a heroic tale himself (427, 436). He enjoys fantasy literature as long as he does not reflect that it is fantastic. The Priest, who had been reading such pastoral works as *The Ten Books of the Fortunes of Love* (61) in addition to books of errantry,[13] is able to excuse himself into reading aloud the "Tale of Foolish Curiosity" by insisting that he only reads out of "curiosity" and for the diversion of the guests (281). The Priest himself sets out disguised in knight-errant fashion, and he parallels Quixote's second thoughts concerning the propriety of his helmet with his own second thoughts concerning which costume he should wear (222). Both Dorothea (251, 252, 266) and the Barber

(223) insist that they need no coaching in the parts they are to play in the rescue of the Knight; evidently they have rehearsed silently for a long time.

Even a character as removed from the Knight's quest as the humanist scholar who accompanies Don Quixote to the region of the cave of Montesinos proves to have significant likenesses to the protagonist. The humanist is, in the first place, "much given to the reading of books of chivalry." Like Don Quixote, he is also given to bolstering his citations "with the utmost precision on the testimony of twenty-five authorities." His work, like Quixote's, is designed specifically to be put into print; ". . . his pursuits and studies were to compose books for the press, all of great profit and entertainment to the commonwealth." And, most important, his work is like Quixote's in its perpetuation of stock emotions: his projected *Book of Liveries* contains no less than 703 "suitable devices" for all occasions—for "the jealous, the scorned, the forgotten and the absent." As he proudly points out, the *Book of Liveries* would spare gentlemen the need to invent their own devices for "their own desires and purposes" (609–611).

The supposition that Quixote is opposed by other characters is shared by these characters themselves, who (like many critics) distinguish sharply between Don Quixote "mad" and Don Quixote "sane." By making such a separation, it is possible to avoid a satiric contamination of the ideals Quixote exhibits when "sane" with those he pursues while "mad." This in turn allows one to take such idealist critical positions as, for instance, that the novel ridicules Quixote's actions but not his ideals,[14] or that his basic sanity marks him as one who is "wise and kind independently of his madness."[15] Thomas Mann put the position well when he said that Quixote is "mad in one single point but in all others a blameless knight."[16] The novel, however, does not observe this neat division; its very point is to violate it. The characters are only too right in their amazement before the sane-mad distinction. For with only a moderate critical effort it would collapse.

The tenuousness of the sane-mad classification is pointed up in the reactions of the Priest and the Barber, who are always astonished and amazed afresh at the Knight's madness (218, 220, 266–267) but who accept equally implausible monologues from Cardenio, Dorothea, and the Knight himself as deeply affecting truths and who are themselves devotees of chivalric literature and of other miraculous literature. When the two men discuss statecraft with Don Quixote, they are pleased to note the "complete possession of his wits" that the Knight displays. But, the previous part of the paragraph casts doubt on their own wits, in the very matter of statecraft: "In the course of their conversation they happened to discuss the principles of statecraft—as they are called— ["en esto que llaman razón de estado"] and methods of government, correcting this abuse and condemning another, each one of the three setting up a fresh legislature, a modern Lycurgus or a brand new Solon" (471).[17] Even the rude Castilian who angrily denounces Quixote is careful to say that it is too bad his "reputed good sense should waste away along the channel of knight-errantry" and that knight-errantry "skims the cream" off the Knight's "intellect" (871). Sampson Carrasco is also sure that Quixote "has an excellent brain if only he can be freed from the follies of chivalry" (892). The ignorant niece responds to Quixote's remarks on vice and virtue with "Good heavens! . . . What a lot you know, uncle!" (505), and to his moralizing use of poetry with "Oh dear! Oh dear! . . . my master's a poet too! He knows everything. He can do everything" (507). The Man in Green is able with all his alleged resistance to impracticality to say that Quixote's "wise speeches" are admirable (581) and that his justification of knight-errantry is "measured on the scales of reason itself" (579). But the "reason" that all these characters admire and accept is Quixote's manipulation of stereotyped concepts. And it is the novel that keeps us aware of how desiccated those concepts are. Unless one is to keep an arbitrary check on response to the novel and obey the imperative suggested by the characters who wish to keep sanity and madness untouched by each other, one is impelled to see that the novel's exposure of the Knight inevitably spills over into an exposure of them too.

The implications of such satiric overflow become particularly clear in part 2,[18] where Quixote, who earlier had made claims to omniscience (100, 212), now generalizes on such topics as poetry, love, marriage, the family, government (as in his advice to Sancho), and war. This outpouring is accepted by one and all as the obvious final truth about reality. Even Sancho consciously resists it very little; at the moment of rejecting his master's Montesinos vision, he specifically excepts from his disbelief all those marks of wisdom that Quixote shows when "offering counsel at every step" (622). His master's conventional advice on marriage wins Sancho's glowing endorsement; ". . . so many things he knows" (609). There is no subject in which his master does not distinguish himself when he offers to "pick at and dip his spoon into" it. Quixote's speech on justifiable war even spurs Sancho to take his master for a theologian (650).

Dulcinea for All Nations

Critics proposing a cautionary interpretation of *Don Quixote* have stressed the amount of upset and harm that results from Don Quixote's interferences. The just rewards of knights may require some drastic steps to ensure their attainment; there are instances of Quixote's wounding other men (144), attacking in a cowardly way (557), justifying homicide itself as long as it is in the interests of knighthood (80). Still, one need not pretend to see wide scale damage in these particular acts, or in the killing of seven sheep as a result of mistaking dustclouds for armies (138), although these passages show that Don Quixote, equipped with normal perception and better weapons, would be a dangerous character. His world of literal chivalry would, if literally fulfilled, represent a social change in its encouragement of more man-to-man combats than normally exist in his actual fictional society. Everyone would duel over Dulcinea. But the fictional society does not need such a resurrection of chivalry, because it already does celebrate and practice a version of the duel-

ing system on a mass basis: in its own stock opposition to those mo-
lesters of Christian womanhood, the Moors.[19]

It is missing the point, then, to exaggerate Quixote's imperious
meddlesomeness into a form of Faustian aggrandizement,[20] but very
much to the point to notice what that meddlesomeness reveals about
a mode of thought he shares with so many others. In the instance of
the sheep taken for battling armies, Quixote had gratuitously interpreted sheep as men and, as men, enemy men and therefore legal
quarry. The commandeering of the barber's basin is not more important than the language Quixote uses as he sees the barber running
away: ". . . the delighted Don Quixote observed that the pagan had
acted most prudently in imitation of the beaver, who when hard-
pressed by the hunters, with his own teeth bites off what he knows by
his natural instinct to be the object of the chase" (162).[21] Other disturbing implications occur in the adventure of the corpse, when, after
wounding several men, Quixote discovers that the dead man being
transported had merely died of the plague: ". . . seeing Who it was
that killed him, there is nothing for it but to be silent and shrug my
shoulders" (145). What appears, out of context, to be the most ordinary commonplace is explicable in the novel at an unusual level of
literalness: Quixote would not interfere with anything done by God,
because God is like one of the great lords of the realm or one of the
kings who is entitled to arbitrary obedience (now that the galley-
slave episode has been resolved a few pages earlier). A single word,
marzipan, connotes in another way the indifference toward life that
the Knight continually evokes despite his professed intentions. The
Canon objects to the way a single youth cuts a giant in two, in the
books of chivalry, as if "he were made of marzipan" (424); Quixote
boasts of how the knights could slaughter the Turks "as if the whole
single lot of them had one single throat or were made of marzipan"
(473); later, infuriated at what he takes to be Moorish infidels, he
nearly slices off Master Pedro's head "as if it had been made of
marzipan" (642).

Such dehumanizations are not strange in a code that regards it as essential to "find some king, Christian or pagan, who is at war and has a beautiful daughter" so that the knight can go to work and earn glory (168). In this formulation, even the pretense that the fight must be in a Christian cause is not maintained very seriously. But eventually, the chivalry-book origin of this attitude is grounded upon a more general and more widely shared ideal: the stereotyped notion of masculine courage. Quixote's verbal defense of chivalric courage is a series of comparisons in which the Knight points out that courage in the abstract is an accepted value; people all admire the "brave sight" of "a gallant gentleman, beneath the eyes of his King," delivering a "well aimed lance-thrust against a brave bull in the midst of a great square" (578); they also admire knights performing military exercises at "the courts of their princes." And since such bravery is to be inculcated, it is not really foolhardy to attack peaceful lions; ". . . in this matter of encountering adventures . . . it is better to lose by a card too many than a card too few, for *such a knight is rash and foolhardy* sounds better in the hearer's ears than *such a knight is timid and cowardly.*"[22] Courage is inculcated in the abstract, tacitly for the benefit of some prince or lordling who is always nearby and ready to honor it, as long as it is within the bounds of convention. Thus the viceroy of Barcelona congratulates his general for a "fine chase" with his slave-powered ship against a pirate vessel, although gratuitous casualties resulted (882).

Although *Don Quixote* does not attempt to reflect all Spanish cultural values, the difference between the ideal of courage for Quixote and for historical Spain is as small as it can possibly be. The *hidalgos* who led the conquest of the New World were in an important sense factual Quixotes for whom reality obligingly cooperated. As J. H. Elliott points out,

their imagination was itself inspired by what they had learnt at home. The coming of printing to Spain around 1473 had given an extraordinary vogue to romances of chivalry, and *Amadís of Gaul* (1508), the most famous of them all, was known in affectionate detail by a vast body of

Spaniards who, if they could not read themselves, had heard them told or read aloud. A society soaked in these works, and touchingly credulous about the veracity of their contents, naturally tended to some extent to model its view of the world and its code of behavior on the extravagant concepts popularized by the books of chivalry. Here was an abundance of strange happenings and heroic actions. What more natural than that the mysterious world of America should provide the scene for their enactment? Uneducated and illiterate as Pizarro, Almagro and their companions may have been, all had heard of and hoped to find the kingdom of the Amazons; and it is recorded that their first sight of Mexico City reminded Cortés's men of "the enchanted things related in the book of Amadís."[23]

The courage of the conquistadores is well known. It is somewhat less well known that the conquest was to a large extent motivated by the opportunity to spread Christianity to new regions and that there were extensive debates in Spain over the proper application of Christian justice to the subjugated Indians. The debates led to elaborate legal codes that gave the *appearance* of creating equity of treatment for the Indians, while the *actual* rule of Spain caused, after the first one hundred years, a 90 percent decline in the native population.[24]

This historical denouement is almost beyond rational grasp. Certainly it cannot be explained in terms of Spanish "greed" or "individualism."[25] Its psychological affinities are more properly those explored in *Don Quixote*, where the main character combines a fine disregard for his own pains with a concomitant disregard for the pains, and even the lives, of others. Thus the Knight's "Discourse on Arms and Learning" (part 1, chapters 37–38) is a coruscating revelation (if it is not automatically classified, as it too often is, as wisdom) of the human implications of an ideology of courage in the abstract.[26] But here again the language is that of nonchivalric discourse, using a theme that was a commonplace in Renaissance literature (as Putnam's and other notes attest). In this discourse, Quixote asserts that "peace" is the aim and object of the profession of Arms, and peace is "the greatest good which men can desire in this life." After giving several biblical quotations to support this statement, Quixote repeats that "peace is the true aim of war; for Arms and war are all one" (340–341). Here once more is an indicator of parody, calling attention to a statement as inane as the equivalence of guaranteed wisdom with the fear of God. It does not matter that the same argument was made by St. Augustine or Castiglione or Dante; it is still inane. Only in the art of *Don Quixote*, however, are we allowed to focus on the inanity. In *De Monarchia*, which Sir Herbert Grierson thought Cervantes must have had on his desk when he wrote this passage,[27] we merely read:

> . . . in the case of anything that is done it is the ultimate end which constitutes the first principle and cause of the whole thing, for it is that end which, in the first instance, sets the agent in motion; so it follows that the whole theory of the means which make for the end must be derived from the end itself. . . . That thing, then, if there is any, which is the goal of the entire civilization of the human race, will give us this first principle, a reduction to which will be held a sufficient explanation of everything to be proved hereafter.[28]

Dante goes on to say that this greatest end is peace.

I am suggesting that the ideological resonances of the speech on Arms and Learning are far-reaching in history and culture. What *Don Quixote* adds to our perception of the problem of the "greatest end" is an ineradicable *critical* use of mind. Thus, although we may agree that peace may be the greatest good, we cannot, in terms of the novel, assume that reference to this goal is "sufficient explanation" for the institutions or ideologies that claim to promote it. In Don Quixote himself, renunciation is the goal, not peace. And when we encounter modern usages of the argument, as in McGeorge Bundy's recourse to it for justification of American military action in Vietnam and the Dominican Republic, we may—and should—connect it with the illuminating quality of *Don Quixote*. Bundy's claim that we are to understand each American intervention with an "awareness that the object of the exercise is peace because the object of our policy as a whole is peace" is, after all, only a very recent variant of Quixote's argument.[29] But in *Don Quixote* allusions to the accepted cultural heritage characteristically produce doubt rather than praise, even in contexts that reach far beyond the period in which Cervantes lived.[30]

The equation of war with peace is not the only notable touch in Don Quixote's discourse on Arms and Learning. There is also the confused but similar assertion, which seems to mean, at best, that the only cure for armed conflict is the profession of Arms:

. . . by Arms, states are defended, kingdoms preserved, cities guarded, the roads kept safe, and the seas swept free of pirates. In short, if it were not for them, states, kingdoms, monarchies, cities, and the highways on land and sea, would be subject to the savagery and confusion which war entails, so long as it lasts and is free to exercise its privileges and powers. (343)

This statement is followed with one of the fundamental assumptions of Dulcineism: ". . . it is a well-known truth that what costs most, is, and should be, the most highly valued." If the cost is carnage, the advocate of Arms will see only noble self-sacrifice. Thus, Quixote effuses over the bravery of the soldier who boards an enemy vessel during close combat:

. . . with undaunted heart, sustained by the honor which spurs him on, he exposes himself as a mark for all their shot, and endeavors to pass along that narrow causeway into the enemy's ship. And, most amazing of all, no sooner does one man fall, never to rise again this side of Dooms-day, than another takes his place; and, if he, in his turn, falls into the sea, which lies in wait for him like an enemy, another, and yet another, takes his place, without a moment passing between their deaths: the greatest display of valor and daring to be found in all the hazards of war. (344)

These juxtapositions of the rationale of war with pictures of its ir-rationality can hardly be read as the kind of beautiful recruiting manual so many critics and commentators see in the passage,[31] although the fact that the critics as well as the characters at the inn, led by the Priest (345), agree here has its significance.

Other passages in which the Knight discourses on war are equally revealing. In attempting to make peace between two feuding villages, he launches into a list of the reasons "prudent men" may go to war; the listing becomes so comprehensive as to furnish cause for almost any war ever designed.[32] But then, perhaps as an afterthought, he juxtaposes the official doctrine of Christian peace, which renders his earlier reasoning inanely beside the point.

Besides, the taking of unjust vengeance—and no vengeance can be just—goes directly against the sacred law we profess, by which we are commanded to do good to our enemies and to love those who hate us, a commandment which may seem rather difficult to obey, but which is only so for those who partake less of God than of the world, and more of the flesh than of the spirit. For Jesus Christ—God and true man—who never lied, nor could, nor can lie, being our law-giver, said that His yoke was gentle and His burden light, and therefore He could not have commanded us to do anything impossible to perform. So, my dear sirs, you are bound to keep the peace by law divine and human.   (650)

But Quixote does not see a contradiction between this argument and his preceding justifications of war. The speech is immediately deflated by Sancho's instinctive mockery, which precipitates violence against himself and his master, on the part of these very villagers. Christian ideals are suitable for constant quotation, but in a society that spends so much effort denying all spontaneity violence is also constantly at hand. At the same time, the sequence, in its very scope of trying to apply ideal doctrine to the patently silly conflict of a couple of villages, is a satiric deflation of Quixote's whole mission. The final comic reversal points to the irrelevance of the doctrine in this specific situation, for the villagers decide afterward not to do battle after all (651), and the great theory of Christian peace is left to find its proper application either in limbo or in our own wars for freedom.

The prologue to part 2 contains Cervantes' apparently serious statement that he has no regrets over being wounded at Lepanto, and he gives some justifications for military virtue that seem to be full-blown Dulcineism. "The wounds a soldier shows on his face and on his breast are stars to guide others to the heaven of honor and to create in them a noble emulation." Or, in an even more stark picture: ". . . a soldier looks better dead in battle than safe in flight" (467). But in the collision-chamber of the novel itself, these sentiments (perhaps part of Cervantes' own conscious mind) are exposed to uncomplimentary view when voiced by a hero who does not comprehend the painful nature of wounds, who does not value the physical body except for idealistic service.[33] In his apostrophe to the young man about to enlist in the infantry, Quixote paints the picture of an honorable early death and repeats the argument that "a soldier looks better slain in battle than alive and safe in flight." Here the supporting argument has its affinity in that indifference to life which has culminated in the Montesinos vision, a chapter earlier. "For supposing you are killed in the first engagement or skirmish, or by a cannon shot or the springing of a mine, what does it matter? It is but death and there is an end" (628; "¿qué importa? Todo es morir, y acabóse la obra . . ."). Patience and shuffle the cards! By early death, the novice is advised, he can avoid an impecunious old age.[34]

The Quixote who makes this speech is no different from the one who declared earlier that "wounds received in battle . . . confer honor" (117), but now his attitude is adorned with full cultural regalia. An enemy, a suitable group of outsiders to fight against, is also provided—the Moors. The Morisco page in *Orlando Furioso* had been the cause of Roland's madness; he had proved sexually attractive to the lady (214–215). The Moors throughout are twitted for their mendaciousness (while the author puts most of his novel into the pen of his ostensible Arabic author, Cide Hamete Benengeli). Late in the novel, there is a glowing description by Don Quixote of "St. James the Moor-Killer," who has often been observed "overthrowing, trampling, destroying and killing the hosts of Hagar" (839, 840).

In *Don Quixote* the Moors, Arabs, and Turks are necessary counter-parts in the division of mankind for a war of implacable ideals that the Dulcineated life implies. One of Quixote's goals is the "chastise-ment of the proud," and one of the characters, a captain, describes the Battle of Lepanto, in which he took part, as the place where the "insolent pride of the Ottoman" received its comeuppance (477, 348). This gentleman's Moorish lady-love would obligingly agree, too, that Moors are all cheats, forgers, schemers, and liars (360–361, 485). As for his own poor success in the holy war, it no more disturbs him than Quixote's failure to reach Dulcinea disturbs the Knight; the Captain says that Heaven has "ordained" this failure for the sins of Christendom and because, in any case, God "ordains that there shall always be some scourge to chastise us" (349). Why did he join up in the first place? Because he would be "thereby serving God and my King" (346–348).

The purest Dulcineism is implied in still another aspect of his tale, for he first narrates a deadly battle with abstract praise for the brav-ery of the combatants and then refers to the two sonnets celebrating this battle, in which the carnage is efficiently idealized into a glo-rious victory over the dastardly enemy. These sonnets win the ap-proval of all those present (351, 353). For Don Quixote, also seated at the banquet table, there is no disparity between all this and his own concept of the unified quest of soldier and knight under God; as he has pointed out long before, "we soldiers and knights carry out what [the priests] pray for, defending it with the strength of our arms and the edge of our swords. . . . We therefore are God's min-isters on earth, and the arms by which His justice is executed here" (98). And it is the Moors who require justice to be done to them, even if the inhabitants of this fictional society require a number of signals from martial music, drums, and cannon shots to evoke the desired reactions. Various combinations of cannons, drums, and Moorish battle cries occur five times in part 2 (chapters 26, 27, 34, 53, and 61).

The exploration of this stock response and of all that goes with it is complex, but the results are hardly a question of unresolved, mutually contrasting perspectives.[35] Instead, *Don Quixote* takes its place as a great forerunner of what Lionel Trilling calls the "bitter line of hostility to civilization," which characterizes much more recent literature.[36] For surely it is not Spain alone that is implicated in Dulcinea's demand for life made right according to received ideals.[37] More radical still is the novel's quite sane comic stance toward the negation of Dulcinea; Cervantes proposes no tears at the deadly lady's unmasking.

The overall quality of his kind of satiric hostility is much different from what the nationalistic material alone might suggest; in *Don Quixote* violent death is usually just around the corner, not in the center of the scene. But because we are made to feel the hovering presence of death, we can take little comfort in the usual fantasy of indestructibility that seems to underlie so much comic art. The interconnections of violent death and Dulcineism are only one of Cervantes' intentions in his gigantic novel; still, these interconnections are far from negligible. It is only that the novel contains the theme of Dulcinea as dealer of death within its greater design of the superficial life.

Paradise Attained

The novel also suggests many likenesses between the idealistic love of Don Quixote for his imaginary mistress and the various romances of the upper-class men and women who (rather than low-life characters) occupy most of those pages that do not deal directly with the Knight.[38] The carry-over is more often implied than made directly, but the aesthetic fusion is made all the more convincing because Cervantes does not depend on omniscient commentary to create it.

A reader as perceptive as Thomas Mann, it is true, failed to cross the barrier between the main story and the juxtaposed tales in *Don Quixote*:

I cannot but shake my head over the single tales scattered through it, so extravagantly sentimental they are, so precisely in the style and taste of the very productions that the poet has set himself to mock. He crams his hosts of readers full to their hearts' content with the very diet from which he would wean them—a pleasant cure! In those idylls he resigns his earlier role, as though to say that if the age wanted that sort of thing, he could give it to them, yes, even be a master at it.[39]

But the lovers in the interpolated tales are no different from those Quixote meets, who in turn are only carrying out, to the best of their ability, Dulcinea's mandates against the sensual and against freedom of perception. They do so with real lovers rather than with purely imaginary ones. If we are to respond to the implications of the unmasking of Dulcinea, we cannot (like Cervantes' early readers) simply turn off these implications when they affect juxtaposed material that is similar in ideological content.

Mann, it so happens, was more than willing to shut off the critical process. As he frankly avows, the novel reveals that Don Quixote is a product of "Christian culture, Christian doctrine, and Christian humanity"; and for Mann there could not possibly exist a critical effort (whether fictional or philosophical) that could truly criticize so crucial a part of the Western tradition. Such critical attacks "can never touch the binding authority of the cultural Christianity of the Western world, which once achieved cannot be alienated."[40] One must retort that it is not for Mann to say how far Cervantes may go. Moreover, I must claim (and with no regrets about it) that Cervantes does indeed rock the great cultural boat, that his tremendous fictional scope in Don Quixote embodies a critical examination of Western culture and its Christian core, and that this examination is fully compelling in the idealistic lovers of the novel.

These lovers are no more hedged in by the paltry probability of reality than is the Knight. Cervantes seems to go to some lengths to show that the love stories accepted for facts are as unreal as any idealist might desire. The luscious Zoraida, for instance, is searched by

French pirates, who rob her of her anklets and of her "rich and precious jewels," but not of her virginity, the most valuable "jewel" of all: for the desires of these pirates, we are assured, "do not extend beyond money" (376–377). The lovely Leandra elopes and is found abandoned in a cave, "clad only in her shift" but sexually inviolate: she "was left in possession of that jewel which, once lost, is beyond all hope of recovery" (448). In part 1, tragic-seeming love affairs are brought to amazingly happy conclusions in the inn that takes on the aspect of "Heaven" itself; for Ferdinand it is a place "where all the ills of the earth are over and done with" (332). Don Quixote eventually gives voice to the same idea, as he invites still another visitor to enter: "Come into this paradise, I say, your worship, for here there are stars and suns to attend the heaven your worship brings with you. Here you will find arms at their zenith and beauty in its prime" (382). And near the end of part 2, the handsome young Don Gregorio is whisked away from a Moorish harem by a special rescue party dispatched from Barcelona, to be reunited with his sweetheart Anna Ricote—much to the delight of all good folk.

It is entirely to the point that the lovely ladies of the miraculous inn in part 1, Dorothea, Lucinda, Zoraida, and Clara, are dormitoried in Don Quixote's attic apartment while he keeps watch over these princesses and the men "stay outside, on guard, as it were" (382, 386). It is equally appropriate that one of the few bawdy passages in the novel seems to imply a complaint of sexual neglect by the landlady of the inn, who demands that the barber return the ox-tail belonging to her husband (which she had lent him for his chivalric disguise): "Give me back my tail, for my husband's what-d'ye-call-it's so kicked about on the floor that it's a shame. I mean his comb that he used to stick into my tail" (277).

Cervantes juxtaposes love literature and love life and shows how the gestures toward love in the novel are snared within the conventions of Dulcineism. The apparently tragic pains of his lovers are revealed as the same kind of sought-for and carefully idealized pains as those of his Knight. What first appears to be a social milieu swarming with passionate lovers eventually emerges as a world in which all passion is contained in predetermined channels. These men and women are busy, not with one another, but with repeatedly playing out the narrow roles Dulcinea prescribes. In "Master Pedro's Puppet Show" and "The Tale of Foolish Curiosity," the novel shows the literary grip of Dulcinea's values upon her audiences; in the pastoral episodes and the love stories of Dorothea and Ferdinand, Cardenio and Lucinda, Zoraida and the captain, and Gregorio and Anna Ricote, the literary connections and controls are shown more indirectly, but always with Dulcinea having the upper hand.

The puppet show of Master Pedro illustrates in miniature the novel's treatment of love as a function of knight-errantry; it also makes use of an accepted folk tradition and of ethnic prejudice. For the story of Gaiferos' rescue of his wife from the Moors comes from Spanish balladry and stems from the Charlemagne legends. It is also "in everyone's mouth and is sung by the boys about the streets" (638). It begins, in the puppet version, with Gaiferos entirely unconcerned about getting his wife back from the Moors; he is more interested in playing backgammon. This of course will not do; Charlemagne soon notifies him that he is "imperilling his honor"; he is hectored into such a rage that he asserts he is "capable of rescuing his wife . . . even though she were imprisoned in the deepest bowels of the earth" (639). Cervantes adds some details to this rescue scarcely to be taken as straight adaptation of the ballads: "Do you observe that Moor stealing up on tiptoe, with his finger to his lips, behind Melisendra's back? Now see him give her a full kiss on the mouth, and see her spit and wipe it from her lips with the white sleeve of her smock. See how she wails and tears her lovely hair in grief, as if she were to blame for his crime" (639). This miscreant is then handsomely provided with two hundred lashes by an understanding Moor (yes, there are exceptions even among the damned!), which makes Melisendra "better and calmer in demeanor," good proto-Dulcinea that she is (640). But now the good guys arrive, and Melisendra exhibits "joyful looks." In another detail probably all his own, Cervantes augments the melodrama; as she tries to mount her husband's horse from the balcony, "see, she is caught by the lace of her skirt on one of the balcony spikes, and is hanging in the air, unable to reach the ground. But see how merciful Heaven sends aid in her sorest need, for Sir Gaiferos comes up, and never pausing to see whether her fine skirt is torn or not, grasps her and brings her forcibly to the ground" (640). A chase ensues, but Quixote, doing what the rest of the audience only thinks of doing, rushes on stage and in a rage tremendous even for him slashes the pursuing puppet-Moors with his sword. Triumphantly, he says: "Consider what would have happened to the good Sir Gaiferos and the fair Melisendra, if I had not been present here" (642). Actually, they would have reached Paris amid much rejoicing, according to the ballad itself, but Quixote is never interested in reaching that kind of consummation.

In fact, he interrupts the puppet performance verbally, before he does so physically, by calling attention to the puppet-show narrator's failure to recount the correct way in which the Moors would have given the emergency signal that Melisendra is trying to escape (641). And in his efforts to assist the lovers, he slices into the head of Melisendra's father, Charlemagne, and cuts nose and eye out of the puppet Melisendra herself (642). It is as if the somewhat erotic details provided by the young boy who narrates the puppet show have caused an extraordinary release (Sancho "had never before seen his master in so outrageous a temper") of the automatically available stock indignation at the Knight's command. And then, having belied his just prior claim to a "mild and compassionate nature" (635), Quixote can seek to distract all critical insight from (and in) himself by a display of generosity in paying for the slashed puppets. The innkeeper is duly "amazed at his liberality" (643–645).

This transaction seems to smooth the way for critics to take an uncritical response toward the puppet show itself, in which all evil is focused upon those Moors, with their persistent habit of bringing to mind sexual matters—which Dulcinea has forbidden anyone to dream of. But the puppet show is not representative of the realm of "art" (as critics too willingly assume); it is counterfeit art in which nothing is risked or explored. Like the talking-ape act with which it is billed, the show is a fraud—but one that can be flattering to one's taste for authoritative statement. Master Pedro's show, the innkeeper declares, "is one of the finest and best-acted . . . we've seen in this part of the kingdom for many a year. He has an ape with him too, with the rarest talents an ape ever had or man imagined" (633; "se imaginó entre hombres"). Such is imagination in Dulcinea's world.

A related fantasy is given in more complex form, and with further interlacing of Dulcineism, in the famous "Tale of Foolish Curiosity," which is read aloud at the inn of paradise. The unhappy case of Anselmo, who has his perfect friend Lothario test his perfect wife's "virtue," is analogous to Quixote's own Dulcineism. When Anselmo is thoroughly deluded into thinking that his Camilla is "virtuous," Cervantes breaks the narrative with the adventure of the wineskins; Quixote rushes in and slaughters these illusory giants and achieves another triumph. But even though Lothario and Camilla seem to the appreciatively peeping Anselmo to be "transformed into the very characters they were acting" (315), and even though "the pair of them made their imposture pass for truer than truth itself" (312), there is something inane rather than ennobling about this form of perspectival subjectivity. The "Tale" surely goes beyond the surface morality critics tend to ascribe to it, which is (however deftly expressed) that Anselmo should not have messed himself up.[41] For at the point of the interruption of the wineskins, Anselmo is a thoroughly happy man, if happiness is defined in Dulcinea's terms, and his happiness lasts for "many months" (316). A mock drama in which the good woman is ready to prove her "purity" by killing herself for "the husband Heaven gave me" (311) proves to be more important than any actual qualities Camilla may happen to have. For him, as for Quixote, the intensified stock virtue is the ultimate reality of paradise. He has not injured himself as yet by his wife-testing, and he has attained, though without the requisite delays and suffering, what the men of the novel want. Appropriately, the listeners to the tale raise no objections to Anselmo's deluded joy.

The complete indifference to the actual qualities in Camilla is dramatized further in a recurrence of Dulcineated poetry. Anselmo offers to assist Lothario in his testing mission by writing some love poems for him, to be presented to Camilla. But Lothario himself proves quite capable of writing these stock sonnets of unrequited love for his compliant lover Camilla, and the resulting sonnets are most pleasing, especially to Anselmo (301–303). In stock emotions, sincerity is easily manufactured.[42] Only Leonela, the maid, who parallels somewhat Sancho's critical role in the main narrative, is able to suggest that love is too varied a phenomenon to be discussed in terms of standardized precepts (304). The ceremonial rhetoric of Lothario (286–293), in which he in effect clears the way for the acceptance of his Lothario role, is a concatenation of commonplace ideals similar to Quixote's advice on government and on war. He begins with references to, and quotations from, poetry on the subject of friendship. But Anselmo and the audience and perhaps Lothario himself are fascinated with a situation in which idealistic mandates are violated: they find that friendship may be used for "purposes offensive to God." Apparently, it is not always enough to believe that "the divine friendship must not be forfeited for a human one," and that "a man without honor is worse than dead." The cautionary tale contains fantasy elements that show a contradictory side of the ideals involved, even though the illumination is consciously available only to the reader and not to the characters.

Lothario goes on to try to intimidate Anselmo by comparing him with the Moors, who also will not understand a thing unless it is proved to them. In fact, he tells Anselmo, "I am even inclined to abandon you to your folly as a punishment for your wickedness." This delicious fantasy cannot be indulged as yet, though; there is more, much more, rhetoric. First a dilemma that is itself full of presuppositions on the nature of women: "If you do not take her for what you say, why do you want to test her instead of treating her as a bad woman, and punish her as you think she deserves? But if she is as good as you think, it will be an impertinence to experiment with truth itself, for when the trial is over, it cannot have a higher value than it had before" (288). But the definition of a good woman as one who is absolutely monogamous is just what prompted Anselmo to make his experiment (285), and just what defined his perfect marriage in the first place. Next come some reflections on fame and glory: it is permissible to gain these only for God or the public weal, never in a personal relationship that is not worthy of "difficult works." This parallels Quixote's own belief in the value of mere difficulty. Anselmo believes that Camilla's value will be increased by her passing "through the ordeal" and being "purged and refined in the fire of temptation and solicitation by someone worthy of her" (286). But such a belief is implicit in both his and Quixote's ideals, and it is Lothario who is "rash" to suggest otherwise.

Lothario now proceeds to launch a series of analogies for purity, embarrassing in their plenitude and rigidity. A pure woman is like a diamond (and another "jewel," comparable to Zoraida, Leandra, and Dorothea), which might break if hit with a hammer; a woman is like an ermine, which will allow itself to be caught rather than dirtied; a woman is like a mirror of "clear and shining glass"; she is "like a beautiful garden full of flowering roses, whose owner does not allow anyone to walk in it or to touch them; enough that they enjoy its fragrance and beauty from afar off through its iron railings" (290–291).

After some additions on the subject of honor and the dangers of being "robbed" of it, the final argument comes. It is the biblical justification: the divine sacrament of marriage, "soluble only by death" and ordaining that the married couple should be "one flesh." The Bible thus forbids Lothario's mission, because in one flesh her dishonor is also his dishonor: "For, just as the whole body feels the pain of the foot or of any other limb, since they are all one flesh; and the head feels the ankle's pain, although it is not the cause of it; so the husband shares his wife's dishonor, being one with her" (292). But these arguments also suggest the spurious head-limb analogy that Don Quixote wishes to impose upon Sancho Panza; a linkage of two people in one flesh denies the individual organism its independent existence. Such a denial, however, is thus shown to be involved in the very concept of Christian marriage. Just as Cervantes grounds his depiction of chivalry upon the more fundamental idealism of Christian asceticism and Western heroism, in "The Tale of Foolish Curiosity" the total idealism of Anselmo is forced back revealingly into its sacred sources.

Finally, the "Tale" is lopped off in a proper ending that mockingly outrages probability. All three guilty protagonists are quickly killed off. Anselmo expires ludicrously in mid-sentence as he writes a confession of his folly; he is found the next day "lying on his face, with half of his body on the bed and the other half on the desk, and with the paper he had written unsealed and the pen still in his hand" (323). But the improbability does not much trouble the Priest or the other listeners to the "Tale"; like Quixote's grabbing of Maritornes, the daydream of being commissioned to seduce another man's beautiful wife can be indulged just as it is repressed. Such vicarious indulgence of sensuality seems to be the only kind available in this fictional world where women succeed in keeping (or are kept) to the ideal pattern of Camilla as she presents it *in appearance* to her husband.

What the Priest does object to (324) is the improbability of any man's trying such an experiment of wife-testing at all. The point is in itself innocent enough, but, when one takes into account the ubiquitous insistence on standard marital virtue and the tacit admission that of course no woman could really be expected to abide by that virtue, the silent acceptance of appearance as the covert ideal becomes reinforced. For readers as well as characters, any intuition into the conventions of story-telling would indicate immediately that the "Tale" will lead to Camilla's departure from virtue, but instead of allowing this fact to suggest an anomaly concerning the ideal of virtue, both characters and readers have hurried on to the cautionary reading that finds Anselmo guilty of daring to put appearance to too strong a test. Anselmo's compulsive daring would be tantamount to Don Quixote's continuing to test his helmet until it really was one, rather than giving up when it appears as one (33–34); it would ultimately parallel a demand that there actually be a flesh-and-blood Dulcinea or a demand that Dorothea genuinely feel her own self-satisfaction in capturing Ferdinand rather than merely emote the culturally requisite sentiments. But the made-to-order ending of the "Tale," which blatantly ignores Anselmo's established ability to remain illusioned as long as he really wants to, comforts everyone (fictional listener and uncritical literary critic) by conveniently "proving" that no such tests or demands need ever be made. Does not Anselmo lose all in his "foolish" attempt?

An apparent (but later disproved) deviation from the pattern of ideal appearance is the cause of Cardenio's highly verbalized grief. In appearance, Cardenio is the most distraught of lovers, but it is a mistake to believe that the atmosphere he evokes simply "translates plastically and novelistically the dramatic character of the occurrence and the state of mind of the individual," as Joaquín Casalduero would have it.[43] Once we listen to Cardenio's words, we must realize the thoroughly stock nature of his grief, its abstract referent, and its irrelevance to anything that might be called "the harmonies of love."[44] Cardenio is more properly described in his own terms, as one who is "turning to stone, void of all knowledge and feeling" (226). However disposed we may be to take his love talk at face value, the novel does not allow it, because if anything is scooped up into the satiric exposure of Don Quixote running through the whole novel, it is the self-revealing use of stock language to describe deep emotion on the part of so many characters. Cardenio, whose affinity in sorrow with the Knight (191–192, for example) has been often noted, is concerned lest he lose Lucinda, "the treasure which I had earned by so many years of love and devotion" (230). Once having lost this treasure (or thinking that he has), he resolves to punish himself rather than do anything else (233–234). For he conceives of himself as a protagonist in an imitation of the tragic story of Pyramus and Thisbe (193). Although his sonnet tells of his grief and "all this sad variety of pain" (184), his words and actions deny either variety or depth. His happy love talk with Lucinda proves to be little more than an exchange of commonplaces: "I would expatiate on my good fortune, thanking Heaven for giving her to me for my mistress, praising her beauty, and extolling her virtue and good sense. She in reply would praise the qualities in me that seemed to her, as my lover, worthy of praise. During these conversations, we amused ourselves with a hundred thousand trifles" (228–229). This passage refers to those instances in which they spoke in person; sometimes it was more enjoyable to do it by mail, as one would with a Dulcinea. The two lovers preferred their "pens, which are more freely used than tongues to express the heart's secrets to the beloved; since often the presence of the loved one confuses and silences the most resolute heart and the boldest tongue. Heavens, how many letters I wrote her! What delicate and modest replies I received! How many songs and love-poems I penned, in which my soul declared and revealed its feelings" (193–194). When Lucinda is for once too upset to speak "another word," Cardenio is "surprised" at such "excess of emotion" and is left "full of confusion and dread" (228–229).

He confides to his friend Ferdinand, who soon becomes enthusiastic over such "virtues" as "Lucinda's beauty, her grace, and wit" (196). When Ferdinand contrives to marry the girl himself, can anyone blame Cardenio for taking drastic action? No, for, as he says himself, "their anger at my violence will turn to pity for my misfortunes" (226). But no, it is better to take to the woods in pastoral mourning, thus to confront "the miserable and dark fate which awaited me" (229). Before going, however, Cardenio conceals himself in her house (231), in order to see with his own eyes the marriage of Lucinda and Ferdinand, curiously like Anselmo's gratifying his compulsive curiosity by concealing himself where he could see Lothario and Camilla. Cardenio's is a sought-for sorrow of pure spirit, only incidentally related to a woman named Lucinda.[45] And the eventual happy resolution of his sad love, his reunification with Lucinda at the heavenly inn, must be understood (in terms consistent with his character) as an acting out of a marriage-to-an-abstraction, similar to Anselmo's ideal marriage to Camilla.

Dorothea, in parallel with Don Quixote himself, reveals certain distinctly sexual (or rather antisexual) connotations and costs of Dulcineism. She is introduced into the narrative, significantly enough, in the midst of her search for some "secret grave" for "the weary burden of my body" (236; "la carga pesada deste cuerpo"). Soon she begins her sad story with an account of her former happiness, conveying only the abstract virtues of a good daughter. To her parents, she had been "the light of their eyes, the staff of their old age . . . sole object of their affections" (239). Now, though, there is nothing to do but "to prove how little I am to blame for falling from that happy state into my present misery" (240). Then follows her account of her resistance to seduction by Ferdinand (the same man who betrays Cardenio), ending with the boudoir scene in which she uses enough arguments, mixed together Lothario-style, to justify going to bed with him. She insists, in this scene, that she is interested only in certain virtuous "qualities" in a husband. In all seriousness, but perhaps with some subconscious doubt, she tells Ferdinand, ". . . though you hold my body in your arms, my soul is secured by the purity of my thoughts."[46]

Finally, she arrives at the ultimate Dulcineated formulation: if she were sure of being married properly, she would sleep with Ferdinand, even "though without pleasure" (242; "aunque quedara sin gusto"). After Ferdinand goes through a lavish oath-taking, using as his Bible an image of Our Lady that Dorothea has in her room, she gives the matter her final consideration:

I thought the matter over briefly at this juncture, saying to myself: "I shall certainly not be the first to rise from low to high estate by marriage . . . Since, therefore, I am doing nothing that has not been done before, it would be as well to accept this honor which fortune offers. For even though his desire may last only until he has had his way, I shall be his wife in the eyes of God all the same. But if I reject him with scorn, I see that he will wickedly force me in the end, and I shall be dishonored and universally blamed. For who could know how innocently I have come into this predicament?   (243–244)

Against these conflicting considerations of what appearances she will evoke, Dorothea's reference to the attractions of Ferdinand's "charm and good looks" is a feeble contrast. The next morning, she solemnly puzzles over the "strange event," for she had not yet made up her "mind if the events of the night had been good or bad" (244).

Evidently they are good if she is married, bad otherwise. Once rebellious instinct overcomes Dulcinea's watchwords, there is nothing for it but to repair the damage. Dorothea's plea for Quixote's aid in recovering her lost kingdom from the "traitor" who "has usurped" it (253) is appropriate to her opinion of her own status, as she explains it to Ferdinand himself later on: "I lived a contented life, enclosed within the bounds of virtue until, at the voice of your persistent and seemingly genuine and loving affection, I opened the gates of my modesty and entrusted the keys of my liberty to you" (327). Marriage alone can restore her into her proper kingdom of virginity; otherwise there is "no possible cure" for the shame that causes her to sentence herself to perpetual banishment from her parents' sight (248).

The Priest and the Barber quite agree with her and with these values. Their minds "were filled with pity and wonder at her misfortunes" (248–249). This is the level of tragedy that they find congenial. And when Cardenio now determines to seek revenge from Ferdinand for Dorothea's sake, the Priest "replied for himself and for her by approving Cardenio's generous determination" (249–250). When the patchwork finally does succeed in repairing the fabric of propriety and the two couples are straightened out, the amount of joy at the inn is hard to overestimate. All virginities are restored, by

the simple expedient of exerting enormous group pressure on the
moderately recalcitrant Ferdinand and by a number of swoonings
and posturings on Dorothea's part, which are as ridiculously apoplec-
tic as that in which the unhappy Anselmo swooned his last. Ferdinand is even assured of her "matchless love"—although this is the
first time Dorothea has mentioned it. In anticipation of the waiting-
woman's daughter in part 2, who is ready to marry *anyone*, Dorothea
says: "If you do not want me for what I am, your true and lawful
wife, desire me at least and have me for your slave. . . . Do not leave
me and abandon me so that my shame becomes the subject of gossip,
or cause my parents a miserable old age" (328). As a last resort, she
argues: "Finally, sir, my last word is that I am still your wife, whether
you like it or not" (328).[47] Ferdinand gives in, and the heavenly
inn thus seems to confirm the pattern of heavenly help Dorothea and
Cardenio have perceived in their misfortunes (247–249); but in the
critical context of *Don Quixote* the miracles of Heaven are only
events that have been labelled as such by characters eager to reassert
their society's moral code. That Ferdinand himself obviously has
little liking for the social norms to which he accedes bothers no one—
or perhaps makes his capitulation all the more gratifying to everyone
else in the episode.

The matchmaking morality has triumphed, and all is smooth until
the crashing punctuation of the brawl in the innyard (406–408)
begun by Quixote, who is fresh from Maritornes' strappado, and
prominently enjoyed by Ferdinand, who has now paid the required
price for his two nights (245) with Dorothea. The juxtapositions
become rich in implications. Ferdinand, who has just agreed to do
the lawful thing, is now beating a law officer of the Holy Brotherhood, in the innyard of the "palace" where the innkeeper is a member of the same Holy Brotherhood (406, 409). Quixote plays his
usual role of the attainer of appearance, this time as peacemaker. He
precipitates the battle by violently taking sides in the dispute (just
after very properly declaring that he has no desire to "interfere in so

perplexed a matter"); he then tries to call a halt by sententiously pointing out how trivial the whole dispute is (405–407). The inn of paradise is equipped with its own aggression chamber, a very necessary appurtenance, if not at all the kind of thing that an ideal world would seem to call for.

It also has other appurtenances for settling disputes (as other aspects of the inn sequence reveal). For a disputed hotel bill, Quixote is able to supply the remedy of peaceful mediation, even though he had hoped and pleaded for the chance to use force; and for a dispute over whether the Mule-Lad should marry the lovely Doña Clara, the Judge supplies a monetary motive for saying yes (401). Finally Cervantes mockingly reports, "Fortune was pleased to complete the task and bring everything to a happy ending" (411). Paradise is thus little more than routine life congratulating itself on its heavenly disguise.

The brawl at the same time punctuates the sugary joy of the fortunate (and unlikely) reunion of the super-patriotic Captive with his brother the Judge. The reunion takes place at the heavenly inn, just after the narration of the Captive's fantastic autobiography. This recognition scene is played for all the sentimentality it is worth by the characters, who conveniently ignore the fact that the Judge, who has not seen or heard from his brother in some twenty-two years, simply *must* soon depart for a colonial position, inasmuch as "it was not possible" for the Judge to give up the trip or even wait for a later ship (386). The Priest eagerly acts as a middle-man in the "experiment" (381) of seeing how the Judge will react to the news of the brother's return (383). The recognition is exploited for full tear-value, first at secondhand as the Priest relates the essential facts to the Judge, and then with a tearful embrace by the two brothers, which causes "most of the company" to weep along with them (383–386). In the fictional milieu of *Don Quixote* fabricated emotional manifestations like these are perhaps needed to offset the absence of spontaneous ones between individuals.

Yet Dulcinea's joy, finally, has to be considered "without pleasure," as Dorothea might put it. And this is not because of the potentially tragic elements in the Captive's story (especially the helpless grief of Zoraida's father [375]), for these are quite forgotten in the gush of sentiment. Nor, of course, is the ultimate joylessness due to the hard fact that the brotherly reunion is only momentary, since that is also brushed over. What is most revealing is the nature of the successful love of the Captive for the Moorish-Christian Zoraida, who is devoted to the Virgin.[48] The extraordinarily prized Zoraida is another of the pure women in *Don Quixote*, a beautiful woman who has refused all prior offers of marriage (360) and for whom the Captive and his co-captives are willing to sacrifice their lives before ever having actually seen her (362). But her purity goes another degree into fantasy. She is a helpless and beautiful *émigré*, unable to take a step in Spain without her husband's help; upon his face "her eyes were always fixed, in absolute dependence" (411). The characters can have things both ways in their enjoyment of this situation: the girl is pure and at the same time her beautiful helplessness connotes a state of total dependence. In other words, under the sugariness lies another dream of revenge against the Moors. Meanwhile, despite the protestations of invincible admiration for Zoraida that the Captive makes, Cervantes quietly points out that it is a question after all of the haves and the have-nots; the Captive is traveling home to find out about the state of his family fortunes before he commits himself to marrying her. Meanwhile, he is traveling with her "as her father and squire, not as her husband" (380).

Some critics take Zoraida as evidence of Cervantes' belief in the workings of Providence, for here a Moorish girl has inexplicably come to be a devotee of the Virgin.[49] This is building too much on a melodramatic lack of motivation. More likely she is Cervantes' way of exploring just such a conception and showing that it entails a fantasy that casts further doubt on the workings of the prescribed ideals of a culture. To be satisfied with a Divine Grace that stops short at the money line is curiously appropriate in a context of chivalric adventure that finds its fulfillment in the rearrangement of appearances within the status quo.[50]

The To-the-Rescue Routine

In part 2, Cervantes ventures one complex episode of romance in which an unidealistic lover, Basilo, who "runs like a deer, jumps better than a goat, and bowls down the ninepins like magic" (589), manages to upset the prevailing patterns. This have-not outfoxes the haves and wins his girl away from the wealthy Camacho, to whom she had been betrothed. Basilio effectively employs all his wit to avoid the state of continual misery in which the other lovers in *Don Quixote* seem to wish to remain. But Basilio's triumph is handled with unusual indirection by Cervantes, who seems to be showing what the episode means to the populace and to Don Quixote, but not what it means to Basilio and Quiteria.

Shortly prior to the Camacho-Basilio-Quiteria episode, Quixote has exuded praise for the thoroughly unoriginal sonnet by the would-be poet, the son of the Man in Green (586), a sonnet on the subject of Pyramus and Thisbe. Quixote then promptly meets two students who tell him of the love of Basilio for Quiteria, "where Love took occasion to revive in the world the now-forgotten loves of Pyramus and Thisbe" (589). It is clear that Dulcinea's love poetry is going to be tried out in a real situation. The populace assumes rather eagerly that Basilio will die of grief, inasmuch as he has been carrying on in pastoral and knight-errant fashion since learning of the impending marriage of Camacho and Quiteria: "He eats and sleeps little; and all he does eat is fruit, and if he does sleep he sleeps in the open, on the hard ground like a wild animal" (590). Therefore, there is great spectator interest; on the day before the wedding, many were "busily raising platforms, from which next day they would be able to see in comfort the plays and dances that were to be performed in that spot, dedicated to the celebration of the rich Camacho's wedding and Basilio's funeral" (594). This fact has a contradictory bearing on the approaching festivities, which have the earmarks of a gay rustic wedding but which are thus impregnated with the expectation of death. Could this combination suggest that the gaiety is not as spontaneous at it appears? One group of peasants, in fact, looks exactly like a paid cheering squad, not like people enjoying themselves: "All were dressed in their holiday best, and each mounted on a fine mare in rich and splendid country trappings with many bells hanging from the harness. These ran in an orderly troop, not once but many times, up and down the meadow, cheering and shouting: 'Long live Camacho and Quiteria. He is rich and she is fair, the fairest maid in all the world!' " (597). Though it would be implausible to suggest that the whole celebration is merely paid gaiety (the text does allude to the train of flatterers who follow the rich [607]), the heavily stressed, unpleasant undercurrent to the celebration cannot be ignored. It is only to be expected that Cervantes should maintain some critical perspective on the common people in a novel that is so critical everywhere else.

Fitting into the mood, Sancho and Quixote have a considerable discussion of Death before the wedding (601–602); there is also, a bit earlier but within the episode, Don Quixote's set speech upon marriage, which agrees entirely with Lothario that marriage is an insoluble union, "right up to the resting-place of Death"—that is, unless "Death's scythe" severs "the Gordian knot" earlier (590).

Sancho, in expatiating on Death, has cited the words of his own village priest. The masque performed by the villagers before Camacho's wedding is also written by a local priest. It is a drama of a last-minute attempt at rescue, fought out by the allegorized figures of Love, Poetry, Good Sense, Good Family, Valor, Interest, Liberality, Gifts, Treasure, and Peaceful Possession. A maiden standing on the battlements of the Castle of Caution is besieged most successfully by Interest, who "took out a big purse, made of a great striped catskin, which seemed to be full of money, and flung it at the castle, whose boards fell apart and tumbled down at the shock, leaving the maiden exposed and defenseless" (599). Love then tries to rescue the maiden and is reconciled with Interest by some innocent and innocuous "savages"; the maiden shuts herself in the castle again, "to the great pleasure of the spectators" (600). The priest's masque has thus preserved the appearance of conflict and has ended with an arbitrary, happy reconciliation that does not criticize the status quo. It is low-tension Dulcineism. Basilio, however, will have it otherwise.

The actual rescue of Quiteria is a melodramatic reversal. Basilio pretends to fall upon his dagger, and everyone sees "the unhappy wretch lying stretched upon the ground, bathed in his blood, and transfixed by his own weapon," which is actually seen sticking out of his back (603–604). In this condition, he manages to extract an avowal of love and consent in marriage from Quiteria, who expects him to die shortly. So, of course, do all the spectators. But, his ruse accomplished, Basilio leaps up in perfectly good health. The marriage is fraudulent, but Quiteria takes the opportunity now to give her consent in earnest.

None of the melodrama is supposed to detract from the beauties of the Basilio-Quiteria union. Quixote seems to speak for the group when he declares, as Basilio lies writhing on the ground, that the young man's request "was very just and reasonable and, what was more, very practicable, and that Sir Camacho would be as honored by receiving the lady Quiteria as the widow of the valorous Basilio as if he were to receive her from her father's side" (604). He seems also to speak for the group when he declares, after the ruse is made known, that "in contests and rivalries of love deceits and plots practised to attain the desired end are justifiable, so long as they are not to the detriment and dishonor of the loved object" (606). This speech allows Camacho a few moments in which to cool off, and thus Quiteria, we are told, is "instantly blotted from his memory" (607). Quiteria, who had not known of the ruse in advance, goes off with Basilio. Basilio's trick, as Thomas Mann said, is a gruesome one: "One cannot imagine a more horrid interruption to a gay and splendid feast."[51] Yet the gaiety seems to continue as if ordered by someone; it simply moves to another village. Even the jilted Camacho goes ahead with his planned wedding feast, sans bride. Could it be that the whole conflict has been of no more depth than that of the two students whom Quixote has recently seen duel with swords and then emerge as "better friends than before"? (592–593). It was these same students who persuaded Quixote to accompany them to the wedding in the first place.

The scene's expectations of death are literally unfulfilled, and Love does seem to win out over Interest. Yet the basis of the rescue, already uncomfortably interfused with melodrama, is now further corroded by an attempt to reform Basilio. Cervantes is careful to show that Quixote's sympathy for Basilio is not one based on a feeling that lovers should choose their own mates, for the Knight expressly declares that the choice of a husband ought to be left not to the daughter, but to the parents; otherwise, the girl might choose some "debauched swashbuckler" (589–590). But since Basilio is something of a trickster and gamesman, it is necessary for the Knight to try to "persuade Basilio to give up practising his arts, for although they brought him fame, they earned him no money" (608). Thus the Knight comes around to the socially prescribed position he had lately berated Sancho for entertaining: that "skills and graces that aren't saleable" are without value (595). What is also interesting is that Quixote's advice to the young couple goes on to two more steps. First, Quiteria is compared to the poor man's precious jewel who is somehow especially valuable because of her ability to resist all manner of temptation; second, Quixote advises that if a woman sins in secret it will not be so disastrous. The first sounds like the all-out Dulcineism of Anselmo, the second is Quixote's customary guarantee of idealistic success: appearance must always be managed (608–609).

One irony in this episode is that Quixote, by fending off the possible attack of Camacho's men, achieves a rare palpable triumph, and he is not regarded as a madman by Basilio. But at the same time Quixote has convinced himself (and tries to convince the couple he has protected) that all is in accord with Dulcinea's values. Quiteria will, he thinks, at least give the appearance of being a chaste jewel, and Basilio will become a proper husband. Yet the young couple remain noticeably silent when they are being lectured at by Quixote, and the text thus permits us to think (though there is no clear implication) that two lovers in the novel have managed actually to reach each other by means of some desperate devices and some strategic silence.

Dulcinea in love and war is shown with further secular enlargements in the remarkable sections, late in the novel, taking place in Barcelona. Here again there is much celebration and illuminating counterpoint. The arrival of the Knight and his squire in that city is an occasion for great rejoicing; but this joy is undercut by the novel as much as the earlier sentimentality at the inn (and more clearly than that at Camacho's wedding). As they enter the outskirts of the city, Don Quixote and Sancho see, for the first time, the bright expanse of the ocean. Immediately they notice the "galleys lying off the strand." The vessels are "decked with streamers and pennants that fluttered in the wind and kissed and swept the water" (866). The apparently joyous people on board begin to join the music-making of the townfolk, who had already begun to herald Quixote's arrival, filling the air with "sweet martial music." There is a "mock skirmish" for the benefit of the spectators, and a serenade of cannons. The sea is described as cheerful, the land as joyous, but the sky, though clear, was "sometimes clouded by the smoke of artillery." Only Sancho, as the paragraph ends, seems to remind the reader of a clouded matter: he could not "imagine how those great bulks he saw moving on the sea could have so many feet." Has joy triumphed, again, only in apperance?

The matter of the galley slaves is soon returned to and explored in a chapter that juxtaposes love and war, entitled: "Of the Disaster that befell Sancho Panza on his visit to the Galleys, and of the strange adventure of the fair Moorish girl" (part 2, chapter 63). In this chapter, Sancho and his master go aboard one of the galleys. Again, there is prearranged rejoicing, with the galley slaves sounding their clarions and giving the Knight three cheers. Sancho, however, is "startled to see so many men bare to the skin" and also to see them working with such frenzy. Then, without warning, the rejoicing is thrown into dark relief by an equally prearranged bit of sadism:

> . . . the last oarsman on the starboard side . . . following his instructions seized Sancho and lifted him up in his arms. Then, all the crew standing ready, starting from the starboard side they sent him flying along from hand to hand and from bench to bench, so fast that poor Sancho lost the sight of his eyes, and imagined no doubt that the devils of hell were bearing him off. . . . The poor fellow was left battered, panting and all in a sweat, unable to imagine what had happened to him.   (880)

Perhaps this prank provides a suitable outlet for the frustrations of slavery and suitable entertainment for the officers who conduct Don Quixote on this tour. When promoted by duly constituted authority, such entertainments are to be taken as just harmless fun.

The crew, having had their entertainment, now return to their functions as automatons, hoisting "the yard with the same speed and clatter with which they had lowered it, and all this in silence, as if they had neither voice nor breath" (880). This sharp silence comments on the noisy appearance of joy in the town's welcome of Quixote.

As the vessel races out to sea, Cervantes does not neglect to mention that the boatswain "began to tickle the crew's back with his whip or hide-strap," and Quixote does not neglect to suggest to Sancho that he sit in with them for the sake of Dulcinea's disenchantment. Sancho expresses sympathy for the victims (880), but Quixote's mind is in affinity with those of the officers. This affinity is assured by his having been "immeasurably delighted to find himself treated in so lordly a fashion" (879), and he now remarks that Merlin might count such well-laid-on lashes at a rate of ten for one in computing the ransom figure for Dulcinea.

Now the news arrives that a small pirate ship is not far off, and the narrative shifts to a brief battle scene. Cervantes moves rapidly from war to love, in a shift that seems deliberately jagged, improbable, and unrealistic. The chase results in the capturing of a pirate captain, who proves to be a distressed damsel in disguise, none other than the Moor Ricote's daughter, Anna, whose religion and love had been discussed previously by Sancho and his friend (822).

Her explanations of how she has been separated from her homeland and from her lover and how she has defended herself against the wicked designs of the Moorish king soon make her captors forget the fact that she is the captain of the pirate ship, and gain her a release from the death penalty about to be invoked for the almost random killing of two Spanish crew-members during the skirmish. In fact, before it is even known that she is a woman, her amazing handsomeness operates as a "letter of recommendation," and, as she tells her sad story, "the tears which filled her lovely eyes drew many from those of her auditors" (885). The Viceroy is especially magnanimous, and "with his own fingers untied the rope binding the Moorish girl's fair hands." He instructs Quixote's host to receive the girl and her father, and to "make as much of them as he could" (887; "los regalase y acariciase cuanto le fuese posible").

This ostentatious indulgence of mercy is followed by much brainstorming over how to retrieve her lover from the Moors. When the retrieval is duly accomplished, all are deeply impressed with the "modest and joyful thoughts" that the two young lovers reveal with their eyes (894). Possibly these two are interested in each other rather than in appearances. But they are not as fortunate as Quiteria and Basilio, because the actual reunion of Anna Ricote and Don Gregorio is dependent on the tender mercies of the central administration in Madrid, who would have to rule that the very Christian and "right-minded" (894; "tan bien intencionado") Ricote and daughter might stay in Spain. In the meantime Don Gregorio is coerced into allowing himself to be separated from Anna; inevitably "there were tears, there were sighs, sorrowings and sobbings." We are not told whether Madrid ever gave its approval, although we see that Anna's father is utterly skeptical concerning the chance of anything being accomplished in those quarters (894–895).

Nonetheless, Quixote adulates Barcelona as "the treasure house of courtesy, the refuge of strangers, the hospital of the poor, the country of the valiant, the avenger of the injured, and the abode of firm and reciprocal friendships, unique in its position and its beauty" (928). The gentry of Barcelona are obviously in agreement with this comfortable estimate. But for a reader of the novel the Barcelona of *Don Quixote* excellently embodies the constant replaying of Dulcinea's terribly limiting formulae: love that cannot be consummated; heroics that bring about an appearance of victory; approved aggression against the infidel, even if the infidel has to be manufactured at home;[52] and a great deal of idealistically produced pain.

Epilogue

In expressing emotion, "most human beings take the channel that is ready made in their culture. If they can take this channel, they are provided with adequate means of expression." So wrote Ruth Benedict in *Patterns of Culture*.[1] I quote this commonplace of anthropological analysis because it centers so well on the very thing at issue in *Don Quixote*, a book in which characters are able to do little else than take the ready-made cultural channel, and yet a book of peculiarly unfulfilled lives. Dulcinea insists that personal expression follow the line of her settled ideals, and the characters (except for much of Sancho) give themselves appallingly to the task, but the result is a failure of expression disguised by the manipulation of appearances as a success. Beyond this pattern is the intimation of the novel that culture cannot cure itself through itself, that the evocation into daily life of the ideals of a high cultural heritage helps not at all, for these ideals are too closely akin to the disease they would cure. It is not fanciful to say that the hope of Matthew Arnold is shown to be empty in 1605–1615 by Cervantes.

Just as disturbing is the novel's revelation of what we all know but will not recognize, for we are surely, in our less guarded moments, aware that the attaining of ideal appearances is a concealment of our embarrassment. Do we not know very well, for example, that the earnest Quixotic stock response that explains our culture's chronic militarism as a mere function of its devotion to peaceful living is a façade? Surely we are somewhere cognizant also that our periodic attempts to catch up with our professed cultural ideals are precisely our greatest efforts to avoid facing their very irrelevance and deadliness.

But although we in a sense do "know" all this, we fear to see it in the clear light Cervantes provides; to do so would be to experience the need to let go, to organize life in a radically different way. We would have to come to terms with the possibilities that *Don Quixote* makes so vivid: that the idealism our culture has for so long wished to attain has in fact long been attained, but only under the aegis of its own self-denying psychology, and that our "justice" is in reality our hope that the need for fair treatment can be made to serve the purposes of that psychology. Equally unsettling is the novel's total deflation of the spiritual and ideal claims traditionally made on behalf of Mind and Imagination. For it associates truly critical thought with the body-based Sancho and uses all its critical force to discredit as sterile and unimaginative the Knight's idealizing of reality.

Hence aesthetics is replete with rules of thumb that conveniently prevent anyone from recognizing any unpleasantly specific critical connections between a seventeenth-century novel of genius and our own historical moment. Instead, literature is required to be contained within the ethereal reaches of an ideal, universal, eternal world of "art"—in other words, in some more elegant version of Don Quixote's "mind." Hence, too, so many cultured minds have a need (a need by now so real that it is akin to Quixote's automatic recourse to the rationalizations of "enchantment") for intellectual twaddle of the war-equals-peace level. We are continually implored, and usually induced, to develop a whole character structure that will politely keep up the appearance that buried somewhere within such twaddle is a viable position.

When John Ruskin realized the seriousness of *Don Quixote*'s ravaging of idealism and thus realized its implicit demand to let go, he concluded that the book threw its huge weight against "the holiest principles of humanity"[2] With far better logic than that of the major critics of *Don Quixote*, Ruskin bitterly rejected the book. Ruskin knew that the novel challenged his idealism; the critics within the three interpretive traditions usually have not been willing or able to reach this point of self-confrontation. Perspectivists refuse all possibility of a challenge, for there is no fictional conflict that they hesitate to explain as a mere fusion of perspectives, a view that in effect labels all resolutions as mere enchantments. Cautionary critics, in their objections to the Knight's conduct, rely unwittingly upon Dulcineated values that are similar to his own and diffused throughout his fictional culture. And the idealist critics continue to find an endorsement of their holiest principles in the very novel that rejects, through its art, their Quixotic loyalties. The novel thus has within it the refutation of these three traditions of criticism, for it explores and explodes their underlying premises.

Ruskin has one way out, and I must grant it its merits, if only to acknowledge that a great work of art may be too upsetting for readers to be able to respond positively toward it. But this way out is surely not the one the book suggests; it is too much like the characters' own determination to preserve ideal appearances, come what may. The challenge to let go of ideals is of course not a stated way out at all; it is an implication embedded in the context of the novel's unremitting insight into the workings of Dulcinea. Yet that crucial implication is a very clear one. What it means, when considered as a real alternative, is nothing less than human life seeking its own impulsive development, which inevitably takes place, when it takes place at all, in opposition to the institutional blockade that now prevents any such rebellion from getting very far. It also requires abandonment of the traditionally favored method of achieving personal and collective change by trying to trap the future within a commitment to one or more of the fixed paths called ideals. To let go in so radical a way is as yet the prerogative of only that small fraction of humankind which has the necessary awareness—by whatever name —of Dulcinea's ways and aims.

But there is still a joker in all this, for *Don Quixote's* creation of laughter is all on the side of the joyous perception of a gigantic cultural farce Cervantes has brought into clarity. The force of the joke is not diminished by our substitution of a new arsenal of Dulcineated concepts for those of the Knight; as Ortega saw, mass culture provides only a somewhat more muffled sound as it tumbles from a less lofty height than does high culture.[3] The *Playboy Advisor* is not so different after all from *Amadís of Gaul*,[4] and *Profiles in Courage* is of the same family as Quixote's speeches on the beauties of bravery in the abstract.

It is a part of Dulcinea's vast farce that James Baldwin brilliantly stumbles upon when he writes: ". . . the major effort of our country until today (and I am talking about Washington and all the way down to whoever heads the Women's Christian Temperance Union) is not to change a situation but to *seem* to have done it. . . . It is hard to begin to understand that the drift in American life towards chaos is marked by all these smiling faces and all these do-good efforts."[5] And it was in another great intimation of Dulcinea's farce that Fielding's Jonathan Wild laid down his rule that counterfeit virtues "adorned the wearer" just as nicely as any others.[6]

Literary criticism and middle-brow as well as popular culture are not the only present-day habitations of Dulcinea. In the realm of "high" culture, I might suggest the example of the fiction of Borges, which is based upon an ideology of perspectivism that is, in a sense, even more Dulcineated than the Knight's own ideal. For whereas Don Quixote admits a test of Dulcinea's value in her "works," Borges places all value upon the movement of his characters toward their self-imposed perspectives and at the same time delights in ironic admissions that all their efforts are futile. In a statement expressive of this futility, he reluctantly admits, "The world, unfortunately, is real; I, unfortunately, am Borges."[7] Perhaps his fictions are intel-

ligible, to a degree, as the creations of someone who had become
"more and more an incredible mind in an ailing and useless body,
much like his character, Ireneo Funes."[8] The personal situation is
recognizably Quixotic. But it hardly explains the attraction felt by
his readers, nor their affinity for the similar idealism that informs
the work of Nabakov, John Barth, and much of the French "New
Novel." Just as if Cervantes never wrote—but often in his name—
recent technically inventive novelists and their readers display a need
or a duty to celebrate a fictional creed that denies the reality of their
own bodily identities.

Dulcinea is virtually everywhere, with her ready-made cultural
channeling of every part of life. But as an individual reader, I align
myself with Cervantes' making of that huge demand to let go. The
rejection of Dulcinea is, in the context of his book, not just Ruskin's
bitter pill; it is also a joyous imaginative act of liberation.

NOTES

The following notes are not simply for purposes of documentation. In them, I have given further consideration to a number of objections to the present reading that inhere in the three critical positions I find defective. Moreover, I have sought to delineate further the relevance *Don Quixote* seems to me to have within our own historical era. As a whole, these notes assume that there is an outer horizon of meaning for *Don Quixote* that can be suggested in definite though not exclusive ways. The immediate meaning of the explication illuminates a closely related extended context. I have argued for such a theory of literary meaning in my discussion of E. D. Hirsch's *Validity in Interpretation*, "Logic, Hermeneutics, and Literary Context," *Genre* 1 (July, 1968): 214–229.

Throughout the present study, commentary concerning specific works of criticism is designed to show the place of certain key arguments within such works in relation to the total framework of the present critical argument. Notes on a given critical work are not intended as full descriptions.

PREFACE

1. Bruce W. Wardropper, "*Don Quixote:* Story or History?" *Modern Philology* 63 (August, 1965): 10.

2. Américo Castro has argued that the novel is indeed a work containing a basic social criticism of Spain, but his case is closely tied to Cervantes' supposed rejection of the doctrine of blood-purity (*limpieza de sangre*). This doctrine was, as Castro points out, a peculiarly Spanish cultural issue, and it is the one issue, he believes, through which Spanish history should be approached. But such an approach to the novel limits its relevance and does so at the cost of building an interpretation upon the

slender basis of the indirect allusions in the text to blood-purity. (There is almost no direct mention of the doctrine in *Don Quixote*.) Furthermore, Castro takes out of context such apparently critical statements as Quixote's advice to Sancho that "virtue has an intrinsic worth, which blood has not" (Miguel de Cervantes Saavedra, *The Adventures of Don Quixote*, trans. J. M. Cohen, p. 738), while I find such statements to be given a radically different meaning through their juxtaposition, in context, with other elements. See Castro, *Cervantes y los casticismos españoles*, especially pp. 84, 100, 125, 347.

3. Salvador de Madariaga, *Don Quixote: An Introductory Essay in Psychology*, p. 55.

4. See, for example, Joseph J. Waldmeir, "The Cowboy, the Knight, and Popular Taste," *Southern Folklore Quarterly* 22 (September, 1958): 113–120; and Américo Paredes, "Luis Inclán: First of the Cowboy Writers," *American Quarterly* 12 (Spring, 1960): 55–70.

5. H. B. Hall, review of Cohen's translation, *Bulletin of Hispanic Studies* 28 (July–September, 1951): 214–216.

6. E. D. Hirsch, Jr., *Validity in Interpretation*, p. 121.

7. Otis H. Green, *Spain and the Western Tradition: The Castilian Mind in Literature from "El Cid" to Calderón*, I, 194 n.

8. Review of Cohen's translation, *Times Literary Supplement*, January 8, 1951.

9. Leland H. Chambers, "Structure and the Search for Truth in the *Quijote*: Notes toward a Comprehensive View," *Hispanic Review* 35 (October, 1967): 309 n.

CHAPTER I. IDEALS AND FICTIONAL PROBING

1. Angel Flores and M. J. Benardete, eds., *Cervantes across the Centuries*, pp. v–vi. Compare the recent estimate of critical progress by Luis Andrés Murillo, "Cervantic Irony in *Don Quijote*: The Problem for Literary Criticism," in *Homenaje a Rodríguez-Moñino*, II, 21–27.

2. And so I have argued at length in my doctoral dissertation, "Satire Denied: A Critical History of English and American *Don Quixote* Criticism" (University of Washington, 1964).

3. For example, Francisco Maldonado de Guevara, *La Maiestas cesárea en el Quijote*, and especially the mammoth (900-page) study by the Thomistic critic, Mario Casella, *Cervantes: Il Chisciotte*. Casella's interpretation "rests completely," as he himself says, on the close analogies that may be drawn between Don Quixote's fictional biography and the pattern

of a Christian quest for union with God, in accordance with the "truth of an absolute reason." ("Critical Realism," trans. Joseph de Simone, in *Cervantes across the Centuries*, ed. Flores and Benardete, p. 207). My own retort here is that such analogies may indeed exist, but that they need to be regarded critically, subject to the novel's exploration and—as it happens—its unmasking.

4. For example, Pavel Novitsky, "Thematic Design," in *Cervantes across the Centuries*, ed. Flores and Benardete, pp. 239–245.

5. Thus Leo Spitzer, in "Linguistic Perspectivism in the *Don Quixote*" (in his *Linguistics and Literary History*, p. 61), affirms that the perspectivism of the novel does not apply to Cervantes' attitude toward God, nor does it imply a perspectivist view of "God's institutions, the King and the State." This is therefore an interpretation in the vein of what I have called cautionary, for God, king, and state rigidly define the limits of Don Quixote's deviation. Ángel del Río, on the other hand, places his nominally perspectivist interpretation over on the idealist side by saying that Don Quixote's ideals are "equally valid for every age" and are "human aspirations good at any time" ("The Equívoco of *Don Quixote*," in *Varieties of Literary Experience: Eighteen Essays in World Literature*, ed. Stanley Burnshaw, pp. 223–224.) This is not to claim, of course, that either Spitzer or Del Río fits entirely into one or another of the three categories of approach I am outlining; my point is merely that *Quixote* criticism consists almost entirely of various combinations of the three approaches, and that nearly all examples emphasize one or another form of a single one of the three.

6. I am concerned, as shall be obvious, with criticism that is not limited to the study of form and technique. I find encouraging the theoretical work of those who would attempt to connect literary insights with our own sense of life: for example, Lawrence W. Hyman's "Moral Values and Literary Experience," *Journal of Aesthetics and Art Criticism* 24 (Summer, 1966): 539–547; and F. E. Sparshott's "Truth in Fiction," *Journal of Aesthetics and Art Criticism* 26 (Fall, 1967): 3–7. To dismiss all such connecting as mere "moralizing" is untenable.

7. Ivan Turgenev, "Hamlet and Don Quixote," trans. William A. Drake, in *The Anatomy of Don Quixote: A Symposium*, ed. M. J. Benardete and Angel Flores, p. 101.

8. Mark Spilka (referring to Parson Adams and Don Quixote), "Comic Resolution in Fielding's *Joseph Andrews*," in *Fielding: A Collection of Critical Essays*, ed. Ronald Paulson, p. 61; P. M. Pasinetti, editorial comment on *Don Quixote*, in *World Masterpieces*, ed. Maynard Mack, *et al.*,

I, 805. The last is José Ortega y Gasset's attitude throughout *Meditations on Quixote*, although Ortega at least does not conceal his belief that *Don Quixote* allows the nemesis to win out.

9. Benedetto Croce, "The 'Simpatía' of Don Quixote," trans. Frederick F. Fales, in *Cervantes across the Centuries*, ed. Flores and Benardete, p. 180.

10. Thus, Joaquín Casalduero, who finds in this passage evidence of Cervantes' respect for virginity as an ideal underlying all other virtues, argues that the irony of the text is merely a way of challenging us to accept the ideal on a basis of willed faith (*Sentido y forma del Quijote [1605–1615]*, pp. 70–71). This is as unanswerable, and as unacceptable a critical ploy as Albert S. Cook's claim that, somewhere behind the action of the novel, the tragic sadness of the Knight rises "mutely"—a term which serves to evade the fact that there is no quotable evidence for its existence (*The Meaning of Fiction*, p. 22; see also p. 16).

11. Thomas Mann, "Voyage with Don Quixote," in *Essays by Thomas Mann*, trans. H. T. Lowe-Porter, pp. 346–347.

12. Edward C. Riley, *Cervantes's Theory of the Novel*, p. 139. Riley's book has been pronounced "quite obviously the best British contribution to Cervantine studies so far" (review by R. D. F. Pring-Mill, *Modern Language Review* 62 [January, 1967]: 149).

13. Edward M. Wilson, "Edmund Gayton on Don Quixote, Andrés, and Juan Haldudo," *Comparative Literature* 2 (Winter, 1950): 72; René Girard, *Deceit, Desire, and the Novel: Self and Other in Literary Structure*, especially chapter 2, "Men Become Gods in the Eyes of Each Other," pp. 53–82; Wilson, "Edmund Gayton on Don Quixote, Andrés and Juan Haldudo," p. 70; Green, *Spain and the Western Tradition*, II, 42–43, and IV, 65–67. Girard argues that Cervantes, Stendhal, Flaubert, Proust, and Dostoyevsky all portray the "ontological sin" indicated in his chapter title, and that in their major novels, all of them show how man's "pride" is sustained by the "lie" of the desire to transcend oneself through the imitation of secular rather than Christian models. Such transcendence has "deviated in the direction of the human" (pp. 74 and 56–58). Compare Chambers, "Structure and the Search for Truth in the *Quijote*," pp. 309–326. Chambers quite properly asserts that Cervantes found ways of "subordinating every traditional idea and literary convention to the needs of the novel." And, "It is typical of Cervantes' technique that the unequivocal ideas are cast into doubt by their contexts and must, consequently, be examined in connection with other related passages" (pp. 310 n, 317 n). But in contrast to these excellent critical principles, Chambers' actual ex-

plication partakes freely of pietistic interpretation instead of critical inspection. Thus, the cause of Don Quixote's recovery from insanity is identified as God, simply because no cause appears in the text (p. 318 n). The novel's characters exhibit confidence in their own motivation "even when doing violence to others," but this merely "implies that God knows and takes account of what is in men's hearts, that He understands the nature of the problems besetting man" (p. 313). Despite the complexity of human choice in the novel, Cervantes at bottom "emphasizes the importance of absolute values to which man can turn for guidance, virtues that are real and accessible" (p. 321). But the evidence for supposing that Cervantes' novel can be said to uphold such values consists largely, in this essay, of simply citing passages that refer to them.

14. Ford Madox Ford, *The March of Literature from Confucius' Day to Our Own*, pp. 680–681.

15. Another arbitrary feature of the cautionary approach is its habit of making the tail wag the dog; that is, the Knight's recantation of chivalry in the last chapter of the novel is made into the apex of the entire book and presumably is sufficient for such readers to cancel any positive involvement they have felt with Quixote's mad imagination through nine hundred pages.

16. See especially Américo Castro, *De la edad conflictiva*, vol. 1, *El drama de la honra en España y en su literatura*, and Castro's masterwork, *The Structure of Spanish History*. Acceptance of Castro's general position leads naturally to an approach to all of Spanish fiction as fundamentally perspectivistic. See, for example, Leon Livingstone, "Interior Duplication and the Problem of Form in the Modern Spanish Novel," *PMLA* 73 (September, 1958): 393–406.

17. Américo Castro, "Prólogo" in the Porrúa edition of *El ingenioso hidalgo Don Quijote de la Mancha*, especially pp. xxiii–xxiv, xl–xli. (This "Prólogo" is also entitled "Españolidad y europeizacion del *Quijote*," but is referred to throughout the present study simply as "Prólogo.") The emphasis on divergent points of view departs from Castro's earlier theory that *Don Quixote* is a harmonious synthesis of Renaissance themes (See Castro, *El pensamiento de Cervantes*, pp. 124, 143, 385).

18. Castro, "Prólogo," p. xxxi. One typical perspectivist *non sequitur* is visible here: because values are created within and through one's personal existence and are not objective entities of the external world, there neither can nor should be any way of evaluating them or of discriminating among them. But in *Don Quixote* these difficult evaluative processes do go on.

19. Murray Krieger, *The Tragic Vision: Variations on a Theme in Literary Interpretation*, p. 242.

20. Martin Heidegger, "The Origin of the Work of Art," in *Philosophies of Art and Beauty*, ed. Albert Hofstadter and Richard Kuhns, pp. 675, 686. The editors point out that, strictly speaking, Heidegger is not an existentialist, but I do not think that this affects the present point. When Heidegger asserts that essential strife is "the surrender of self to the secret originality of the source of one's own being" and not "the fixing of self in some contingent circumstance" (p. 675), he is speaking in the same spirit as the Américo Castro of later years. For example: *"El Quijote es un taller de existencialidad uno de cuyos primarios artífices fue la tensión-opresión del propio existir"* (*"El Quijote, taller de existencialidad," Revista de Occidente* 5 [July, 1967]: 14). That Castro can go on to warn against equating this "existencialidad" with existentialism is appropriate to his faith (never, to my knowledge, argued on its merits by him) that the imitation of literary roles by characters in *Don Quixote* sufficiently expresses and accommodates the need for self-creation of a human being's own existence. The darker themes of existentialism are not required; the rock of Sisyphus, in this myth, moves efficiently uphill—and only uphill. See Castro's use of Michel Foucault's *Words and Things* (*"El Quijote, taller de existencialidad,"* pp. 15–17), as well as his comments on Cervantes' own self-creation (pp. 5, 17–31). Ortega's nemesis of physical reality is thus overcome without being confronted.

21. Dorothy Van Ghent, *The English Novel: Form and Function*, p. 15; W. K. Wimsatt, Jr., *The Verbal Icon: Studies in the Meaning of Poetry* (see also Wimsatt's defense of a "tensional" theory of cognition in literary criticism in *Hateful Contraries: Studies in Literature and Criticism*, pp. 35–48); Northrop Frye, *Anatomy of Criticism*, pp. 234, 306; Lionel Trilling, *Beyond Culture: Essays on Literature and Learning*, p. 221.

22. See Manuel Durán, *La ambigüedad en el Quijote*.

23. John Dewey, *Art as Experience*, p. 37.

24. Harold Rosenberg, *The Tradition of the New*, p. 32. Rosenberg, however, seems to see the "constant no" solely as an advantage to the artist. *Quixote* critics do not, it is true, argue so strenuously as this against all resolution; what they seek to avoid is *critical* resolution, in which one value is shown to be in any sense superior to another.

25. To forestall a misunderstanding, I hasten to add that I am aware that there is no single simple belief here, but a whole set of modern theories, which I am not attempting to outline comprehensively. José Ortega y Gasset's claim that "reality happens to be . . . possessed of an infinite num-

ber of perspectives, all equally veracious and authentic" (*The Modern Theme*, pp. 91–92) may serve as a convenient epitome of these theories. All I am claiming, in this elementary broaching of the matter, is that a number of modern intellectual interests in fact intersect and help to prevent the recognition of nonperspectivist possibilities in *Don Quixote* interpretation, and that to encourage this prevention is an act of dogmatism. For some objections to the perspectivist attitude in general, see Benjamin DeMott, "The Little Red Discount House," *Hudson Review* 15 (Winter, 1962–1963): 551–564.

26. Compare E. M. Forster's comment on Belief, which suggests very well the sense of faith that is Dulcineated: "Faith, to my mind, is a stiffening process, a sort of mental starch, which ought to be applied as sparingly as possible. I do not believe in it, for its own sake, at all" ("What I Believe," in *Two Cheers for Democracy*, p. 67). But, as John J. Allen points out, Don Quixote is an exemplar of faith in the tradition of St. Paul; and such faith Allen identifies as "the prime heroic ingredient" in the Knight's make-up (*Don Quixote: Hero or Fool? A Study in Narrative Technique*, p. 85).

27. The distinction is argued in Isaiah Berlin's pamphlet, *Two Concepts of Liberty*.

28. Arnold Hauser, *Mannerism: The Crisis of the Renaissance and the Origin of Modern Art*, I, 323, and I, 245–246. *Don Quixote* is therefore a work to which some of the descriptions of Neo-Marxist aesthetics can be applied: it "projects" a demand that the repressive order it critically delineates be overcome; on the other hand, it can hardly be contained within "the prevailing unfreedom in which it was born and from which it has been abstracted" (Herbert Marcuse, *Eros and Civilization*, chapter on "The Aesthetic Dimension", and *One-Dimensional Man*, p. 228).

29. Mann, "Voyage with Don Quixote," p. 343.

30. This is to reject such radical separations of parts 1 and 2 as that proposed by Joaquín Casalduero, who goes so far as to say that if we should keep in mind the adventures of part 1 when reading part 2 we shall be left in "complete confusion" ("The Composition of 'Don Quixote,'" trans. Esther Sylvia, in *Cervantes across the Centuries*, ed. Flores and Benardete, p. 87). The novel itself asks us to make just the sort of cross-references that Casalduero forbids; for example, the Knight's explanation of why he thinks Dulcinea is enchanted in part 2, chapter 32, hinges on facts he draws from his own "enchantment" in the latter portions of part 1 (Cohen, p. 682). Similarly, Quixote refers at the end of part 2, chapter 44, to his encounter with Maritornes in part 1, chapter 16.

31. *Don Quixote* does not fit Alvin Kernan's thesis that satire is always "a fantastic jumble of men and objects," but any definition of satiric plot is too narrow, surely, if it fails to take in *Don Quixote*. See Kernan, *The Plot of Satire*, p. 68.

32. Thus John Ormsby noted in 1885 that few of the Spanish critics seem to enjoy the humor of the novel, and Américo Castro, in 1960, says that nothing in *Don Quixote* is "enteramente risible," or at least not for long. See Ormsby's introduction to his translation, *The Ingenious Gentleman Don Quixote de la Mancha*, p. lxxi; and Castro, "Prólogo," p. li, and also p. xii, where Castro lumps comedy in with a list of qualities he regards as secondary.

33. Philip Rahv, "Fiction and the Criticism of Fiction," in *The Myth and the Powerhouse*, p. 45. The problem of comedy is complicated by modern theories, which, as W. K. Wimsatt has pointed out, are singularly unfriendly toward laughter ("The Criticism of Comedy," in *Hateful Contraries*, pp. 90–107). *Don Quixote* does not fit the theoretical expectations of a comic, regenerative "green world" (as Northrop Frye would sometimes have it) so much as it implies a joke in which the situational punchline is an unexpected reassertion of the insanely mechanical behavior Bergson saw in comedy. But Bergson's theory, too, is too narrow for *Don Quixote*, if only because the exposure of the ridiculous in Cervantes' novel is not premised on an acceptance of the norms of the fictional social life with which it deals; instead, Cervantes eventually renders these forms as ridiculous as Quixote's own automatic responses in the face of comic perversity.

34. Ricardo Quintana, "Situational Satire: A Commentary on the Method of Swift," *University of Toronto Quarterly* 17 (January, 1948): 133.

35. For example, Oscar Mandel, "The Function of the Norm in *Don Quixote*," *Modern Philology* 55 (February, 1958): 160–161.

36. Irwin E. Edman, Introduction to *Don Quixote: The Ingenious Gentleman of La Mancha*, p. 9.

37. "Primeramente ¡oh hijo! has de temer a Dios; porque en el temerle está la sabiduría, y siendo sabio no podrás errar en nada." See the commentary on this sentence by Samuel Putnam, in his translation, *The Ingenious Gentleman Don Quixote de la Mancha*, p. 1013.

38. For example, Donald W. Bleznick, "Don Quijote's Advice to Governor Sancho Panza," *Hispania* 40 (March, 1957): 62–65. The Marxist critic, Ludovick Osterc, has emphasized a parallel statement of advice in a political conduct-book by the humanist, Alfonso de Valdés (*El pensa-*

miento social y político del Quijote, p. 262). But even this supposed proof of Cervantes' serious intention in the advice to fear God does not explain the incongruous juxtaposition of Don Quixote's wording. Both Marxists and believers in democracy have tried to invest Sancho's learning experience under Quixote with a positive value that the novel does not allow it to have.

39. George Meredith, "An Essay on Comedy," in *Comedy*, ed. Wylie Sypher, p. 44. But as David Worcester has pointed out, Meredith's essay is heavily weighted against all satire (*The Art of Satire*, p. 7). So is Dorothy Van Ghent's account of "the juxtaposition of the two companions" (*The English Novel*, p. 14).

40. Casalduero, "The Composition of 'Don Quixote,'" in *Cervantes across The Centuries*, ed. Flores and Benardete, p. 63. Some other examples of the habit of reducing all difference between Quixote and Sancho are: Samuel Putnam, who declares that Sancho's "attitude toward reality is essentially the same as that of his master" in *The Portable Cervantes*, p. 33; Richard L. Predmore, *The World of "Don Quixote"*; Casella, "Critical Realism," in *Cervantes across the Centuries*, ed. Flores and Benardete, p. 208; and Chambers, "Structure and the Search for Truth in the *Quijote*," p. 312.

41. The exaggerated suspension of action may also refer to such writers as Pulci and Ariosto. For discussion of the overall problem, see Knud Togeby, *La composition du roman "Don Quichotte*,*"* pp. 25–26; also, Raymond S. Willis, Jr., *The Phantom Chapters of the "Quijote*.*"* But I doubt the validity of Togeby's statement that the break between chapters 8 and 9 is a device for arousing the reader's curiosity concerning the outcome of the narrative; if anything, the passage is mocking such cheap suspense.

42. The story is continued in the guise of a manuscript found by Cervantes, translated from the original by a "Spanish-speaking Moor" whom he ran into in Toledo, but written by "Cide Hamete Benengeli, Arabic historian" (Cohen, pp. 76–77). Hence arises Cervantes' pose as the mere "step-father" of Don Quixote (prologue to part 1). Although the pretended translator and historian continue to interject various comments in the novel, the ultimate effect is not a Jamesian complexity of story-telling narrators within narrators; if anything, the realism of the protagonists is heightened by Cervantes' disclaimer of authorial responsibility. This disclaimer, moreover, serves to destroy any reliance on the "authority" of the narrator's evaluations of the action (such as his praise or doubt of Don

Quixote's exploits) and thus to force the reader to derive meaning solely from context. This is the most important function of the narrator.

George Haley has argued that the oblique narrative method has the cumulative effect upon the "discreet reader" of showing that literature must never be confused with life (as Don Quixote confuses it during the puppet show); the reader recognizes that literature is fictional illusion ("The Narrator in *Don Quijote*: Maese Pedro's Puppet Show," *Modern Language Notes* 80 [March, 1965]: 160–165). No critic, however, denies that *the usual convention*, which would have us accept the factual account of the narrator(s) concerning the actions and utterances of the characters (including those of the Knight and his squire), *applies throughout the length of the novel*. As John J. Allen concludes, in his study of the novel's implied "authors," there are only "negligible" reservations to be made concerning authorial "reliability" in *Don Quixote* (*Don Quixote: Hero or Fool?* p. 27). Despite Haley's observation that Cervantes is calling attention to the "possibility of error" in any allegedly "true" account, there is no doubting this convention, and indeed there hardly could be if there is to be any data at all upon which to ground one's perceptions of the novel. Even the critic most committed to giving the narrator a primary role, Ruth El Saffar, admits that "in the case of *Don Quijote* the characters' claim for the exclusive interest in the novel is especially strong." Yet she goes on to maintain that the narrator, about whom "the reader knows much less," admittedly, than he does about the Duke and Duchess of part 2, shares with Don Quixote an "opposition . . . that forms the basis of the novel" ("The Function of the Fictional Narrator in *Don Quijote*," *Modern Language Notes* 83 [March, 1968]: 167–171, 175).

43. Castro, "Prólogo," pp. xxi–xxii, xxiv, xxxiii. The present study is not an attempt to see *Don Quixote* without its historical context (I have used, wherever I found them relevant, the standard historical tools); it is an attempt that stems, in part, from dissatisfaction with the particular concepts of historical context employed by most Hispanists. I seek to discover the context of the novel within history. It has seemed to me that specialist interpretations of the novel are in a contradictory position of having reconstructed what they claim to be the critically appropriate *Weltanschauung* of the period (though they disagree whether idealist, cautionary, or perspectivist emphases should govern this reconstruction), while at the same time they are unable to show that *any* of Cervantes' contemporaries actually read the novel in terms of this reconstruction. Indeed, the overwhelming evidence points to a disinclination of the period to take the novel as a serious art object. It has been shown many times that the serious

interpretations arose only much later. See, for example, "The Image of the *Quijote* in the Seventeenth Century," a dissertation by Daniel E. Quilter (University of Illinois, 1963); see also P. E. Russell, "*Don Quixote* as a Funny Book," *Modern Language Review* 64 (April, 1969): 319. The supposed historical interpretation thus itself appears to be seriously ahistorical.

The last point is complicated by the tacit adoption by scholars of a dubious paradigm of literary creation: authors of the Golden Age are assumed to have written in willing conformity with the conservative ideology of the age. A paradigm of the writer as not necessarily aware of the radical implications of his work seems to me far more responsive to such data as we have concerning literary creation (see my argument in "Logic, Hermeneutics, and Literary Context," *Genre* 1 [July, 1968]: 214–219; this is part of a symposium on E. D. Hirsch's book, *Validity in Interpretation*). Surely "historical context" is defined too narrowly if it is taken to mean interpretations possible within the prevalent ideologies contemporary with the work in question.

An important indication of a needed redefinition of historical context is given in one of Ralph Cohen's conclusions to his exhaustive study of criticism of Thomson's *The Seasons*. Cohen finds that it is "self-contradictory to attempt to interpret 'The Seasons' merely in terms of its own period." Contemporary critics of works as conceptually innovating as *The Seasons* (or, even more so, of such a work as *Don Quixote*) are not likely to be equipped for the criticism they seek to do; the period lacks just the innovative concepts that the work suggests (*The Art of Discrimination: Thomson's "The Seasons" and the Language of Criticism*, p. 443).

CHAPTER II. THE BENUMBED KNIGHT

1. Ortega y Gasset, "The Hero," in *Meditations on Quixote*, p. 149.

2. As Castro points out, "Prólogo" pp. xxii, lviii.

3. Samuel Taylor Coleridge, "Don Quixote. Cervantes." in *Complete Works*, ed. W. G. T. Shedd, VI, 267–268; William Hazlitt, "Standard Novels and Romances," in *Collected Works*, ed. A. R. Waller and Arnold Glover, X, 29–30.

4. For example, Castro, "Prólogo," p. xxv.

5. Castro, "Incarnation in *Don Quixote*," in *Cervantes across the Centuries*, ed. Flores and Benardete, pp. 136–178; see especially 165–166. Also Castro, "La palabra escrita y el *Quijote*," in *Hacia Cervantes*, 3d edition, pp. 359–409.

6. Castro, "Prólogo," p. xxv, and "Incarnation in *Don Quixote*," p. 139.

7. Castro, "Incarnation in *Don Quixote*," pp. 137, 159.

8. Cook, *The Meaning of Fiction*, p. 9.

9. Castro, "Prólogo," pp. liv–lv, lix; see also William J. Entwistle, *Cervantes*, pp. 154–155.

10. An interesting Freudian analysis that connects Don Quixote's old and new egos is Helene Deutsch's "Don Quixote and Don Quixotism," in her *Neuroses and Character Types: Clinical and Psychoanalytical Studies*, pp. 218–225. Some of Deutsch's key points parallel speculations of Miguel de Unamuno's in *The Life of Don Quixote and Sancho*, pp. 59–67, 98–99, 243–253. Deutsch and Unamuno suggest, in their different ways, that Don Quixote's new life is a sublimation, not a magical transformation. On the other hand, the Catholic theologian and *Quixote* commentator, Ambrosius Czako, is happy to say simply that by creating Dulcinea, Don Quixote "becomes a perfectly new man inwardly" (*Don Quijote: A Commentary*, p. 31).

11. Entwistle, *Cervantes*, p. 159. Compare Robert Alter's comment in *Rogue's Progress: Studies in the Picaresque Novel*, p. 109: ". . . the picaroon lives by ear; Don Quixote lives by the book."

12. *The Life of Saint Teresa of Ávila by Herself*, trans. J. M. Cohen, p. 37. In light of this and other passages, it is amusing that Denis de Rougemont can find no sign of sublimation or inhibition in St. Teresa's personal make-up (*Love in the Western World*, p. 163).

13. Compare Durán, *La ambigüedad en el Quijote*, pp. 242–243: "Los hombres son hijos de sus obras, no esclavos del destino o de la pre-determinación divina. Los ideales aparecen en el *Quijote* . . . como formas teóricas de vida que los incitan a la acción, y, a través de esta acción, a crearse a sí mismos como personajes." The point is in a way a natural concomitant of Castro's interpretation, which Durán accepts, but it is never used to begin an evaluation of different kinds of "works," probably because the conception of creative action that the position involves does not permit discriminations. The same failure to discriminate lies behind the habit of equating a conscious awareness that one is acting out a role with "artistic quality." For an example of this fallacy in *Quixote* criticism, see Herman Meyer, *Poetics of Quotation in the European Novel*, p. 66.

14. The particular proposal that Quixote advocates here (a revival of chivalry in order to carry out renewed hostilities against the Turks) may, among other things, recall the well-known fate of Sebastian I of Portugal, who became "obsessed with imperial delusions of knight-errantry" and led his forces in 1578 on an utterly suicidal foray into Morocco, where

some eight thousand were killed and fifteen thousand were taken into slavery or held for ransom (Harold Livermore, *A History of Spain*, pp. 236–237, 245–246; see also William C. Atkinson, *A History of Spain and Portugal*, p. 159).

The proposal itself is consistent with the Knight's overall bent toward institutionalized concepts of self-aspiration. Chivalric adventure simply becomes a variant of nationalism. As Joseph Bickermann pointed out, Quixote's whole notion of knight-errantry is premised on an institutional basis that was absent from European chivalry. (*Don Quijote y Fausto*, pp. 166–170). When Quixote departs from the precise models given in his corpus of books, he usually arrives at a more rigid and routinized outcome.

15. Américo Castro's emphasis (as in *The Structure of Spanish History*) on the internal, subjective life of Spaniards, which implies that empirical confirmation was of almost no importance to the Spanish mind, does not really accord with the character of Don Quixote, who is content with purely subjective evidence for the merits of chivalry only when no other evidence can be found. In fact, the Knight's purpose in descending into the cave of Montesinos is to "see with his own eyes whether the marvels related about it thereabouts were true" (Cohen, p. 609). We too easily forget that there did exist in the Spanish culture of the time an "empirical approach" to the world; J. H. Elliott speaks of the "inherent tendency of the Castilian mentality to concern itself with the concrete and the practical" (*Imperial Spain: 1469–1716*, p. 380). He notes also the implicit focus on practicality in St. Teresa's maxim, "The Lord walks among the pots and pans."

Richard L. Predmore's *The World of "Don Quixote"* reaches conclusions concerning characters in Cervantes' novel that (as he recognizes) are in accord with Castro's theory of Spanish national character. Predmore emphasizes the problematical features of the "reality" that the characters of the novel must face and that they are prone to interpret subjectively. The problems of reality are to some extent, however, creations of the types of critical argument. Cervantes is said to be "showing us how difficult it can be to read aright the face of reality" (p. 31), but a philosophically supported, commonsense theory of reality hardly would postulate any such ability to "read," with immediate visual scrutiny, the nature of things seen, as Predmore appears to suppose.

Some of Predmore's examples of problematical reality seem to be especially of the critic's own making. For instance, Cervantes writes that the exposed leg of Dorothea really "seemed" to be of white alabaster;

Predmore regards this as an instance of an appearance that can justify the characters' making misinterpretations (p. 82). But is it not preposterous to suggest that the Priest and the Barber, when they observe this leg, literally think it is made of alabaster?

A more general point concerns Predmore's claim that the verb *parecer* ("to appear, or seem") is emphasized by its frequency in the novel; similarly, he stresses the conjectural phrase *deber de* ("must"). No doubt there is potential value to such word studies, but the results become dubious when one consults the counted totals of *all* the words in the novel. For one then learns that *saber* ("to know") occurs even more frequently than *parecer* and that *deber* occurs far less frequently than either. Other words discussed by Predmore also prove to have lower frequencies than one would surmise from his studies, whereas verbs that he does not study, such as *ser, haber, decir, hacer,* and *tener,* occur with much greater frequency than any of those previously mentioned. Admittedly, these are all common verbs, but some of them become inexplicable if we accept the conclusion that the language of the novel (considered in terms of word frequencies) shows that reality is basically problematical for the characters (see the statistical study by Carlos Fernández Gómez, *Vocabulario de Cervantes,* pp. 1103–1136).

16. Cohen, pp. 258–259. The 1607 Brussels edition of *Don Quixote* gives "desgracias" rather than "gracias," the word that is translated here as "whims." The Brussels text would denote instead "misfortunes," which makes sense. (I am indebted to Mack Singleton for this point.)

17. Note Erich Auerbach's difficulties with this speech, which he first finds to be both subjectively appealing and a fine example of elevated style. But, as he goes on to say, the elevated style does not fit with the undoubtedly comic treatment of the entire scene. Any tragic possibilities for the speech are immediately denied in the novel (Auerbach astutely points out) by the fact that Quixote "instantaneously and as it were automatically takes refuge in the interpretation that Dulcinea is under an enchantment." Don Quixote, Auerbach finally decides, is "not possibly but unqualifiedly conceived not with an undertone of ridicule but as ridiculous through and through." I concur with him here, but not with his conclusion that the novel can be taken only as "a dance of gay and diverting confusion" (*Mimesis: The Representation of Reality in Western Literature,* trans. Willard R. Trask, pp. 339–345, 358).

18. The only prominent modern critic I can recall who takes this position concerning reality is Georg Lukács (other critics in the Marxist tradition probably would concur with him). See his interesting theoretical

statements in *Realism in Our Time*. Lukács' arguments are long overdue for consideration. Yet his own criticism of *Don Quixote* is a disappointing mixture of the usual idealist and cautionary approaches, tucked under the heading of "social reality." See his preface to a Hungarian edition, translated in *Communist Review* (1951), pp. 265–271, under the title "Don Quixote."

19. Unamuno, *The Life of Don Quixote and Sancho*, pp. 76–77.

20. Quixote of course idealizes Spanish history here; in point of fact, Christian kings during the long reconquest sometimes did marry "Muslim princesses and gave their own daughters in marriage to Islam" (Atkinson, *A History of Spain and Portugal*, p. 60).

21. Emilio Goggio, "The Dual Role of Dulcinea in Cervantes' *Don Quijote de la Mancha*," *Modern Language Quarterly* 13 (September, 1952): 285–291; see also K. K. Ruthven, "The Composite Mistress," *AUMLA*, no. 26 (1966), pp. 198–214.

22. José Ortega y Gasset, "Spanish Letter: July 1924," in *A Dial Miscellany*, ed. William Wassertrom, p. 212.

23. W. H. Auden believes that this shows that Quixote's triumph is merely ironic, for the stated goal was to be a hero, not a madman (*The Dyer's Hand and Other Essays*, p. 136). But whereas Auden feels sure that "Don Quixote is perfectly aware that he has failed to do anything which he has set out to do," Cervantes only shows that Quixote is often pleased with his exploits in part 1, and that he takes at face value the interest in his career as a knight that is shown by the Duke and Duchess in part 2.

24. It was Bishop Richard Hurd who first expressed the fear that Cervantes, in having Don Quixote defend the truth of chivalry books by comparing them to the ancient epic, was thereby implying that both literary forms were lacking in essential truth (*Hurd's Letters on Chivalry and Romance, with the Third Elizabethan Dialogue*, ed. Edith J. Morley, p. 161).

25. Quoted from Samuel Putnam's translation, *The Ingenious Gentleman Don Quixote de la Mancha*, p. 547. The Spanish is "los que viven, sin que merezcan otra fama ni otra elogio sus grandezas." The passage is part of Don Quixote's longest speech on the subject of lineages. Yet this speech is ignored by Américo Castro, who claims to discern a rejection of the conventional value of lineages in Don Quixote's words (see especially *Cervantes y los casticismos españoles*, pp. 93–94, 100). Had Castro dealt with this indispensable passage, he would have had to face the fact that the "virtue" Don Quixote extols is one that is defined and

validated by public opinion, not (as Castro maintains) one that opposes the collective mind. Everyone who sees the virtuous man will praise him, Don Quixote says, "since praise has ever been the prize of virtue, and the virtuous cannot fail to be praised" (Cohen, p. 506). Nor is the virtue that Quixote has in mind the personal, spiritual kind that Castro claims a "new Christian" sensibility implies: it is defined in Quixote's own conventional examples in this speech, both of which concern donating money to charity. Although Quixote stresses that it is as virtuous for a poor gentleman to give his two "maravedis" as it is for a rich man to give greater amounts, the group approval that people have always enjoyed for this sort of charitable giving can hardly be mistaken for a revolutionary or spiritual value.

26. D. H. Lawrence, *Lady Chatterley's Lover*, p. 19; see also pp. 55, 70–71. I am aware that Don Quixote sometimes expresses distrust of appearances himself, most notably in the Waggon of Death episode (Cohen, p. 535). But to say that his occasional remarks in this vein demonstrate a realization on his part of "how problematical" reality might be (as Predmore claims in *The World of "Don Quixote,"* p. 34) is to be misled by the literal. It is in fact *after* the Waggon of Death episode that the lengthy sequence of deceptions at the Ducal palace takes place; Quixote does not question these appearances of chivalric reality, even though he has formally admitted that one must do so. His characteristic method of explanation of discrepancies between appearance and reality—namely, that the differences are caused by enchanters—would conveniently invalidate any method of probing appearances. But, in any case, he is scarcely interested in such a probe. For him to recognize that appearances may be deceptive serves, not as a skeptical, but as a relieving function. He is free to believe anything that appears and then to disclaim responsibility if the appearance is revealed as a deception.

To be sure, Quixote deeply desires that others share his perceptions and accept them as true. But this does not show that he has an interest in probing truth itself. The novel instead shows that group agreement would take the place of any such interest. The phenomenologist Alfred Schutz, by taking literally the Knight's commitment to "the spirit of truth, the defense of which is the first task of the knight errant," mistakenly equips Quixote with an epistemological conscience and an insight into the nature of "inter-subjectivity" ("Don Quixote and the Problem of Reality," in *Collected Papers,* ed. Arvid Broderson, II, 148–156). I agree that Quixote does not want to place credence in his vision of Montesinos if he has to believe that it was only a dream, but there is no basis in the text for supposing that he therefore concludes that perhaps all his perceptions had been illusory.

27. Miguel de Unamuno, "Don Quixote in the Contemporary European Tragic-Comedy," in *The Tragic Sense of Life*, p. 302. Unamuno is wise in silently assuming that the Knight's affinity for suffering has a far greater ideological resonance than a mere imitation of courtly love and its narcissistic sense of pain would afford. For this reason, purely psychoanalytical intuitions into courtly love, as in Melvin W. Askew's "Courtly Love: Neurosis as Institution," *Psychoanalytic Review* 52 (Spring, 1965): 19–29, parallel some aspects of the present study of Don Quixote's character without suggesting the vital ideological connections that give the novel its special impact. The notion of courtly love does not provide a wide enough base for the literary love patterns Cervantes explores. Certainly Christian marriage is involved as well, and probably, too, the suffering lovers of *Don Quixote* may be traced back through the whole stream of literary pseudoeroticism that began with Achilles Tatius. See Alex Comfort's essay on the latter tradition, "The Rape of Andromeda," in *Darwin and the Naked Lady: Discursive Essays on Biology and Art*, pp. 74–99.

28. The contexts of the novel suggest in any case that this ending, like others, need not be taken straight. Cervantes, in such instances as the "Tale of Foolish Curiosity" and the multiple happy endings at the inn in part 1, is a master at making neat endings appear so preposterous that they must be regarded with critical skepticism rather than simply accepted as resolution of the story. Note also that Predmore, who accepts the theory that Quixote's death is due to his loss of cherished illusions, is forced simply to improvise reasons for the Knight's unexplained failure to push ahead with his elaborate plans for pastoral imitation, developed just before the death scene (*The World of "Don Quixote,"* pp. 124–125). For a detailed (and I think very plausible) interpretation of the ending in terms of irony, see Margaret Jimmie Canfield, "Don Quixote Sets out to Die," *Paunch*, no. 32 (August, 1968), pp. 23–38.

29. Rocinante's choosing the way is so prominent a feature of part 1 that Knud Togeby has explicated that whole part as structurally centered on the Knight's horse. Togeby regards Rocinante as having greater comic import, and as offering greater resistance to the Knight, than anything offered by Sancho (*La composition du roman "Don Quichotte,"* pp. 15–33, especially p. 18).

30. See John Ormsby's translation, *The Ingenious Gentleman Don Quijote de la Mancha*, I, 98 n.

31. Otis Green points out that the Spanish romances of chivalry were

much less titillating and much more properly moral than were others in Europe (*Spain and the Western Tradition*, I, 164). Nonetheless, Spanish moralists did rage, and the matter of sexual propriety in chivalry books leads, in *Don Quixote* itself, to a battle between Quixote and Cardenio (Cohen, p. 198).

32. Harry Levin is thus misled to take Quixote's account of a knight being greeted by a "lovely group of maidens" who "strip him as naked as his mother bore him, and bathe him in warm water" (Cohen, p. 441) as evidence that Don Quixote's drive toward romance is akin to Freud's pleasure principle ("The Example of Cervantes," in *Society and Self in the Novel*, ed. Mark Schorer, p. 8). Salvador de Madariaga, who locates in Quixote's chivalry books a dream of "free instinctive pleasure" is similarly mistaken (*Don Quixote: An Introductory Essay in Psychology*, p. 50). And the psychoanalyst Helene Deutsch overlooks the fact that Quixote's re-creation in his chivalric dream world of "the megalomanic self-importance" of the child does not entail a revivification of infantile sexuality ("Don Quixote and Don Quixotism," in *Neuroses and Character Types*, p. 221).

33. The one outright exception to the pattern is Don Quixote's little speech in favor of procuring (Cohen, p. 174). This seems so out of character to me (even after many readings) that I must bypass it. Nor do any of the annotations remove this difficulty of interpretation.

34. Otis Green, following Pedro Salinas, points out that regardless of what reply Sancho brings for Don Quixote's message to Aldonza-Dulcinea, the Knight "has determined ahead of time the solution of his . . . predicament." For Green and Salinas, Quixote is all the "more admirable" because he can leap "to the safety of his own personal logic, across all the barriers of common sense," even though Sancho's reply brings out the illogicality of Quixote's position (*Spain and the Western Tradition*, I, 196–197). But if one follows out Quixote's "personal logic" in its fuller implications (as I propose to do), it is hardly possible to regard it as ultimately admirable, except by adopting an ideology something like that expressed in Borges' fictions.

35. Prose translations supplied by Mack Singleton.

36. The report of a deathbed retraction of the whole vision, put into the mouth of the ostensible author (and not actually rendered in the deathbed scene) is equivocal: ". . . he finally retracted it on his death-bed and confessed he had invented it since it seemed to him to fit in with the adventures he had read of in his histories" (Cohen, p. 624; the Spanish is: "por

paracerle que convenía y cuadraba bien con las aventuras que había leído en sus historias").

37. Critical reactions to this grotesque revelation tend to be more or less preposterous. Dorothy Van Ghent calls it "a consummatory vision, peaceful and beautiful" (*The English Novel*, p. 10). Harry Levin is pleased to find that Don Quixote has established contact with "the deep well of the past," but Levin neglects to add that this only shows how deadly that past is ("The Example of Cervantes," pp. 22–23). Joaquín Casalduero is aware of serious imperfections in the dream of delight but insists that these are caused by the novel's involvement with social reality in part 2, which automatically corrupts the Knight's purity. This hardly explains, however, why society's values need be present at the deepest levels of Quixote's unconscious mind or why the Knight should express such delight at the results (*Sentido y forma del Quijote*, pp. 271–274). Salvador de Madariaga regards the incident of the cut-out heart as comic and even "merry" realism but takes the association of Dulcinea's image with money as "cruel realism" (*Don Quixote: An Introductory Essay in Psychology*, pp. 160–162).

38. Durán, "La aventura de la cueva de Montesinos," in *La ambigüedad en el Quijote*, pp. 210–228; Madariaga, "The Inner Enemy of Don Quixote," in *Don Quixote: An Introductory Essay in Psychology*, pp. 109–115.

39. Durán, *La ambigüedad en el Quijote*, pp. 219–220. Though Durán is perhaps technically correct in calling Quixote's resistance to the meaning of the vision a conscious act, it would be a distortion to say that Quixote really thinks the matter out and then resists. His resistance is automatic, conventional. He shows no sign at this point of having learned anything about himself in Montesinos. Hence it is extravagant to argue (as Gloria M. Fry does) that the cave episode is the key moment of the Knight's "catharsis by progressive steps" toward his final resumption of his old role as Alonso Quixano ("Symbolic Action in the Episode of the Cave of Montesinos from 'Don Quijote,'" *Hispania* 48 [August, 1965]: 468–474). Fry, whose critical approach derives from Kenneth Burke, concedes that the alleged catharsis contains no "shock of recognition" on the part of the Knight, nor does it very intimately involve the reader.

The cautionary approach to *Don Quixote* not only fails to show why the reader should regard the prearranged cure of the Knight's madness as viable fictional progression; it also leaves unexplained both the absurdity of a catharsis virtually unnoticed by the one who supposedly undergoes it, Don Quixote (a "tragic" character whose ability to *experience* tragedy thus remains invisible), and the preposterous final leap from chivalry to Christian cure in one final chapter. The present study attempts to demonstrate that the leap is from the outset a short one, and that the novel shows us just what this shortness implies.

Predmore, in the final chapter of *The World of "Don Quixote,"* has assembled evidence to support the theory that the Knight becomes aware of his madness and evinces a desire to be cured prior to the death scene. But these details are inconclusive, especially in view of the mass of conflicting evidence in which the Knight, to the very last chapter, shows no sign of such self-awareness. Even the apparent indication in part 2, chapter 58, where Don Quixote briefly expresses a desire to be cured, is equivocal inasmuch as it is expressed in connection with a desire for Dulcinea to be disenchanted. This is hugging the disease while hoping for its remission.

It seems most unsatisfactory to argue (as Otis Green does) that Quixote's occasional questions concerning the reality of his vision in the cave of Montesinos show him to be "haunted" by that problem; or that all Don Quixote's varied misfortunes and melancholy from part 2, chapter 10, to the end of the novel constitute a "sequence of disasters" (actually, many of them are little different from previous misfortunes, and Green even transfers one of the earlier incidents—the suspension by strappado in part 1, chapter 43—to part 2, as part of his case); or that all the events that are not misfortunes or melancholy in this alleged sequence are simply instances of "the hero's backsliding" (*Spain and the Western Tradition*, IV, 63, 67–69).

40. Pedro Salinas, in his chapter, "La tradición de la poesía amorosa" (in *Jorge Manrique, o tradición y originalidad*, pp. 9–43), describes the conventions that I maintain *Don Quixote* is critically undermining; see especially "El amor al amor imposible" (pp. 28–30). De Rougemont also traces a literary pattern in which the lovers suffer for the sake of suffering, but the separation from Christian piety that he finds in the sentimental love-religion seems to differentiate that literary pattern from what is shown in *Don Quixote*. If he is right about this separation, De Rougemont is also right to give only a brief passage to Don Quixote (*Love in the Western World*, p. 189).

41. Manuel Durán concedes that psychoanalysis could bring us to a deeper interpretation of certain details in the Montesinos episode, but he declines to go further than this remark (*La ambigüedad en el Quijote*, p. 216). The Thomist Mario Casella purchases safety by insisting with great frequency that no rational, material, or empirical explanations of

motive are to be attempted for Don Quixote ("Critical Realism," in *Cervantes across the Centuries*, ed. Flores and Benardete, pp. 197–210 *passim*). On the other hand, those attempts which have come from psychiatry rather than literary criticism treat the novel too narrowly; for example, see Eduardo Urzaiz' analysis of Quixote as simply a paranoid type ("Don Quijote ante la psiquiatría," in *Exégesis Cervantina*, pp. 11–26).

42. Auerbach, *Mimesis*, pp. 348–349.

43. Otis Green's attempt to explain Don Quixote's malady in terms of the psychology of humors is not only reductive ("the derangements were produced by excessive heat of the brain, caused by such agents as lack of sleep and aggressive emotions"), but it posits airtight compartments within the Knight's character ("intermittent derangements" versus "recurring lucid intervals") that serve to prevent an adequate understanding of the relationship of his "madness" to his society's "sanity" (*Spain and the Western Tradition*, IV, 260–261). The relationship of sanity and madness in the novel is discussed especially in chapter 4 of the present study. What I must insist upon here is a suspension of two assumptions about madness: that which derives from Romantic ideology and finds madness to be somehow right and that which derives from conservative tradition and finds madness to be an obviously valueless deviation from the normal.

44. Arnold Hauser's observation on the particular genius of Renaissance literature is appropriate here: "The real discovery of the age . . . was not the world of fantasy, but that of psychology. . . . Shakespeare and Cervantes became the founders of the new psychology . . . because of their possession of a new key to the mechanism of the mind and their discovery of the ambivalence of mental attitudes" (*Mannerism*, I, 315).

45. In addition to the Christian and epic-heroic strands in Don Quixote's character, there are elements of medieval character typology, as well as reflections of the Renaissance courtier. William J. Brandt has pointed out that "regardless of the exact list of attitudes one proposes" as the set of ideal qualities prized by the medieval aristocrat, all relationships were governed by purely external conceptions of status; thus the alleged "personalism of the medieval aristocracy was actually very impersonal" (*The Shape of Medieval History: Studies in Modes of Perception*, p. 109). The same sort of external definition of self is true of Don Quixote. And the contrast between the medieval knight and the Renaissance courtier, usually supportable on the grounds that the courtier (unlike the knight) was expected to be a master of a great many skills and familiar with a great many aspects of knowledge (E. R. Chamberlin, *Everyday Life in Renais-*

sance Times, pp. 48–49), does not hold for Don Quixote, whose claims to near-universal aptitudes and knowledge are stressed by Cervantes, especially in part 2.

46. It has been noted that Quixote also uses more uncomplimentary epithets on Sancho here than anywhere else in the novel. See Helen Phipps Houck, "Substantive Address Used between Don Quijote and Sancho Panza," *Hispanic Review* 5 (January, 1937): 60–72.

47. Note Voltaire's quip: "Don Quichotte qui adorait Dulcinée du Toboso dans les bras de Maritorne" (quoted in Walter Starkie's translation, *Don Quixote of La Mancha,* p. 249 n.). Coleridge's intuition here was far less happy: "Don Quixote's age of fifty," he says, "may well be supposed to prevent his mind from being tempted out of itself by any of the lower passions" ("Cervantes. Don Quixote," p. 266). The misperception is duplicated by W. H. Auden, who writes that Don Quixote "is past the age when sexual love means anything to him" (*The Dyer's Hand,* p. 453).

It was Andreas Capellanus who spelled out the guaranteed sexual wisdom of chivalry when he said that the courtly lover becomes chaste in thought as well as in deed, "For when he thinks deeply of his beloved the sight of any other woman seems to his mind rough and rude" (*The Art of Courtly Love,* p. 4).

48. Note that Quixote's well-known speech on liberty is set in the context of a flight from Altisidora (rather than from the supposed ease of the Ducal palace in general): "When Don Quixote found himself in the open country, free and disembarrassed of Altisidora's attentions, he felt himself in his element, with his spirits reviving for the fresh pursuit of his scheme of chivalries" (Cohen, p. 837).

49. She quotes with facility the hideous lines from a ballad about King Rodrigo, who is attacked by reptiles: "Now they eat me, now they eat me, in the part where I most sinned" (Cohen, p. 688). This seems to be the extent of her interest in poetry. Note also how she "defends" all waiting-women by comparing their bodies to dunghills (p. 712). Her beloved husband had died of a shock that resulted from his being dismissed by his aristocrat employer, and from the ridicule he received from boys in the streets—but not, apparently, from the deep stab his mistress gave him with a long pin or bodkin into his loins. Some chapters later, Tosilos the lackey receives an appropriately Dulcineated visitation from Cupid, and hence offers to marry Doña Rodriguez' daughter: ". . . the little blind boy, who is generally called Love in these parts . . . ran a six-foot dart into the poor lackey's left side and pierced his heart through and through" (pp.

777, 831). The imagery of pain cannot fail to give a grotesque twist to the Knight's uncritical chivalric assistance for the widow, quite aside from the Duke's bullying interference in the project.

50. As Otis Green points out, *Spain and the Western Tradition*, I, 196.

51. Czako, *Don Quijote: A Commentary*, p. 47.

52. Delfín Carbonell y Basset, "Don Quijote desde un punto de vista existencio-fenomenológico," *Duquesne Hispanic Review* 2, no. 1 (1963): 30, 32. Compare the concluding sentence of Predmore's book, which declares that Cervantes has created, "above all, an open world whose rare freedom serves not the triumph of matter but the revelation of spirit" (*The World of "Don Quixote,"* p. 129).

53. G. K. Chesterton, "The Divine Parody of *Don Quixote*," in *A Handful of Authors: Essays on Books and Writers*, pp. 24–27. Ludovick Osterc, however, finds that Don Quixote's aim is the establishment of, or at least the articulation of, a historically and humanly superior kind of primitive communism. Hence his justice is far from being hare-brained. For Osterc, the Knight's words of social defiance aimed at the state troopers (at the end of part 1, chapter 45) constitute the key passage of the entire novel (*El pensamiento social y político de Quijote*, pp. 250–251). But to take the Knight's words here as a true description of his mission is to deny the juxtapositional undermining that the whole novel provides.

54. Turgenev, "Hamlet and Don Quixote," pp. 105, 107, 112.

55. Van Ghent, *The English Novel*, pp. 11–12. That Van Ghent is making the issue more abstract than it is even to Don Quixote is indicated by Quixote's use of a physical basis (for once) in his reproach to the rich Haldudo, who has complained that Andrew owes him for some shoes and for some medical services: "But set the shoes and the blood-lettings against the undeserved flogging you have given him. For, if he broke the leather of the shoes you gave him, you have broken the skin of his body, and if the barber let his blood when he was sick, you have done the same now, when he is well. On that score he owes you nothing" (Cohen, p. 48). Here Quixote seems tacitly to accept a requirement that Andrew really be helped, in a physical sense, rather than merely be utilized for a perspectival discussion of justice. See the comments by Wayne Burns in "The Panzaic Principle," *Paunch*, no. 22 (January, 1965), pp. 17–19, which effectively refute Van Ghent on this scene.

56. The inequities are further marked if one considers two things not mentioned in the text but no doubt well known in Spain at the time: Quixote himself could not have been tortured or sentenced to the galleys

by the king, because his status as a don makes these steps illegal (J. H. Elliott, *Imperial Spain*, p. 104), and the Spanish monarchy, here so prim about such matters as a stolen basket of linen, was itself hopelessly riddled with graft and bribery, a fact that is alluded to in certain passages concerning Sancho's governorship in part 2.

57. A. A. Parker, *"Don Quixote* and the Relativity of Truth," *Dublin Review* 220 (Autumn, 1947): 9. On the contrary, there is little that Quixote need hesitate about. The elaborate Spanish legal code certainly would not be able to do a better job than he does by releasing the prisoners, and it does appear as if he is substantially right in his analysis. Even Américo Castro has pointed out that for a moment there is little cause for the reader to find contradictory perspectives; the galley slaves, the guards and Don Quixote agree that this justice is a fraud ("Prólogo," p. xl).

58. Hence Luis Rosales is suggestive but misleading when he describes the aftermath of the freeing of the slaves as a clash between their idea of liberty and Quixote's idea. Quixote's overt goal is to get everyone perfectly into conformity with Dulcinea; his covert one is to get everyone involved in a futile effort at sensual renunciation and to call the appearance of success in the project a real achievement. Neither goal could be called "liberty." But Rosales, in his gigantic study, mistakes Don Quixote for Cervantes' ideal man (*Cervantes y la libertad,* I, 177–178, and II, 304).

59. Castro has said that Cervantes, in this scene, is a forerunner of the Spanish anarchists ("Prólogo," p. xl), and I am attempting to spell out somewhat more fully what this might mean in terms of Cervantes' novel. For an example of modern theory that is skeptical of the ideal of justice (though not concerned with the study of Cervantes), see Otto Kirchheimer, *Political Justice: The Use of Legal Procedure for Political Ends.*

60. Northrop Frye has gone so far as to place Quixote's imagination on a par with that of William Blake ("The Imaginative and the Imaginary," in *Fables of Identity: Studies in Poetic Mythology,* pp. 151–167). And for Américo Castro, Don Quixote's belief that a barber's basin is really the helmet of Mambrino is on a par with the imaginative use of physical objects in the creative process of Joan Miró ("Prólogo," p. xvii).

61. For an interesting account of critical reactions to Hobbes's remark, see Stuart M. Tave, *The Amiable Humorist: A Study in the Comic Theory and Criticism of the Eighteenth and Early Nineteenth Centuries,* especially p. 46.

62. In Wilhelm Reich, *Listen, Little Man!* The cartoon by William Steig faces the title page.

CHAPTER III. THE POSSIBILITIES OF THE SQUIRE

1. Ormsby, Introduction to his translation, *The Ingenious Gentleman Don Quixote de la Mancha*, p. lx. Leif Sletsjöe finds a dissociation between Sancho's critical role in part 2 and what Sletsjöe takes as a much less developed role in part 1. (*Sancho Panza: Hombre de bien*, pp. 62–70, 91). But there is more evidence of Sancho's critical mind in part 1 than Sletsjöe would allow, and the wider depiction of Sancho's family relationship in part 2 is to be explained not as a change in Cervantes' intention (as Casalduero also thought), but as a normal function of the character revelation that the novel gives: it moves not by slow build-up, but by sudden glimpses in depth. Character is revealed in quantum-theory chunks, as it were, but it is not dissociated because of this. We must also recall that in part 1 (beginning with chapter 20), Sancho is partially muzzled by his master and so cannot speak as freely as he would. The fact that Sletsjöe does recognize that Sancho operates with a good deal of verbal freedom in the novel is encouraging, but, instead of attempting to trace out the value of Sancho's critical side, Sletsjöe, like Hipólito R. Romero Flores before him, is too preoccupied with Sancho's conventional goodness (compare Romero Flores, *Biografía de Sancho Panza: Filósofo de la sensatez*). A similar predilection dominates the long article by Lucio Pabón Núñez, "Sancho, o la exaltación del pueblo español" (*Cuadernos Hispanoamericanos* 58 [June, 1964]: 541–580), although this contains interesting resistance to the usual glossing over of the differences between Quixote and his squire. Even Dámaso Alonso, who does not accept the equation of Sancho's values with those of his master, finally does little more than claim that Sancho is only in some ways and at some times engaged in the pursuit of his ideal island. That Sancho has a critical function in relation to the Knight is not brought out ("Sancho-Quijote; Sancho-Sancho," in *Del siglo de oro a este siglo de siglas*, pp. 9–19). Nor is this critical function noticed in Raymond Willis' recent existential interpretation, "Sancho Panza: Prototype for the Modern Novel," *Hispanic Review* 36 (January, 1969): 207–227. In Willis' eyes, Sancho only "witnesses" and "shares" his master's "dialogue" with the material world (p. 217).

2. Aubrey Bell, who had an intense admiration for the Spanish peasant, was never very happy with Sancho, who, he thought, lacked the proper dignity of the Spanish people (*Cervantes*, pp. 104, 140–141, 146).

3. E. C. Riley (following Hiram Haydn's *The Counter-Renaissance*) classifies Sancho as one of the literary "wise fools" who are humble, simple, and pious (*Cervantes's Theory of the Novel*, p. 69). But this does not fit.

More likely predecessors are suggested by Jack Lindsay, in *A Short History of Culture from Prehistory to the Renaissance*, pp. 432–434, 448–449, 475–478, 485–486. But even these scarcely suggest Sancho's precise make-up or fictional role. Walter Kaiser's claim that in *Don Quixote* "the world is on the fool's side for the first time, and the fool acts as spokesman for that world against his master" unfortunately obscures the vital difference between the idealistic upper-class characters of the novel's society and Sancho (*Praisers of Folly: Erasmus, Rabelais, Shakespeare*, p. 285). But Kaiser's quoting of Philaréte Chasles, who placed Sancho in the company of Panurge and Falstaff, a trinity who form a "mocking chorus, a complete critique of all that carries man beyond the limits of material life," is certainly appropriate.

Heinrich Heine, in *The Romantic School* (1833), briefly suggested that Sancho brings into the novel the insight of back and belly, but the idea was not developed. In an introduction to *Don Quixote* that Heine wrote a few years later, the idea does not even reappear. The introduction does criticize severely the values of Spain and Don Quixote, but Heine insists that he will always regard Dulcinea with ideal eyes (*Werke und Briefe*, ed. Hans Kaufmann, V, 87, 406–427, especially p. 409).

4. Sancho does, it is true, join in the request that the Priest read the "Tale of Foolish Curiosity," but he then apparently does not stay to hear it out, and goes off instead to see what his master is up to (Cohen, pp. 282, 316).

5. Predmore, *The World of "Don Quixote,"* especially chapters 2, 3, and 4.

6. Bell, *Cervantes*, p. 131.

7. Sancho is particularly effective as argumentative catalyst in the Sierra Morena scenes. See Cohen, pp. 199–209, especially.

8. As shown by Wayne Burns in his important essay, "The Panzaic Principle." Contrast the comments on this episode by either Predmore or Willis, in which the problem of Sancho's insight is hardly considered (Predmore, *The World of "Don Quixote,"* p. 44; Willis, "Sancho Panza: Prototype for the Modern Novel," pp. 220–221).

9. Such statements of direct opposition toward the respectable people in the novel are, however, rare. One asks whether Cervantes considered that the sheer weight of realism would not allow a peasant character to be so "smart" toward his betters, or whether Sancho's function is to criticize *directly* only the Dulcineism of the somewhat declassed Knight. The effect, in any case, is to allow Sancho great critical scope but at the same time to

make him appear merely entertaining to many of the other characters, who cannot see themselves in Don Quixote.

10. Actually Sancho has already been accepted as dinner companion by the Knight, this coming about naturally in their wanderings. At the end of the previous chapter, it is reported that "the two of them ate their dinner peacefully and companionably" (Cohen, p. 84). James Russell Lowell noticed that the offer of equality is simultaneously denied, because Quixote reminds Sancho that the favor "is granted by one who is his natural lord and master" ("Don Quixote," in *Lowell: Essays, Poems, and Letters*, ed. William Smith Clark III, p. 179). The point is missed by Mark Van Doren, who admires uncritically the Knight's granting of pseudo-equal status to Sancho (*Don Quixote's Profession*, pp. 18, 85–87).

11. Walter Starkie, in his translation of the novel, somehow manages to "correct" this error. See Starkie's version, *Don Quixote of La Mancha*, p. 590.

12. Willis has shown that Cervantes' use of the chapter break is integral to the art of *Don Quixote*, although Willis' analysis of this particular break suffers from the attempt to apply Castro's perspectivist interpretation to the novel (*The Phantom Chapters of the "Quijote,"* p. 31).

13. Probably, though, the remark also conveys some sense of the widespread fears of contaminating "Old Christian" blood, rather than being limited to a sexual reference.

14. Madariaga, *Don Quixote: An Introductory Essay in Psychology*, especially pp. 137–156.

15. Thus Northrop Frye, in his few pages of practical criticism on *Don Quixote*, assumes that Sancho's following Don Quixote is some sort of guarantee of moral worth in the latter (*Fables of Identity*, p. 165). Herbert Grierson also thought that Quixote's hold over Sancho is "the greatest proof of Don Quixote's courage, sincerity, and goodness" ("*Don Quixote*: Some Wartime Reflections on Its Character and Influence," in *The Background of English Literature: Classical and Romantic*, p. 50).

16. The notion that a man might gain himself a kingdom is not as far-fetched as it might sound. *Tirante the White*, one of the chivalry books spared from Don Quixote's library (Cohen, p. 60), is based on the feats of a group of Catalan mercenaries under Roger de Flor, who eventually "seized the duchy of Athens and there maintained themselves as a sovereign state from 1322 to 1386" (Atkinson, *A History of Spain and Portugal*, p. 96). John Ormsby noted that *Tirante the White*, unlike most books of chivalry, did treat "its readers as rational beings" (Ormsby's translation of *Don Quixote*, II, 537). Another, and perhaps more pertinent, analogue

is that of Cortés (who is mentioned in *Don Quixote*, on page 517 of the Cohen translation), a man who conquered some eleven million inhabitants of Mexico with a force of a few hundred men. "Cortés, like any *caballero* of mediaeval Castile, aspired to obtain a fief and vassals, to secure a title, and to make a name for himself in the world—and all of these ambitions he attained through his conquest of Mexico" (J. H. Elliott, *Imperial Spain*, p. 54). Bernal Díaz del Castillo, in admitting that the Spaniards had come to Mexico "to serve God and the king, and also to get rich" (quoted by Elliott, *Imperial Spain*, p. 53), was speaking in the spirit later invoked by Don Quixote to induce Sancho to help attack the windmills: "With their spoils we will begin to get rich, for this is a fair war, and it is a great service to God to wipe such a wicked brood from the face of the earth" (Cohen, p. 68). Sancho is not above getting rich, even though he cannot be talked into attacking windmills. Note that Sancho's wife, far from regarding him as necessarily mad because of his involvement with the Knight, is interested mainly in his material success: "Bring your money, good husband . . . I don't care where you gained it" (Cohen, p. 932).

17. As Entwistle pointed out, Sancho is in all likelihood sometimes tricked by "collusive testimony" (see his discussion in *Cervantes*, pp. 138–144). Such trickery deprives the incident of its perspectivist luster. Even under pressure of such deceptive testimony, Sancho delays considerably before using the word *baciyelmo*, and then is immediately threatened with bodily harm if he should change his mind: " 'Whoever says anything to the contrary,' said Don Quixote, 'if he is a knight, I will teach him that he lies, and if he is a squire, that he lies a thousand times' " (Cohen, pp. 402–403). As an underling, Sancho is certainly not free in the novel to say or not say just what he pleases; the Barber even threatens to accuse Sancho of robbing and murdering Don Quixote if Sancho should fail to give certain information demanded by the Barber and the Priest (Cohen, p. 218).

It is even possible that Sancho is playing a trick rather than being tricked, for, in his speech just prior to the utterance of the term *baciyelmo*, Sancho reveals a dawning awareness of the shakiness of his claim to possession of the basin on the grounds that it is just the fair spoils of chivalric adventure. He may find it convenient, now, to pretend that it is a helmet as well.

But for critics of perspectivist persuasions, the squabble over the barber basin and packsaddle is evidence that the philosophical problem of "the objective and the subjective" is here being "dealt with explicitly" (Jorge

Luis Borges, "Partial Magic in the *Quijote*," in *Labyrinths: Selected Stories and Other Writings*, p. 194).

18. Van Ghent, *The English Novel*, pp. 17–18. For an even more mechanical alignment of Sancho with his master, see René Girard, who declares that just as soon as Quixote influences Sancho's desire, the squire's "sense of reality is lost" and his "judgment is paralyzed" (*Deceit, Desire, and the Novel*, p. 4).

19. Rather than becoming more and more sure that enchantment is a reality, Sancho begins to ferret out the nature of all this mock enchantment by paying attention to certain suspicious loose ends (Cohen, p. 747).

20. Auden, *The Dyer's Hand*, p. 137.

21. Northrop Frye is one of the more recent major critics to read the governorship sequence in this light (*Fables of Identity*, pp. 165–166).

22. Sancho's rulings here are a reflection of the Spanish penchant for mixing moral with economic reforms, which was to lead to several attempts at so-called sumptuary legislation. But to identify such absolutist measures as just those which Cervantes himself would have favored (as scholars sometimes do) is to ignore the deeper vision of the comic artist who knew very well that human reality is not amenable to such straight-jacketing.

23. Yet Mark Van Doren regards Sancho's handling of this case as the most impressive evidence of his "sanity, not to say his maturity" (*Don Quixote's Profession*, p. 90).

24. Self-knowledge connoting self-control is emphasized in Castiglione, Du Bartas, Sir Thomas Elyot, and other Renaissance authors. Sir John Davies' *Nosce Teipsum* is almost contemporary with *Don Quixote*. The saying itself has, of course, a long history.

25. The attitude is sometimes duplicated by critics. Brander Matthews, for instance, thought that Quixote's beatings cause resentment in us, but not those received by Sancho, who is somehow compensated by being of "stout heart" and by having a store of proverbs ("Cervantes, Zola, Kipling & Co.," *Cosmopolitan Magazine* 14 [March, 1893]: 612). Some later critics even imply censure of Sancho's failure to honestly undergo the 3,300 lashes. For example, Togeby, *La composition du roman "Don Quichotte*," p. 54; Green, *Spain and the Western Tradition*, I, 197; Theodore Holmes, "Don Quixote and Modern Man," *Sewanee Review* 78 (Winter, 1970): 58. Hipólito R. Romero Flores has remarked that in Spain the traditional opinion of Sancho is approximately that of the niece and housekeeper in *Don Quixote* (part 2, chapter 2)—Sancho is a mon-

ster, glutton, and villain (*Biografía de Sancho Panza*, pp. 85–86). Even Américo Castro reveals a strong bias against Sancho in his remark that persons of Sancho's type are satisfied with their "inert" lives (*Cervantes y los casticismos españoles*, p. 157; see also p. 154). But the efforts of Romero Flores, along with those of Manuel Socorro (*La ínsula de Sancho en el reino de Don Quijote*), to elevate Sancho's dignity by emphasizing his alleged "education" under Don Quixote are subtly more denigrating than the traditional opinion.

It is worth noting, in this regard, that there are extremely few source studies on the unworthy Sancho; the only one of recent years is by Francisco Márquez Villanueva, "Sobre la génesis literaria de Sancho Panza," *Anales Cervantinos* 7 (1958): 123–155.

26. Robert Martin Adams notices that the Knight often is indifferent to human suffering ("Two Lines from Cervantes," in *Strains of Discord: Studies of Literary Openness*, p. 77).

27. Auden, *The Dyer's Hand*, p. 138.

28. But Mark Van Doren takes it straight, as evidence of the great friendship of master and man (*Don Quixote's Profession*, pp. 88–89).

29. *estiércol*; or manure.

30. I intend my analysis of Sancho as a method for comprehending Sancho's own critical powers within the novel. The figure at the center of the novel is, of course, Don Quixote. My own interests in, and sympathy for, a greater acceptance of the human body as a literary subject with positive importance are not intended as a recommendation for modeling lives after Sancho's way of life. One need only read the ghastly use of proverbial, or "good-soldier," wisdom in Jakov Lind's story, "Soul of Wood," to be reminded that Sancho's way is defined by its own context (*Soul of Wood and Other Stories*, p. 60).

CHAPTER IV. A WORLD ALREADY CONQUERED BY DULCINEA

1. Appeal to immediacies is one of the more bothersome forms of critical dogmatism, as Stephen C. Pepper points out (*The Basis of Criticism in the Arts*, pp. 5–6).

2. Quixote's treatment by those who wish to cure him is poor psychiatry and equally poor Christianity, but it is scarcely a series of horrors, as those who admire the Knight's trials sometimes imply. He is treated better than a madman usually is (whether in Renaissance bedlams or in twentieth-century shock-treatment palaces). The Priest does at least pay for

some of the damages Quixote does (Cohen, p. 411) and argues against the troopers who want to arrest the Knight.

3. The mock invasion by the Moors, acted out by the Duke's servants, is so convincing as to seem to intimidate even the Duke, although he is in on the secret (Cohen, pp. 695–696). Artificially induced emotion is at a premium in both Ducal and Quixotic personalities. Of course, this artificially induced emotion may be genuinely intense; probably it evokes depths of response commensurate with melodrama. The same can be said of Don Quixote's conversion of pain into a literary response. I am not denying (in fact I am insisting) that the superficial appearances upheld in various aspects of Dulcineated behavior require deep psychic involvement from the characters involved. See my article, "Technology and the Future of Art," *Massachusetts Review* 7 (Autumn, 1966): 686.

4. Oscar Mandel, typifying the cautionary approach, accepts all the alleged humor of the Ducal pranks as a form of Cervantes' own commentary on Quixote, no matter how sadistic these pranks may be. He also typifies the cautionary taste for incomplete satire (using *Don Quixote* as an excuse to belabor "enthusiasm" but nothing more) by insisting that Don Quixote is a neatly split personality whose idealistic speeches are Cervantes' own thoughts ("The Function of the Norm in *Don Quijote*," pp. 154–163). But a proper critical reading would consider both the presented comedy and the possibility of *forced comedy* on the part of the characters. A critic must accept responsibility for ascertaining the experienced impact of satire, rather than merely following the instructions for reading that he may derive from statements made by the narrator. Mandel insists that we read to order. He thus exemplifies the weakness of the approach recommended in Wayne Booth's *The Rhetoric of Fiction*, where, in fact, Mandel's article is endorsed (see Booth, p. 183 n).

John J. Allen has developed the approach suggested by Mandel, Booth, and like-minded critics in a manner that depends upon "contextual" and stylistic "disclosure" rather than upon authorial commentary. But the concepts used by Allen are almost all limited to the traditional cautionary range of "pride," "presumptuousness," "punishment," and "purification." Thus, when the Knight verbosely and mistakenly boasts of his physical prowess, Allen's hypothetical reader is almost automatically "disposed" to laugh at any ensuing physical distress, including even Don Quixote's torture, being strung up from his wrist (*Don Quixote: Hero or Fool?* p. 40, 29–57 *passim*). Such "disclosure" has little to do with experiencing the full impact of a fictional context; it merely converts the entire text into a somewhat disguised moral commentary combined with the rhetorical manipulation of a pretended "reader." Allen avoids dealing with the stereotyped quality of what is "disclosed" through his procedure, partly by labeling it Cervantes' (rather than Allen's own) "maintenance of the balance of justice in the novel" (*ibid.*, p. 51).

5. The text also says that this adventure gives Sancho "a subject of talk for ages," but this is of lesser significance. Sancho's overall characterization indicates that he would never settle for the pleasures of mere talk; he would become critical in his talking and would want more than verbal rewards.

6. For this reason, it is critically disastrous to take the speech on poetry as Cervantes' own and attempt to interpret the novel from there. Whatever Cervantes may have written elsewhere, Cervantes as novelist in *Don Quixote* is working against this concept of poetry. Hence, I must reject the view of E. C. Riley, *Cervantes's Theory of the Novel*, pp. 74–75, 97–98.

7. Cohen, p. 542. The Spanish is:

> Dadme, señora, un término que siga,
> Conforme a vuestra voluntad cortado,
> Que será de la mía así estimado
> Que por jamás un punto del desdiga.

8. Carrasco's animus against the Knight is not simply resistance to Dulcineism, but also an urge to get some sort of revenge for the way Quixote unhorsed him and knocked him unconscious, "in complete safety and without the slightest risk" (Cohen, p. 557).

9. The whole subject of poetry must have been ambivalent for Cervantes, who probably wanted to be a much better poet than he actually was. But I see no reason to think that his comic genius could have placed any stock in an uncritical acceptance of Don Quixote as "ejemplar poeta," whose greatest creation is Dulcinea, the woman who represents things as they should be. The latter is the position of Jean Krynen, "Don Quixote, ejemplar poeta," *Anales Cervantinos* 7 (1958): 1–11.

10. As Dalai Brenes has pointed out in "The Orthodoxy of Cervantes," *Hispania* 15 (September, 1957): 312–316.

11. It is plain that the fictional society of *Don Quixote* lives within a mythic consciousness, for, as Northrop Frye argues, myths "seem to provide a containing form of tradition, one result of which is the obliterating of boundaries separating legend, historical reminiscence, and actual history that we find in Homer and the Old Testament" (*Fables of Identity*, p. 31). What Frye would not care to say, however, is that Cervantes manages to be totally critical regarding this mythic consciousness, and that his novel

finally negates it. Compare my exchange with Robert Hapgood, "Shakespeare's Negated Myths?" *Paunch*, no. 27 (October, 1966), pp. 5–12. In this context, one may assert that the prefatory verses to part 1 of the *Quixote*—which take the form of mock sonnets addressed to the Knight, to his squire, or to Dulcinea, and which are sent, ostensibly, by such notables as Orlando Furioso, Amadís of Gaul, and the Lady Oriana—show that Cervantes was quite able to conceive of the intermingling of legend and belief in farcical terms. The would-be hero may establish contact with mythic predecessors, but these models may have nothing to offer him but their own inherent silliness.

12. Américo Castro points out that this particular book was much influenced by Erasmian concepts of the subjective value of religious experience ("Erasmo en tiempo de Cervantes," in *Hacia Cervantes*, pp. 236–252). But there is no reason to suppose that the Knight, in recommending the book, means any more than his stereotyped language would suggest.

13. One of these, *El monserrate*, by Cristóbal de Virués (1587), contains considerable violence bordering on the sadistic. This book is a source of Matthew Lewis' *The Monk*. The Priest finds *El monserrate* to be one of the "richest treasures of poetry Spain possesses."

14. Even Ramiro de Maeztu, who is one of the few Spanish critics to resist the elevation of Don Quixote into a complete model of the national ethos, made this reservation (*Don Quixote, Don Juan y la Celestina: Ensayos en simpatía*, pp. 63, 68, 72, and elsewhere).

15. Auerbach, *Mimesis*, p. 347. Even Florenz Rang, who saw many defects in Don Quixote (and who interpreted the novel as a criticism of Imperial Spain), believed that Don Quixote was fundamentally good, that "soul and character are independent of one another." Such a separation is surely artificial. The somewhat similar interpretation by Joseph Bickermann maintains that the speeches of Quixote on various general topics are merely Cervantes' own inserted opinion, not part of what the novel is satirizing. See Lienhard Bergel, "Cervantes in Germany," in *Cervantes across the Centuries*, ed. Flores and Benardete, pp. 338–339 and 340–341, in whose useful summaries of Rang and Bickermann these details may be found.

16. Mann, "Voyage with Don Quixote," p. 335. Compare Gloria M. Fry's statement that the Knight is "calm, reasonable, and so admirably logical in his thinking and argumentation" in part 2 ("Symbolic Action in the Episode of the Cave of Montesinos from 'Don Quijote,'" p. 471). Or, for a more ponderous statement of the same position, see René Girard, who finds that Quixote shares in his society's "ontologically healthy de-

sire" during his lucid intervals (*Deceit, Desire, and the Novel*, p. 141). Even Theodore Holmes, who regards both Quixote and his fictional society as mirrors of each other's sinfulness and pride, classifies the Knight's discourses as "eminently sane" ("Don Quixote and Modern Man," p. 43).

17. J. H. Elliott points out that there were many *arbitristas*, or projectors, in the reign of Phillip III, who proposed schemes, "both sensible and fantastic," for national recovery (*Imperial Spain*, pp. 294–295). Cervantes clearly is poking fun at this whole *arbitrista* frame of mind.

18. Note Robert C. Elliott's statement: "Let the conscious intent of the artist be what it will, the local attack cannot be contained; the ironic language eats its way in implication through the most powerful-seeming structures" (*The Power of Satire: Magic, Ritual, Art*, p. 274).

19. The fascination with Moslem enemies in the novel cannot be explained as a reflection of Spanish national interest. During Cervantes' whole life, Spain had been embroiled in wars with other enemies quite as dangerous as the Moors, despite the crisis at Lepanto in 1571; indeed it was the abundance of other military problems that made it impractical for their Spaniards to press their victory there.

20. Bickermann, *Don Quijote y Fausto*. Bickermann's cautionary approach is one of the more interesting ones in this vein, but its central point —that Cervantes is trying to show through Don Quixote that reality is not constructed in accordance with the demands of idealism—is ultimately a depletion of the novel's juxtaposed elements and a reversal of its meaning. For, in actual context, reality is a much too cozy embodiment, not a refutation, of Quixote's dreams.

21. This remark refers to the legend concerning the beaver, whose sex glands were once used to make castoreum.

22. The speech on courage thus defines Quixote's limitations as once again conventional, even in his victory over the lion (which it follows). The effect is retroactive; what had at least looked like a totally idiosyncratic gesture of impractical valor now becomes narrowed to an ideal out of Dulcinea's general locker.

23. J. H. Elliott, *Imperial Spain*, pp. 52–53.

24. There are few historians who doubt this figure, according to Irwin R. Blacker, writing in a review (*New York Times Book Review*, May 8, 1966, p. 7) of J. H. Parry's authoritative work, *The Spanish Seaborne Empire*. For accounts of the great Spanish debate over the treatment of the Indians, see J. H. Elliott, *Imperial Spain*, pp. 57–64; Otis H. Green, *Spain and the Western Tradition*, III, 89–93. Elliott (p. 286) treats the death of most of the Indian population as a "demographic catastrophe"

that had unfortunate effects on the Spanish economy, whereas Green neatly balances appearance and reality by saying that the high-sounding laws of 1547, "whatever their lack of success in practice, do honor to Spain as a colonizing nation" (p. 90).

Both writers are probably concerned to avoid the Ku Klux Klan mentality of the *leyenda negra*, in which everything of Spanish, Catholic, and monarchical origin is automatically condemned in self-righteous tones. The concern to avoid this legend has gone so far that some historians wonder whether another legend, a *leyenda blanca* of "Spanish altruism and tolerance" has not been promulgated (Benjamin Keen, Introduction to *Spain in America: 1450–1580*, by Edward Gaylord Bourne, p. x). But the depletion of 90 percent of a population is no figment of historical distortion; it is a fact too enormous ever to be explained as only one facet of the rich complexity of Spanish Renaissance culture. Nor can it be explained away as a result of the poor medical knowledge of the time, even if most Indian deaths were the result of plagues. Decimation of native populations has been a consistent feature of the Western (not just the Spanish) adventure in "civilizing" the natives. In South America, Protestant missionaries of our own time, though aware that their efforts will certainly lead to the wiping out of native cultures, do not turn back from their Dulcineated missions. See Peter Matthiesson, *The Cloud Forest: A Chronicle of the South American Wilderness*, pp. 111, 138–139.

25. Similarly one must reject the theory of M. A. S. Hume, who thought the Knight a reflection of the excessive individualism of Spanish character and hence of Spanish imperialism ("The National Significance of *Don Quixote*," *Fortnightly Review* 88 [October 1, 1907]: 652–665).

26. *Don Quixote* is comparable, in a limited way, to Cervantes' novella, "Rinconete and Cortadillo" (in *The Portable Cervantes*, trans. Samuel Putnam), which portrays a community of thieves who employ a great deal of traditionally pious language as they carry on their forays among the populace.

27. Grierson, "*Don Quixote*: Some Wartime Reflections on Its Character and Influence," pp. 48–50.

28. *The Portable Dante*, ed. Paolo Milano, pp. 640–641.

29. McGeorge Bundy, "The Uses of Responsibility," *Saturday Review* 48 (July 3, 1965): 13–14. To deny this type of connection for the novel is to encourage the pretense that *Don Quixote* is relevant only to Spain of the Golden Age. I, of course, can see no theoretical or factual grounds for supposing such a limitation to be legitimate. My examples of Vietnam and the Dominican Republic are not intended as the only ones possible,

although they are specific rather than hypothetical instances of the novel's unavoidable relevance.

30. For an analysis of this form of argument as a piece of rhetoric, see Kenneth Burke, *A Grammar of Motives and a Rhetoric of Motives*, p. 544.

31. Quixote goes on to consider the effects of the rise of gunpowder on chivalry, but it is hardly correct to take this as a protest on his part against the effects of modern warfare. What he is really worried about, what "grieves him to the heart," is that "powder and lead may deprive me of the chance of winning fame and renown by the strength of my arm and the edge of my sword, over all the known earth. But let heaven do what it will. If I achieve my purpose, I shall be the more highly esteemed for having faced greater dangers than did the knights-errant of past ages" (Cohen, pp. 344–345).

32. Compare the pulpit rhetoric of Ribadeneyra, who helped prepare Spain for mounting its attempted invasion of England in 1588: "Every conceivable pretext for a just and holy war is to be found in this campaign. . . . This is a defensive, not an offensive, war: one in which we are defending our sacred religion and our most holy Roman Catholic faith; one in which we are defending the high reputation of our King and lord, and of our nation; defending, too, the land and property of all the kingdoms of Spain, and simultaneously our peace, tranquility and repose" (quoted in J. H. Elliott, *Imperial Spain*, p. 282).

33. Many scholars and critics have found it convenient to take Cervantes' assurances of loyalty as a touching picture of his indefatigable idealism. But in view of the king's refusal to help the Cervantes family ransom their son after he had been captured in the line of duty, the subsequent refusal to give Cervantes a good job in the colonial service, the arrest and jailing of Cervantes' whole household for a week in 1605 (six months after part 1 of *Don Quixote* had been published), and the rejection of the author's application for a post in Naples as late as 1610, it would be strange indeed if Cervantes were so totally imbecilic as to have nothing but love for his country.

34. The passage is commonly taken as an expression of Cervantes' bitterness over the poor treatment afforded to veterans in the Spain of his time, and this is certainly possible. But Quixote only adds that poverty and hunger are possible outcomes of an honorable military career as part (Cohen, p. 629) of a longer speech that, in context, undermines military valor itself.

35. Nor can a responsive reading accept such a convenient way out of disturbing insight as Casalduero's position that social life in *Quixote* is

bound to be corrupt because anything that is not purely ideal must thereby be part of man's sinful natural life, and therefore must sully the purity of any ideals it happens to touch ("The Composition of *Don Quixote*," in *Cervantes across the Centuries*, ed. Flores and Benardete, p. 83).

36. Trilling, *Beyond Culture*, p. 3.

37. For an argument that it is characteristic of the West to combine idealism with organized violence, see the first chapter of *The Politics of Hysteria: The Sources of Twentieth-Century Conflict*, by Edmund Stillman and William Pfaff. Note also the use of this book by Geoffrey Barraclough, in a recent review of studies in medieval history ("Deus le Volt?" *New York Review of Books* 14 [May 21, 1970]: 12).

38. It is difficult to make any sense (even on quantitative grounds) of Samuel Putnam's belief that the novel is at its best with lower-class characters (Introduction to *The Portable Cervantes*, pp. 18, 23).

39. Mann, "Voyage with Don Quixote," p. 343.

40. *Ibid.*, pp. 355–356. The undeniable associations and connections between Quixote's mission and the ideals of Christianity have been seen by such diverse writers on Cervantes as Unamuno, Casella, Auden, Predmore, and Otis H. Green. José Vasconcelos argued that every Christian is a Quixote, for every Christian serves an ethic that contradicts nature and puts him above it (*Discursos 1920–1950*, p. 263).

41. Thus Bruce W. Wardropper (to take one critic among many) thinks that the "Tale" is designed to prove that certain truths, particularly the truth of Camilla's virtue, cease to be true if they are put to experimental test; Anselmo's error, therefore, is in making the test ("The Pertinence of 'El Curioso Impertinente,'" *PMLA* 62 [September, 1957]: 599–600). This position, however, would automatically protect idealistic truth as long as it remained a belief not tested. Hence the argument is self-confirming.

Francisco Ayala varies the usual cautionary interpretation by insisting that Anselmo's desire is a sexual perversion ("Los dos amigos," *Revista de Occidente* 3 [September, 1965]: 287–305). But Ayala's gross clinical label is not very enlightening.

42. Compare the hilarious passage in Cervantes' "Dialogue of the Dogs," in which one of the dogs tells how he managed to attract a new master by means of a well-planned "performance" of humility, meekness, and other virtues (in *Six Exemplary Novels*, trans. Harriet de Onis, pp. 13–14).

43. Casalduero, "The Composition of *Don Quixote*," in *Cervantes across the Centuries*, ed. Flores and Benardete, p. 70.

44. *Ibid.*, p. 59.

45. Salvador de Madariaga's explanation of Cardenio's action is that

"indignation, suppressed by cowardice, turns against the coward and burns up his reason" (*Don Quixote: An Introductory Essay in Psychology*, p. 102). The explanation is especially amusing in view of the subtitle of Madariaga's book.

46. Cervantes elsewhere has one of his characters piquantly ridicule those women who "wish their husbands to respect them because they are chaste and decent, as if their perfection of character lay in that and in nothing else; and they do not notice the leaks that siphon off the cream of a thousand other virtues that they lack." See "The Judge of the Divorce Court," in *The Interludes of Cervantes*, trans. S. Griswold Morley, p. 13.

E. H. Templin interprets Dorothea as one who consciously attempts to build up sympathy for herself, after half-inviting Ferdinand to make his seductive advances. Dorothea thus moves up from her own class of wealthy farm-girl to being the wife of a very rich nobleman ("'Labradores' in the 'Quijote,'" *Hispanic Review* 30 [January, 1962]: 49). The interpretation is plausible, and a welcome relief from the usual idealizing of Cervantes' already ideal women, but it does not allow sufficiently for the way Cervantes shows his characters to be caught in a scheme (Dulcinea's) greater than any of their own. Because every nook of Dorothea's character, as we see it in the text, is occupied with manipulating Dulcinea's categories, one must regard Dorothea as a person whose rise in social class is of no help in actually changing her life, nor is it ever intended by her as such a fundamental change.

47. Casalduero thinks all this is designed to show how sexual desire must be channeled into social ideal ("The Composition of *Don Quixote*," in *Cervantes across the Centuries*, ed. Flores and Benardete, pp. 73–74). But in context Dorothea's story is one in which the basic social ideal is rendered preposterous by showing how people are reduced to frantic stereotypes by the very effort to placate it.

Casalduero, however, even regards the Priest's assistance in manipulating Dorothea's marriage to Ferdinand as "literary creation." See his article, "La creación literaria en el 'Quijote' de 1605," in *Homenaje ofrecido a Dámaso Alonso*, I, 307–319. There is no limit to what one can call literary creation if one ignores the question of quality.

48. This is convenient for everyone in the novel to believe, in another sense, too, since it reinforces the notion that Moors really want to be converted and ignores all the pressure put upon them. Castro, alluding to Zoraida (*Cervantes y los casticismos españoles*, p. 93), falls into the characteristic liberal trap of assuming that approval and acceptance of sincere converts to a dominant ideology (in this case, to Christianity) is equal to

genuine acceptance of human differences. The same general fallacy underlies his positive emphasis on Don Quixote's admiration for the life story
of St. Paul (*ibid.*, pp. 101–102, referring to Quixote's remarks in part 2,
chapter 58, to be found in Cohen, p. 839).

49. Casalduero thus believes that Zoraida shows the beauty of the Im-
maculate Conception, and Leo Spitzer sees in her story the drama of
"Divine Grace working against all possible handicaps" (Casalduero, "The
Composition of *Don Quixote*," in *Cervantes across the Centuries*, ed. Flores
and Benardete, p. 77; Spitzer, "Linguistic Perspectivism in the *Don
Quixote*," in *Linguistics and Literary History*, p. 65).

50. As E. H. Templin points out, "real class lines are rarely crossed" in
Don Quixote, despite a great deal of concern for equal treatment of persons within a class structure (" 'Labradores' in the 'Quijote,' " p. 51).

51. Mann, "Voyage with Don Quixote," p. 349. One scholarly explanation of the way in which Quiteria is instantly expunged from Camacho's
memory is that Camacho is in reality a wealthy convert to Christianity,
who is in a position to purchase a bride like Quiteria but who has no
real attachment to her. Nevertheless, even if we waive the problem of the
factual adequacy of this account of Camacho's background, the explanation remains superficial. Since when are ostentatious people, newly established in social status, content to give up politely the objects (human
or other) they have acquired?

52. Even the extremely sympathetic account of the Spanish Golden Age
by R. Trevor Davies fully concedes that the internal Morisco menace was
produced by the operation of Spanish idealism itself, which was characteristically more interested in enforcing an appearance of Christian practice
in the Moorish minority than in actually integrating that minority into the
national life (*The Golden Century in Spain: 1501–1621*, p. 253; also pp.
54 and 242–247).

EPILOGUE

1. Ruth Benedict, *Patterns of Culture*, p. 103.
2. John Ruskin, *Lectures on Architecture and Painting*, in *Works*, ed.
E. T. Cook and Alexander Wedderburn, XII, 56.
3. Ortega y Gasset, *Meditations on Quixote*, p. 163.
4. As Nelson Algren well shows, in his book, *Who Lost an American?*
(pp. 286–335), the *Playboy* "bunny" is an obverse side of a long tradition
that divides all women into an infinitely idealizable type and a drastically
circumscribed "physical" type.

5. James Baldwin, "The Artist's Struggle for Integrity," in *Seeds of Liberation*, ed. Paul Goodman, p. 387.

6. Henry Fielding, *The Life of Mr. Jonathan Wild the Great*, p. 216.

7. Borges, *Labyrinths*, p. 234.

8. James E. Irby, Introduction to Borges' *Labyrinths*, p. xvii.

LIST OF WORKS CITED

WORKS BY CERVANTES

Castro, Américo (intro.). *El ingenioso hidalgo Don Quijote de la Mancha.* Mexico City: Editorial Porrúa, 1960.

Cohen, J. M. (trans.). *The Adventures of Don Quixote.* Harmondsworth, Middlesex: Penguin Books, 1950.

de Onis, Harriet (trans.). *Six Exemplary Novels.* Great Neck, N.Y.: Barron's Educational Series, 1961.

Morley, S. Griswold (trans.). *The Interludes of Cervantes.* Princeton: Princeton University Press, 1948.

Ormsby, John (trans.). *The Ingenious Gentleman Don Quixote de la Mancha.* 2 vols. New York: Thomas Y. Crowell and Co., 1896.

Putnam, Samuel (trans.). *The Ingenious Gentleman Don Quixote de la Mancha.* New York: The Viking Press, 1949.

———— (ed.). *The Portable Cervantes.* New York: The Viking Press, 1951.

Starkie, Walter (trans.). *Don Quixote of La Mancha.* New York: New American Library, Signet Classics, 1964.

WORKS BY OTHER AUTHORS

Adams, Robert Martin. *Strains of Discord: Studies in Literary Openness.* Ithaca: Cornell University Press, 1958.

Algren, Nelson. *Who Lost an American?* New York: The Macmillan Co., 1963.

Allen, John J. *Don Quixote: Hero or Fool? A Study in Narrative Technique.* Gainesville, Fla.: University of Florida Press, 1969.

Alonso, Dámaso. *Del siglo de oro a este siglo de siglas.* Madrid: Editorial Gredos, 1962.

Alter, Robert. *Rogue's Progress: Studies in the Picaresque Novel.* Cambridge, Mass.: Harvard University Press, 1964.

Askew, Melvin W. "Courtly Love: Neurosis as Institution." *Psychoanalytic Review* 52 (Spring, 1965): 19–29.

Atkinson, William C. *A History of Spain and Portugal.* Harmondsworth, Middlesex: Penguin Books, 1960.

Auden, W. H. *The Dyer's Hand and Other Essays.* New York: Random House, 1962.

Auerbach, Erich. *Mimesis: The Representation of Reality in Western Literature.* Translated by Willard R. Trask. Princeton: Princeton University Press, 1953.

Ayala, Francisco. "Los dos amigos." *Revista de Occidente* 3 (September, 1965): 287–305.

Baldwin, James. "The Artist's Struggle for Integrity." In *Seeds of Liberation,* edited by Paul Goodman. New York: George Braziller, 1964.

Barraclough, Geoffrey. "Deus le Volt?" *New York Review of Books* 14 (May 21, 1970): 12–17.

Bell, Aubrey. *Cervantes.* New York: Collier Books, 1961.

Benedict, Ruth. *Patterns of Culture.* New York: New American Library, Mentor Books, 1957.

Bergson, Henri. "Laughter." In *Comedy,* edited by Wylie Sypher. New York: Doubleday and Co., Anchor Books, 1956.

Berlin, Isaiah. *Two Concepts of Liberty.* Oxford: The Clarendon Press, 1958.

Bickermann, Joseph. *Don Quixote y Fausto.* Barcelona: Casa Editorial Araluce, 1932.

Blacker, Irwin R. Review of J. H. Parry, *The Spanish Seaborne Empire.* *New York Times Book Review,* May 8, 1966, p. 7.

Bleznick, Donald W. "Don Quijote's Advice to Governor Sancho Panza." *Hispania* 40 (March, 1957): 62–65.

Booth, Wayne. *The Rhetoric of Fiction.* Chicago: University of Chicago Press, 1961.

Borges, Jorge Luis. *Labyrinths: Selected Stories and Other Writings,* edited by Donald A. Yates and James E. Irby. New York: New Directions, 1964.

Bourne, Edward Gaylord. *Spain in America: 1450–1580.* Introduction by Benjamin Keen. New York: Barnes and Noble, 1962.

Brandt, William J. *The Shape of Medieval History: Studies in Modes of Perception.* New Haven: Yale University Press, 1966.

Brenes, Dalai. "The Orthodoxy of Cervantes." *Hispania* 15 (September, 1957): 312–316.

Bundy, McGeorge. "The Uses of Responsibility." *Saturday Review* 48 (July 3, 1965): 13–14, 47.

Burke, Kenneth. *A Grammar of Motives and a Rhetoric of Motives.* Cleveland and New York: The World Publishing Co., Meridian Books, 1962.

Burns, Wayne. "The Panzaic Principle." *Paunch*, no. 22 (January, 1965), pp. 2–31. [Reprinted in Burns's *Towards a Contextualist Aesthetic of the Novel*, edited by James Flynn, Gerald Butler, and Evelyn Butler. Seattle: Genitron Books, 1968. Copies in the possession of Wayne Burns, Department of English, University of Washington, Seattle, Washington 98105.]

Canfield, Margaret Jimmie. "Don Quixote Sets Out to Die." *Paunch*, no. 32 (August, 1968), pp. 23–38.

Capellanus, Andreas. *The Art of Courtly Love*, edited by Frederick W. Locke. New York: Frederick Ungar Publishing Co., 1957.

Carbonell y Basset, Delfín. "Don Quijote desde un punto de vista existenciofenomenológico." *Duquesne Hispanic Review* 2 no. 1 (1963): 21–32.

Casalduero, Joaquín. "La creación literaria en el 'Quijote' de 1605." In *Homenaje ofrecido a Dámaso Alonso*, vol. 1. Madrid: Editorial Gredos, 1960.

———. *Sentido y forma del Quijote (1605–1615).* Madrid: Ínsula, 1949.

Casella, Mario. *Cervantes: Il Chisciotte.* 2 vols. Florence: Felice Le Monnier, 1936.

Castro, Américo. *Cervantes y los casticismos españoles.* Madrid-Barcelona: Alfaguera, 1966.

———. *De la edad conflictiva.* Vol. 1, *El drama de la honra en España y en su literatura.* Madrid: Taurus, 1961.

———. *Hacia Cervantes.* 3d edition. Madrid: Taurus, 1967.

———. "*El Quijote*, taller de la existencialidad." *Revista de Occidente* 5 (July, 1967): 1–33.

———. *El pensamiento de Cervantes.* Madrid: Hernando, 1925.

———. "Españolidad y europeización del *Quijote*." Prólogo" to *El ingenioso hidalgo Don Quijote de la Mancha,* by Miguel Cervantes Saavedra. Mexico City: Editorial Porrúa, 1960.

———. *The Structure of Spanish History.* Princeton: Princeton University Press, 1954.

Chamberlin, E. R. *Everyday Life in Renaissance Times.* New York: G. P. Putnam's Sons, 1965.

Chambers, Leland H. "Structure and the Search for Truth in the *Quijote*:

Notes toward a Comprehensive View." *Hispanic Review* 35 (October, 1967): 309–326.

Chesterton, G. K. *A Handful of Authors: Essays on Books and Writers.* London and New York: Sheed and Ward, 1953.

Cohen, Ralph. *The Art of Discrimination: Thomson's "The Seasons" and the Language of Criticism.* Berkeley and Los Angeles: University of California Press, 1964.

Coleridge, Samuel Taylor. *Complete Works,* edited by W. G. T. Shedd, vol. 6. New York: Harper and Row, 1884.

Comfort, Alex. *Darwin and the Naked Lady: Discursive Essays on Biology and Art.* London: Routledge and Kegan Paul, 1961.

Cook, Albert S. *The Meaning of Fiction.* Detroit: Wayne State University Press, 1960.

Czako, Ambrosius. *Don Quijote: A Commentary.* Winnipeg: The Christian Press, 1943.

Davies, R. Trevor. *The Golden Century of Spain: 1501–1621.* New York: Harper and Row, Torchbooks, 1965.

Dante Alighieri. *The Portable Dante,* edited by Paolo Milano. New York: The Viking Press, 1947.

Del Río, Ángel. "The Equivoco of *Don Quixote.*" In *Varieties of Literary Experience: Eighteen Essays in World Literature,* edited by Stanley Burnshaw. New York: New York University Press, 1962.

DeMott, Benjamin. "The Little Red Discount House." *Hudson Review* 15 (Winter, 1962–1963): 551–564.

De Rougement, Denis. *Love in the Western World.* New York: Pantheon Books, 1965.

Deutsch, Helene. *Neuroses and Character Types: Clinical and Psychoanalytical Studies.* New York: International Universities Press, 1965.

Dewey, John. *Art as Experience.* New York: Minton, Balch, and Co., 1934.

Durán, Manuel. *La ambigüedad en el Quijote.* Xalapa, Mexico: Universidad Veracruzana, 1960.

Edman, Irwin E. Introduction to *Don Quixote: The Ingenious Gentleman of La Mancha.* New York: The Heritage Press, 1951.

Efron, Arthur. "Logic, Hermeneutics, and Literary Context." *Genre* 1 (July, 1968): 214–229.

———. "Satire Denied: A Critical History of English and American *Don Quixote* Criticism." Ph.D. dissertation, University of Washington, 1964.

———. "Technology and the Future of Art." *Massachusetts Review* 7 (Autumn, 1966): 677–710.

Efron, Arthur, and Robert Hapgood. "Shakespeare's Negated Myths?" *Paunch*, no. 27 (October, 1966), pp. 5–12.

Elliott, J. H. *Imperial Spain: 1469–1716*. New York: St. Martin's Press, 1964.

Elliott, Robert C. *The Power of Satire: Magic, Ritual, Art*. Princeton: Princeton University Press, 1960.

El Saffar, Ruth. "The Function of the Fictional Narrator in *Don Quijote*." *Modern Language Notes* 83 (March, 1968): 164–177.

Entwistle, William J. *Cervantes*. Oxford: The Clarendon Press, 1940.

Fernández Gómez, Carlos. *Vocabulario de Cervantes*. Madrid: Real Academia Española, 1962.

Fielding, Henry. *The Life of Mr. Jonathan Wild the Great*. New York: New American Library, Signet Classics, 1962.

Flores, Angel, and M. J. Benardete, eds. *Cervantes across the Centuries*. New York: The Dryden Press, 1948.

Ford, Ford Madox. *The March of Literature from Confucius' Day to Our Own*. New York: The Dial Press, 1938.

Forster, E. M. *Two Cheers for Democracy*. New York: Harcourt, Brace and Co., 1951.

Fry, Gloria M. "Symbolic Action in the Episode of the Cave of Montesinos from 'Don Quijote.'" *Hispania* 48 (August, 1965): 468–474.

Frye, Northrop. *Anatomy of Criticism*. Princeton: Princeton University Press, 1957.

——. *Fables of Identity: Studies in Poetic Mythology*. New York: Harcourt, Brace and World, 1963.

Girard, René. *Deceit, Desire, and the Novel: Self and Other in Literary Structure*. Baltimore: Johns Hopkins Press, 1965.

Goggio, Emilio. "The Dual Role of Dulcinea in Cervantes' *Don Quijote de la Mancha*." *Modern Language Quarterly* 13 (September, 1952): 285–291.

Green, Otis H. *Spain and the Western Tradition: The Castilian Mind in Literature from "El Cid" to Calderón*. 4 vols. Madison: University of Wisconsin Press, 1963–1966.

Grierson, Sir Herbert. "*Don Quixote*: Some Wartime Reflections on its Character and Influence." In *The Background of English Literature: Classical and Romantic*. New York: Barnes and Noble, 1960.

Haley, George. "The Narrator in *Don Quijote*: Maese Pedro's Puppet Show." *Modern Language Notes* 80 (March, 1965): 145–165.

Hall, H. B. Review of J. M. Cohen's translation of *Don Quixote*. *Bulletin of Hispanic Studies* 28 (July–September, 1951): 214–216.

Hayden, Hiram. *The Counter-Renaissance.* New York: Charles Scribner's Sons, 1950.

Hauser, Arnold. *Mannerism: The Crisis of the Renaissance and the Origin of Modern Art.* 2 vols. New York: Alfred A. Knopf, 1965.

Hazlitt, William. *Collected Works,* edited by A. R. Waller and Arnold Glover, vol. 10. London: Dent, 1902–1906.

Heidegger, Martin. "The Origin of the Work of Art." In *Philosophies of Art and Beauty,* edited by Albert Hofstadter and Richard Kuhns. New York: Random House, 1964.

Heine, Heinrich. *Werke und Briefe,* edited by Hans Kaufmann, vol. 5. Berlin: Anfbau-Verlag, 1961.

Hirsch, E. D., Jr. *Validity in Interpretation.* New Haven: Yale University Press, 1967.

Holmes, Theodore. "Don Quixote and Modern Man." *Sewanee Review* 78 (Winter, 1970): 40–59.

Houck, Helen Phipps. "Substantive Address Used between Don Quijote and Sancho Panza." *Hispanic Review* 5 (January, 1937): 60–72.

Hume, M. A. S. "The National Significance of *Don Quixote.*" *Fortnightly Review* 88 (October 1, 1907): 652–665.

Hurd, Richard. *Hurd's Letters on Chivalry and Romance, with the Third Elizabethan Dialogue,* edited by Edith J. Morley. London: Henry Froude, 1911.

Hyman, Lawrence W. "Moral Values and Literary Experience." *Journal of Aesthetics and Art Criticism* 24 (Summer, 1966): 539–547.

Kaiser, Walter. *Praisers of Folly: Erasmus, Rabelais, Shakespeare.* Cambridge, Mass.: Harvard University Press, 1963.

Kernan, Alvin. *The Plot of Satire.* New Haven: Yale University Press, 1965.

Kirchheimer, Otto. *Political Justice: The Use of Legal Machinery for Political Ends.* Princeton: Princeton University Press, 1961.

Krieger, Murray. *The Tragic Vision: Variations on a Theme in Literary Interpretation.* Chicago: University of Chicago Press, Phoenix Books, 1966.

Krynen, Jean. "Don Quijote, ejemplar poeta." *Anales Cervantinos* 7 (1958): 1–11.

Lawrence, D. H. *Lady Chatterley's Lover.* New York: The Modern Library, n.d.

Levin, Harry. "The Example of Cervantes." In *Society and Self in the Novel,* edited by Mark Schorer. New York: English Institute Essays, 1961.

Literary Criticism." In *Homenaje a Rodríguez-Moñino*, vol. 2. Madrid: Castalia, 1966.

Ortega y Gasset, José. *Meditations on Quixote*. Translated by Evelyn Rugg and Diego Marín. New York: W. W. Norton, 1961.

―――. *The Modern Theme*. Translated by James Cleugh. New York: Harper and Row, Torchbooks, 1961.

―――. "Spanish Letter: July, 1924." In *A Dial Miscellany*, edited by William Wasserstrom. Syracuse, N.Y.: Syracuse University Press, 1963.

Osterc, Ludovick. *El pensamiento social y político del "Quijote."* Mexico City: Ediciones de Andrea, 1963.

Pabón Núñez, Lucio. "Sancho, o la exaltación del pueblo español." *Cadernos Hispanoamericanos* 58 (June, 1964): 541–580.

Paredes, Américo. "Luis Inclán: First of the Cowboy Writers." *American Quarterly* 12 (Spring, 1960): 55–70.

Parker, A. A. "*Don Quixote* and the Relativity of Truth." *Dublin Review* 220 (Autumn, 1947): 28–37.

Parry, J. H. *The Spanish Seaborne Empire*. New York: Alfred A. Knopf, 1965.

Pepper, Stephen C. *The Basis of Criticism in the Arts*. Cambridge, Mass.: Harvard University Press, 1963.

Predmore, Richard L. *The World of "Don Quixote."* Cambridge, Mass.: Harvard University Press, 1967.

Pring-Mill, R. D. F. Review of E. C. Riley, *Cervantes's Theory of the Novel*. *Modern Language Review* 62 (January, 1967): 146–149.

Quilter, Daniel E. "The Image of the *Quijote* in the Seventeenth Century." Ph.D. dissertation, University of Illinois, 1963.

Quintana, Ricardo. "Situational Satire: A Commentary on the Method of Swift." *University of Toronto Quarterly* 17 (January, 1948): 130–136.

Rahv, Philip. *The Myth and the Powerhouse*. New York: Farrar, Straus and Giroux, 1965.

Reich, Wilhelm. *Listen, Little Man!* New York: The Noonday Press, 1948.

Riley, Edward C. *Cervantes's Theory of the Novel*. Oxford: The Clarendon Press, 1962.

Romero Flores, Hipólito R. *Biografía de Sancho Panza: filósofo de la sensatez*. Barcelona: Editorial Aedos, 1951.

Rosales, Luis. *Cervantes y la libertad*. 2 vols. Madrid: Sociedad de Estudios y Publicaciones, 1960.

Rosenberg, Harold. *The Tradition of the New*. New York and Toronto: McGraw-Hill, 1965.

Lind, Jakov. *Soul of Wood and Other Stories*. New York: Fawc
Library, Crest Books, 1965.

Lindsay, Jack. *A Short History of Culture from Prehistory to th
sance*. Greenwich, Conn.: Fawcett World Library, Premier Boo

Livermore, Harold. *A History of Spain*. New York: Grove Press,

Livingstone, Leon. "Interior Duplication and the Problem of For
Modern Spanish Novel." *PMLA* 73 (September, 1958): 393–4

Lowell, James Russell. *Lowell: Essays, Poems, and Letters*, ec
William Smith Clark III. New York: The Odyssey Press, 1948.

Lukács, Georg. "Don Quixote." *Communist Review* (1951), pp. 2
———. *Realism in Our Time*. New York and Evanston: Harper ar
1964.

Mack, Maynard, *et al.* (eds.), *World Masterpieces*. 2 vols. Nev
W. W. Norton, 1956.

Madariaga, Salvador de. *Don Quixote: An Introductory Essay in P
ogy*. London: Oxford University Press, Galaxy Books, London, 1

Maeztu, Ramiro de. *Don Quijote, Don Juan y la Celestina: Ensa
simpatía*. Buenos Aires: Espasa-Calpe, 1945.

Maldonado de Guevara, Francisco. *La Maiestas cesárea en el Q
Madrid: Instituto "Miguel de Cervantes" de Filología Hispánica,

Mandel, Oscar. "The Function of the Norm in *Don Quixote*." *M
Philology* 55 (February, 1958): 154–163.

Mann, Thomas. "Voyage with Don Quixote." In *Essays by Thomas I
translated by H. T. Lowe-Porter. New York: Random House, Vi
Books, 1957.

Marcuse, Herbert. *Eros and Civilization*. New York: Random House,
tage Books, 1962.

———. *One-Dimensional Man*. Boston: Beacon Press, 1964.

Márquez Villanueva, Francisco. "Sobre la génesis literaria de Sa
Panza." *Anales Cervantinos* 7 (1958): 123–155.

Matthews, Brander. "Cervantes, Zola, Kipling & Co." *Cosmopolitan M
zine* 14 (March, 1893): 609–614.

Matthiesson, Peter. *The Cloud Forest: A Chronicle of the South Amer
Wilderness*. New York: Pyramid Books, 1966.

Meredith, George. "An Essay on Comedy." In *Comedy*, edited by W
Sypher. Garden City, N.Y.: Doubleday and Co., Anchor Books, 1ç

Meyer, Herman. *The Poetics of Quotation in the European Novel*. Tra
lated by Theodore and Yetta Ziolkowski. Princeton: Princeton Univ
sity Press, 1968.

Murillo, Luis Andrés. "Cervantic Irony in *Don Quixote*: The Problem

Ruskin, John. *Works*, edited by E. T. Cook and Alexander Wedderburn, vol. 12. London: George Allen, 1903.

Russell, P. E. "*Don Quixote* as a Funny Book." *Modern Language Review* 64 (April, 1969): 312–326.

Ruthven, K. K. "The Composite Mistress." *AUMLA*, no. 26, (1966), pp. 198–214.

Salinas, Pedro. *Jorge Manrique, o tradición y originalidad.* 2d edition. Buenos Aires: Editorial Sudamericana, 1952.

Shutz, Alfred. *Collected Papers*, edited by Arvid Broderson, vol. 2. The Hague: Martinus Nijhoff, 1964.

Sletsjöe, Leif. *Sancho Panza: Hombre de bien.* Madrid: Insula, 1961.

Socorro, Manuel. *La ínsula de Sancho en el reino de Don Quijote.* Las Palmas, Grand Canary Island: Imp. España, 1947.

Sparshott, F. E. "Truth in Fiction." *Journal of Aesthetics and Art Criticism* 26 (Fall, 1967): 3–7.

Spilka, Mark. "Comic Resolution in Fielding's *Joseph Andrews*." In *Fielding: A Collection of Critical Essays*, edited by Ronald Paulson. Englewood Cliffs, N.J.: Prentice-Hall, 1962.

Spitzer, Leo. *Linguistics and Literary History*. Princeton: Princeton University Press, 1948.

Stillman, Edmund, and William Pfaff. *The Politics of Hysteria: The Sources of Twentieth-Century Conflict.* New York, Evanston, and London: Harper and Row, 1964.

Tave, Stuart M. *The Amiable Humorist: A Study of the Comic Criticism of the Eighteenth and Early Nineteenth Centuries.* Chicago: University of Chicago Press, 1960.

Templin, E. H. " 'Labradores' in the 'Quijote.' " *Hispanic Review* 30 (January, 1962): 21–51.

Teresa, Saint. *The Life of Saint Teresa of Ávila, by Herself*, translated by J. M. Cohen. Harmondsworth, Middlesex: Penguin Books, 1957.

Times Literary Supplement. Review of J. M. Cohen's translation of *Don Quixote.* January 8, 1951.

Togeby, Knud. *La composition du roman "Don Quichotte."* Copenhagen: Librairie Munksgaard, 1957.

Trilling, Lionel. *Beyond Culture: Essays on Literature and Learning.* New York: The Viking Press, 1965.

Turgenev, Ivan. "Hamlet and Don Quixote." In *The Anatomy of Don Quixote: A Symposium*, edited by M. J. Benardete and Angel Flores. Reprint edition. Port Washington, N.Y.: Kennikat Press, 1969.

Unamuno, Miguel de. *The Life of Don Quixote and Sancho*. New York: Alfred A. Knopf, 1927.

———. *The Tragic Sense of Life*. New York: Dover Books, 1954.

Urzaiz, Eduardo. *Exégesis Cervantina*. Mérida: Universidad de Yucatán, 1950.

Van Doren, Mark. *Don Quixote's Profession*. New York: Columbia University Press, 1958.

Van Ghent, Dorothy. *The English Novel: Form and Function*. New York: Harper and Row, Torchbooks, 1961.

Vasconcelos, José. *Discursos 1920–1950*. Mexico City: Ediciones Botas, 1950.

Waldmeir, Joseph J. "The Cowboy, the Knight, and Popular Taste." *Southern Folklore Quarterly* 22 (September, 1958): 113–120.

Wardropper, Bruce W. "*Don Quixote*: Story or History?" *Modern Philology* 63 (August, 1965): 1–11.

———. "The Pertinence of 'El Curioso Impertinente.' " *PMLA* 62 (September, 1957): 587–600.

Willis, Raymond S., Jr. *The Phantom Chapters of the "Quijote."* New York: Hispanic Institute, 1953.

———. "Sancho Panza: Prototype for the Modern Novel." *Hispanic Review* 36 (January, 1969): 207–227.

Wilson, Edward M. "Edmund Gayton on Don Quixote, Andrés, and Juan Haldudo." *Comparative Literature* 2 (Winter, 1950): 64–72.

Wimsatt, W. K., Jr. *Hateful Contraries: Studies in Literature and Criticism*. Lexington, Ky.: University of Kentucky Press, 1965.

———. *The Verbal Icon: Studies in the Meaning of Poetry*. New York: Noonday Press, 1964.

Worcester, David. *The Art of Satire*. New York: Russell and Russell, 1960.

INDEX